Reviews of Paul Wright's Widely Acclaimed
THE LITERARY ZODIAC

THIS IS SUPERB. *It is beautifully written and its content is worth being studied by the most experienced astrologer as well as the student. . . . This is a first class book. Paul Wright must be congratulated. This will surely become an astrological classic.*—Considerations Magazine

Very impressive! If there were universities that gave degrees in astrology, the author would have a Ph.D. by now.—Stephen Arroyo

Extremely interesting, well researched and original. . . . I found his analysis deep and insightful.—Liz Greene

The Literary Zodiac is an important contribution to the field of astrology and to the study of creative writing. It is easy to recommend The Literary Zodiac to just about anyone.—Welcome to Planet Earth Magazine.

ASTROLOGY IN ACTION

Paul Wright

CRCS PUBLICATIONS
Post Office Box 1460
Sebastopol, California 95472
U.S.A.

Library of Congress Cataloging-in-Publication Data

Wright, Paul.
 Astrology in action / Paul Wright. — 1st ed.
  p. cm.
 Includes index.
 ISBN 0-916360-44-X : $12.95
 1. Astrology. 2. Horoscopes. I. Title.
 BF1708.1.W77 1989
 133.5--dc19
                                                                    89-30050
                                                                       CIP

First Edition
International Standard Book Number (ISBN) 0-916360-44-X

First published in USA and Canada by CRCS Publications
Originated and published in Great Britain by Anodyne Publishing

Distributed in UK/Eire by Airlift, and in USA, Canada,
 Australia and New Zealand by CRCS Publications

Chart diagrams by Shanna and Galen Song.

CONTENTS

Part 1: Introduction

Part 2: Astrology in action at the individual level

Astrological profiles. Birth charts and biographies of well-known individuals.

(continued over)

Part 3: Astrology in action at the collective level
The outer planets

Addendum
Fourteen more astrological profiles

Introduction

Astrology for a new age.

The value of astrology is perceived differently by different people. Some value it primarily as an aid to therapy or individual growth (comparatively modern usage). Others see it primarily as an oracle, as a way of divining the meaning of the moment and using this information as a basis for decision making (a more traditional use). Some seek from it knowledge of the future, be this a life's destiny or the outcome of a horse-race. Some regard it as nothing more than a fascinating parlour game put here for our amusement and to help fill the vacancies of attention. Indeed, it may be valuable to a greater or lesser degree in any or all of these areas. But what is not so often mentioned is its potential value as a universal language and as a basis for a vocabulary of consciousness.

A universal language.

What contemporary thought lacks is universals. The evidence of this is the prevailing confusion. We have fragmentation in all disciplines of thought; plurality rather than singularity. The Tower of Babel is a fitting symbol, a myth that focuses on the difference between universal truth and partial, 'man-made' truth.

A work like *Theories of Personality* by Hall and Lindzey[1] demonstrates this. This is an interesting, useful and well-written book that summarises the work and ideas of a number of psychologists. But we are struck by the range of ideas, the shades of opinion, in some cases the contradictions between individual psychologies, and are left wondering how they can all be right. This isn't to demean the work of psychologists but simply to put it into perspective. Creative thought in any sphere always brings down something of the universal. This is why we recognise the zodiacal symbolism of Leo in Jung's work, or of Taurus in Freud's. Reich was not wrong in his ideas of the energy of the universe being released through individuals. He was an Aries Sun, living and expressing his own truth and the essential meaning of the sign. But as astrologers we know that Aries is only part of the picture, no more or less important, certainly no more 'right' or 'wrong' than any other part. To use another fable, an individual in any field may describe the elephant's leg very lucidly, but it is still not the elephant, which is all and none of its individual parts.

Astrology, on the other hand does describe the elephant. It is a universal system of knowledge and not the product of an individual mind. The truth embodied in the astrological symbols emanates from higher levels than the individual mind. Astrology embraces partial truths; they can all be contained within it. It is Truth as opposed to truths (and bear in mind that an individual's thought doesn't necessarily constitute a partial truth. We must distinguish between creative and simply clever or idle thought.) If we lose sight of these differences between individual and universal truth, if we stray that far, as contemporary Western Man has done, that we can not even countenance the existence of universals such as astrological symbols, then we start talking in tongues, or, like the Lilliputians go to war over a difference of opinion as to how to break an egg.

A vocabulary of consciousness.

Consider the problem that faced David Livingstone in his work in Africa amongst the Makololo people. In their language there was no distinction between *agape* and *eros*. Love and sex were synonymous. And the closest word this tribe had for 'sin' also meant cow-dung. One can imagine the confusion Livingstone's preaching caused and it is small wonder that in all his time in Africa he made only one convert (who was later to relapse). Communication can be a problem if the vocabulary is inadequate.

In the West we are just emerging from a very materially oriented epoch, one where the collective focus has been the understanding and manipulation of the outer world. Because of this, vocabulary has developed in a particular way. For example, we have words to distinguish between thousands of minerals. Not only that, we have invented more words for the 92 types of basic matter — the natural elements — that constitute these. Our medieval ancestors were content to call it all 'earth', or 'rock'. However, while we are able to discriminate between many kinds of matter, we tend to rely on broad and often vague terms like 'soul', 'spirit' or 'mind' to cover vast areas of inner experience. If indeed, as many feel, we are embarked on a new era in which inner awareness and consciousness will attain greater significance then it is important that there is an appropriate vocabulary, one far more refined than the one in current, common usage. I believe astrology is pertinent here. Terms like 'mind' when viewed through an astrological lens are shown to be multifaceted. Moreover, the revealed facets can be readily labelled, so we have a Lunar mind, a Mercurial mind, a Jupiterian mind and so forth.

The basic symbols of astrology constitute in effect a universal algebra of consciousness, a sort of *lingua franca* for comprehending non-material dimensions of life. Part of the intention of *Astrology in Action* is to demonstrate the power of astrology to describe both individual and collective consciousness; its capacity to isolate those patterns that underpin behaviour, motivation and the course a life takes. While most astrologers are aware of this power, many who pursue parallel disciplines such as sociology, psychology, or philosophy, or who follow a path of self-development, are not. I hope to show in these chapters that we have no need for neologisms. That in astrology we have a self-consistent set of metaphors wholly adequate to describe the complexity of life.

Real astrology.

A sub-title to this book might be 'Real Astrology'. What is regarded as real and what not varies from time to time and culture to culture, and it is not my intention to enter into metaphysical debate on the point. But I use the term 'real' to indicate that the book represents an empirical and down-to-earth approach to the subject. For although astrology is a celestial art, and one that can not be wholly contained by rationalism or empiricism, it still has to be brought to earth. Its ultimate test is how it works in practice. *Astrology in Action* demonstrates just how it does, through examples drawn from extensive biographical and historical research, and through the use of accurate birth charts.

My first book, *The Literary Zodiac*, attempted to illuminate the symbolism of the signs and planets. This current work attempts the same, although with a significant difference. *The Literary Zodiac* delineated these meanings as they operate at a broad and abstract level — this because they were drawn from the rarefied level of creative literary minds. But *Astrology in Action* focuses on the same principles as they manifest at a more obvious and immediate level. Hence the sub-title 'real'.

Contemporary astrology tends to be two-dimensional. It is often not made plain that a particular principle will manifest one way on the individual level, another on the collective; one way on the creative level, another on the behavioural, and so on. Other systems of knowledge, notably Cabala and I Ching recognise different 'worlds' or levels of being. The latter, for example, distinguishes between a World of Thought and a World of Senses, the first representing existence at a more abstract level than the second; a level of potential rather than actuality. The World of Thought represents a level of fluid energy patterns or 'ideas' underlying the sensate manifest world of space, time and experience. In these terms, then, *The Literary Zodiac* is concerned more with astrology at a World of Thought level, *Astrology in Action* with the World of Senses.

The work comprises three main sections. An introduction, which includes a summary of the meanings of the astrological symbols as they manifest at the two levels described, and a discourse on chart synthesis. The second section looks at astrology at the individual level through 50 or more astrological profiles of famous men and women. These profiles demonstrate how complex personalities can very often be broken down and understood in terms of three or four major chart factors. In part three the focus changes to astrology at the collective level, with an emphasis on the meaning of the so-called modern planets Uranus, Neptune and Pluto. The chapter on Pluto additionally highlights the hereditary dimension of astrology, a largely untapped but potentially fruitful area of research. There is an addendum, which contains a further 14 astrological profiles plus an astrological cross-referencing index.

Biography and astrology.

In *The Literary Zodiac* I demonstrated that literature provides a valuable source of astrological insight. This is so because a novel, a poem or a play represents the deepest and most honest account a person can give of his or her essential self. In *Astrology in Action* I demonstrate a second valuable way of learning more about astrology, that is, the use of biography. Good biography represents a repository of thoughtful, insightful and (generally) objective observations regarding an individual's behaviour and character. Biography is often an account of a life realised. It translates the potential and possibility symbolised in a horoscope to the actuality of a life lived. Considering this is what interpretation essentially is, it is surprising that biographical study is not recommended more often than it is to students of astrology.

Astrology is learned through the conscientious study of many charts. There are no short-cuts or substitutes. This has often been said, but is no less true for it. The majority of astrologers, and particularly novices, do not have a burgeoning clientele. The supply of friends and acquaintances is soon exhausted so biographical study represents a good way of increasing both number and variety of charts. We learn by observation and feedback, by comparing the chart with the individual before us. In some respects face to face readings have an advantage over biography, for we are dealing with a person and not an abstraction of one. But there are many regards in which biography represents a better method of acquiring feedback. It is only a small minority of astrologers who enjoy on-going client relations, and it is not easy in my experience to learn much about a person in a one hour session. Even if they are forthcoming and self-aware they are not always honest. People, I find, are often too polite to tell you when you are wide of the mark in your interpretation.

Moreover, in a one-off session we only get a snapshot of a person. We get a certain side of a person at a certain point in his or her life. The various facets of a person's nature generally only become apparent over time and with familiarity. But biography, good biography, presents a panorama rather than a snapshot. It condenses the broad meaning of an individual life; it catalogues development and the different phases of a life; it presents a private self and a public self. It often provides a cross-section of opinions and impressions (and indeed it is true that an individual is experienced differently by different people). Importantly, biography is free from astrological bias. Biographers are not attempting to fit individuals into a preconceived mould and so we avoid the trap of self-perpetuating astrological misconceptions. Biography thus represents a useful tool for research, a way of discriminating between what is true and what false in contemporary astrological lore (and this remains a pressing task).

Biography provides a touchstone against which astrological *statements* — rather than astrological truths — can be tested. We must distinguish between the two. It is, for example, one thing to show and say that Neptune relates to music and the 12th house; another to say that musicians tend to have these factors emphasised in some way, and then to base a judgement on this tenet. It might be hoped that the one would follow from the other, but this is an assumption which may or may not be true. The statement is much easier to test empirically than the truth. In fact, based on a study of my own of a hundred or so Scottish musicians I would say that the second statement is not true. In this sample there is not a real emphasis on Neptune or the 12th house. However, this finding does not preclude the possibility that the first statement is true, that in some abstract way Neptune is related to music (and in such a way that precludes the possibility of empirical testing).

It should be said that if biography does tend to show up shortcomings in the contemporary astrological wisdom then it does on balance leave one with a deeper conviction of the potency of astrology. It is unusual to find cases where a life is not clearly described by the symbolism of the chart. We read about Sir Thomas Callender, the Scottish Industrialist, that 'his outstanding characteristics were his tremendous driving force and energy'[2] and are not surprised to learn that he had Sun conjunct Mars in Aries. Reading the following about James Clyde, a past Lord Justice General of Scotland, most astrologers will have no difficulty in guessing a predominant chart influence:

> He loved battle, and like a good fighter he was always prepared to take as good as he gave ... He was always the dominant figure in any gathering. His appearance, his manner, even his walk suggested, as was the fact, that he was endowed with an immense store of vitality and power.[3]

Most astrologers will have no difficulty here in recognising the Mars principle in action, and I think most would opt for Scorpio. And rightly so. In fact, his chart shows Sun, Mercury, Jupiter and Mars in Scorpio.

Such apposite quotes are not hard to find and, indeed, I list around 300 in connection with the individual profiles. I have attempted to avoid simply selecting quotes that seem to 'fit', and instead list statements that are very definite or precise in their tone, or which reflect in the biographer's opinion the salient and significant characteristics of the subject. Both the quotes above, for example, are quite specific, and in the first case we are informed that the trait described is a fundamental constituent of the subject's personality.

To sum up. I think we can do much to clarify some of the confusion in contemporary astrology only through detailed case study. Biography represents a valuable source of such case studies. I think consensus on meaning is more likely to come working with 'public' lives like this rather than the private lives of astrologers' clients (although these also have a value). I hope the astrological profiles presented in this book will impart a greater understanding of the astrological symbols.

The individuals profiled are well-known individuals, although I have avoided over-used examples. In some instances I believe the charts have not been published elsewhere, or at least are not widely known. In all cases those individuals selected exemplify astrological principles in a marked, sometimes vivid and unusual way. To some extent, however, choice has been limited by the availability of reliable birth time and informative biography.

Interpretation and synthesis.

There are many schools of thought regarding chart interpretation. There are a variety of systems and little agreement as to which is the best. The number of chart factors available to the practising astrologer has multiplied over the last twenty years or so; harmonics, fixed stars, midpoints, alternative zodiacs, nodes, parts, astronomic and geocentric points, asteroids. All have their champions. At the same time, it is probably true to say that the majority of astrologers still firmly base interpretations upon ten planets, twelve houses, twelve signs, and half a dozen major aspects. I class myself amongst these, for practical and theoretical reasons.

It is just not possible to take everything into account, and I have not the time to empirically test every new method that is proposed (and, yes, I must own to a strong streak of Earthy scepticism, and a disinclination to accept information on trust). My main reservation, however, is the belief that the proliferation of technique and chart factors in contemporary astrology is simply an outcrop of the Western way of looking at the world, a world-view that is essentially alien to the spirit of astrology. There seems to be the unspoken assumption that truth builds in an inductive way, in jigsaw puzzle fashion from the piecing together of facts, and the more pieces the more complete the picture. This is a very comforting philosophy for the novice with a stack of astrological 'cookbooks' or computer software at his or her disposal. But, as Swift pointed out three centuries ago, this Lilliputian piecemeal approach to truth is only half the matter.

The wisdom, and the interpretive power, of astrology reside in the depths of its symbols, and not in the particular way you care to arrange these. There is no meaning in methodology. If there were, then there would only be one astrology. As it is, we have cultural variations — Hindu, Chinese, etc — each of which seems to work for its own culture. A technique is two-dimensional, a symbol three. Symbols are protean, but this doesn't mean that they can be distorted or twisted to mean anything. They are very precise in their way, although this meaning has to be grasped intuitively, as a whole. Indeed, the art of astrological interpretation is being able to recognise the meaning of a symbol, that is, a sign or planet, as it manifests in many guises. Symbols can be peeled for levels of meaning and yield in proportion to the quality of the consciousness that contemplates them. They challenge us to grow in awareness, although too often in astrology this challenge is not taken up, and instead the easier course is followed, of fabricating something else at the same level of awareness. Thus do we get a two-dimensional proliferation of chart factors.

It may well be that a new methodology will evolve, one that can be seen to focus astrological meaning effectively and consistently. And one that belongs to the twentieth century West, for it is indeed a property of Truth that it has to be constantly redefined in terms of the times. However, none of this can come about until there is adequate understanding of the meanings of the fundamental symbols, the signs and planets. Until there is this understanding there is no way of even testing the efficacy of a new system, for however you care to juggle and arrange, at the end of the day you still have to interpret. I also believe that once the astrological symbols come to be more fully understood then it will become plain that there is not a need for all these new factors. The signs and planets, in the depths of their symbolism contain all human and collective life. My aim in *Astrology in Action* (and in *The Literary Zodiac*) is to contribute to an overall deeper grasp of astrological meaning, and both works should be approached with this in mind.

Prime factors.

It is my experience that a clear and fundamentally accurate picture of an individual can be drawn from a limited number of chart factors. Some astrologers employ a great arsenal, but I find that beyond a certain number diminishing returns soon set in, with each addition then tending to cloud and confuse rather than clarify.

The signs of the Sun, Moon and ascendant are generally the most important factors in a chart. In some cases a person will mirror all three equally but in other cases one or other will dominate. I don't think it is possible to tell simply looking at a chart which will be the case. Planets conjunct an angle (up to ten degrees either side) almost always constitute a major overtone of a person's life. There seems to be little difference which angle; it is the nature of the planet involved that is important. Likewise the meaning of any planet conjunct the Sun or Moon generally describes a significant part of an individual's make-up. Of lesser importance than these, though still contributing to the individual timbre of a life are certain planetary conjunctions, any close aspect to the Sun or Moon, planets involved in T-squares or grand trines, planets in their own sign, or stationary planets. The importance of the latter has probably been understated. I have often found it the case that the energy symbolised by a planet that is stationary is quite apparent in a person's make-up. However, it is an area where more research is needed.

I don't ignore houses, but experience shows me that in natal astrology at least they are not as valuable as the conventional wisdom suggests. Certainly they do not always work in the straightforward way that many texts suggest they do. I have examined the accurately timed charts of many vocational groups and have found, for example, that the religious profession do not have the 9th or 12th house especially emphasised; and creative people on balance do not have strong 5th houses. Again, such results do not show that houses are invalid; they simply cast doubt on some of the statements made about them. Houses do seem to me to have some validity but when studying biographical accounts of individuals their influence is not as *apparent* as the other factors I have listed. The real significance of the diurnal circle seems to lie in the angles themselves, and the planets highlighted thereby. However, where biographical description does seem to relate to traditional house interpretation I note it, and also whether by equal or by quadrant division. The evidence of this study is that the one can not be judged better than the other.

Transits and progressions.

Biography often isolates the significant times in a person's life and it is informative to examine the prevailing transits and progressions. Once more, we are faced with a choice of technique, and no real consensus as to which is the best. I limit myself to transits and secondary progressions. I have found a most reliable indicator to be the progressed angular relationship between Sun and Moon, the so called lunation cycle[4]. The time corresponding to a progressed new Moon is very often a critical phase in the life.

I think it is the experience of many astrologers that these dynamic techniques are not as reliable as once held. Sometimes there is nothing in a life to correspond to what is classed as significant planetary activity. Conversely, there are sometimes consequential developments, or major events, for which there is no appropriate celestial mirror. It may be that I err in my choice of available technique, but it may also be that the universe is not as regular as we would like it to be. I think as astrologers we must remain aware of another shortcoming of our scientific, Mercurial age: an overweening attitude that thinks it knows everything. The craft of astrology as much as rationalist science is a human invention and as such limited, imperfect and approximate. It is remarkable it works to the extent it does, but we should perhaps not insist on perfection.

An important point to remember when dealing with transits and progressions is that we are concerned with meaning*ful* rather than meaning*less* coincidence. Planetary patterns coincide with events all the time but there must be an essential concordance between the two. If Mars is involved in the pattern then the earthly event or development must be an essentially Martial one. Whether it is in human terms profound or trivial is not the point; it must simply be apt. This is what we mean by meaningful coincidence, and I provide many examples in parts 2 and 3 of this book. An example of meaningless coincidence is the following.

Tottenham Hotspur are a famous football team. They have won the English FA Cup more times than any other team. They first won it in 1901, a year when Saturn and Jupiter were conjunct in the sky. They next won it in 1921, again a year of a Saturn-Jupiter conjunction. The year 1941 the same conjunction again, but in the affairs of Man a world war, and no FA Cup competition. However, in the year of the next Saturn-Jupiter conjunction, 1961, Tottenham again won the cup. They won the following year also. About the middle of 1981 there was a Saturn-Jupiter conjunction. In May 1981 Tottenham won the FA Cup for the sixth time. They won it in 1982 also, when the two planets were not far separated. All in all this is a highly unlikely coincidence. In terms of correlation of planetary pattern and very specific earthly event it is one of the more impressive I have come across. At the same time I'm not convinced it's at all meaningful. It is perhaps in the same mould as those quirky tricks of chance that used to haunt Jung. I think the whole question of chance or randomness is not as sewn up as the statisticians would have us believe.

A note on birth times.

One encouraging trend in contemporary astrology is the increasing awareness of the need for reliable birth data. Astrology is based on the birth chart and a spurious birth time can not be compensated by even the astutest interpretation. Thanks to the laudable efforts of individuals in both America and Europe a substantial body of reliable birth data has been accumulated and this represents a great boon for all working astrologers.

In *Astrology in Action* I have endeavoured to use only what I believe to be accurate data, and in all cases I cite a source. The great majority of the data used in this book originates from official sources. I have drawn on the bodies of data collected by other workers, such as the Gauquelins, but just over half the times I have researched myself. In some cases this represents data hitherto unpublished (or at least not widely so). A valuable source of raw data for the British astrologer is Register House in Edinburgh. The recording of births, including the time, has been statutory since 1855. Copies of birth certificates of all those born in Scotland from this time are stored under one roof in the capital and, what is more, for a small fee, available for public scrutiny. I have used this facility regularly over the years and in all have retrieved the birth data of some 1200 individuals.

The fact that a time has been recorded does not guarantee its accuracy (and this applies to official and unofficial records). Not every culture has been as obsessed with measurement and precision as our own. Not so long ago a league was a standard measure of distance, this being about three miles or the distance a man could comfortably walk in an hour. Today we are much more abstract and define distance in terms of the wavelength of light and to the nearest nanometre. I'm not quite sure why. Likewise with time. It is generally true to say that we have become more meticulous and precise over the years. With pre-fifteenth century births there is often uncertainty regarding the year, let alone day or time. In the sixteenth century, in this country, royal births are being recorded although there is a tendency to state the time only to the nearest hour. We note that even in the nineteenth century in the civil records of Europe times are very often rounded to the hour.

In Scotland the times have become more precise with the years.

Times today are sometimes noted to the nearest minute. But this has not always been the case, at least this is what I have concluded from a study of my own of 700 recorded births between 1855 and 1964. Within any hour we would expect a more or less random distribution of birth times. There is no reason I can think of why births should congregate around the hour or half-hour. But this is what we tend to find. There are more times recorded on the hour or half-hour than would be expected. This is most noticeable the further back we go. By the early decades of this century a more random distribution is evident, suggesting that the times are at least being recorded more precisely. It tells us nothing about the accuracy of the information conveyed to the registrar.

However, we need not dismiss a chart because it has been rounded to a half-hour, so long as we bear in mind the degree of uncertainty. A chart based on a time rounded to half an hour is accurate to plus or minus fifteen minutes, which makes for an uncertainty in ascendant (in Scottish latitudes) of about two to three degrees for a slow rising sign, and nine degrees or so for a fast one like Aries. These are the maximum errors. There are one or two cases where the ascendant for the given time seems less appropriate than one for a few minutes earlier or later. Thomas Hardy seems more late Cancer than early Leo; Earl Mountbatten early Leo rather than late Cancer; Kenneth Grahame early Cancer rather than late Gemini; and Norman Mailer early Aries rather than late Pisces. However, in all cases I have gone by the given time and not attempted any rectification.

Signs and planets, the astrological building blocks.

The following section presents a summary of the meaning of the astrological symbols, the basic building blocks from which chart synthesis and interpretation must be constructed. It is only a summary. I refer the reader to *The Literary Zodiac* for a more detailed and reasoned exposition, and the profiles which follow in section two will flesh out the bare bones of the summary. Nor is the account here exhaustive but, rather, concentrates on those characteristics that are mentioned most frequently in biographical description. I do not include Uranus, Neptune or Pluto here for they are dealt with in more detail in section three. Each of the symbols, or principles, is dealt with at a 'World of Thought' and 'World of Senses' level.

To prevent repetition, a planet and the sign it rules are discussed under one heading, although distinction is made when necessary. It is widely acknowledged within the astrological fraternity that, for all intents and purposes, there is a fluid equivalence between certain of the parameters that constitute the astrological vocabulary. So that, for example, we can talk about a 'Mars' overtone in a chart when we wish to indicate that either the planet or the signs it rules are in some way accented. There are differences between a sign and a planet but from a practical point of view these differences seem to blur. This method of reducing a related sign, house and planet to a single principle is a valuable shorthand and one that facilitates chart synthesis. The example charts in this book will make it plain just how it works in practice.

Aries Mars Scorpio

World of Thought: Mars relates to the principle of focalisation in one form or another; to the idea of the individual as a focus of the life energy of the universe (and thus, a connection with birth, rebirth and Nature). Mars is a symbol of the organic lifeforce that withdraws into the earth in autumn (Scorpio) and reappears in spring (Aries).

Aries represents the awareness one *is,* rather than the knowledge of what or who one is. It is the urge to render or intensify consciousness by interaction of self with life, or with what is not the self. Particularly in Aries the world can be seen as something hostile, something to be conquered rather than adjusted to — although this is the real challenge facing Aries. Mars and both its signs equate to 'be-here-now' and existential philosophies, to the idea that we are alone in the universe and there is no superintending, divine providence.

Mars is the natural counter to Jupiterian excess. Mars symbolises applied justice. Mars by nature is assertive and selfish, given to authority and domination rather than compromise. It is embodied in the politics of the far Right, and in acerbic, war-like cultures like ancient Sparta.

At the abstract level Scorpio relates to the idea of regeneration, or initiation into a greater life. In another sense, the breaching of ego-barriers to bring about a sense of oneness with others (usually accompanied by an infusion of compassion). Scorpio has to learn that human welfare is more important than dogma or abstract theory. This sign also relates to the recognition of evil and darkness in human beings, and to the awareness that this has to be in some way embraced and redeemed rather than simply censured or legislated away.

World of senses: When Mars or its signs are manifesting in a character it is usually quite obvious; it is probably the most visible energy. There is often strong presence, intensity of being, magnetism. We find energy, vigour, incisiveness. There is great capacity for work and, particularly with Aries, marked ambition. In Scorpio the energy is more disciplined, and there is more tenacity and persistence. There is often a sharp and quick mind. There can often be a brusque or abrasive manner, a domineering or bullying side. Mars is disciplinarian by nature, both toward self and others. With Martial characters there can be insensitivity, or more broadly a difficulty in gauging their own impact on those around them. The urge for relationship is strong in both signs, but harmony doesn't come naturally. Mars is essentially selfish and tends to see others in terms of its own needs. Aries tends to bore easily, and seek fresh conquests.

With Aries particularly there is impatience and impetuosity, and a tendency to stir things up if they are a little dull. Mars is about action, about doing. In both signs there is a liking and capacity for dealing with crisis and emergency. Both thrive on challenge and the overcoming of it. There is courage with Mars and its signs, although in the case of Aries it is often the courage of ignorance. In both signs there can be an attraction to, or fascination with the seamier side of existence, with life in the raw.

Mars types are often independent, capable of going it alone or taking things on. Self-reliance is a marked trait, particularly in Scorpio. Both signs are autocratic, and more given to conflict than compromise. There is often self-assurance. In Scorpio there is often strong pride; sometimes aloofness and arrogance.

There is a certain naive quality about Mars, most evident in Aries. It tends to see things simply and can be unrealistic accordingly. This is linked to a championing side. Both signs have a taste for combat, but particularly when there is an injustice to redress. Aries sees things very black and white and generally is in no doubt as to who is the dragon and who St George.

With Scorpio, reticence is often marked. Taciturn rather than shy, there is generally a secretive quality, a reluctance to expose feelings, or to talk about things that really matter to them. This is in contrast to Aries. With this sign there is often a refreshingly frank and open nature.

Taurus
Venus
Libra

World of Thought: Venus represents a bridge between force and form. It exists in tandem with matter as a sort of patterning template. Venus orders by establishing right relationship. It creates cosmos from chaos, music from noise. Venus also relates to that power in the individual to form images that are representative of some spiritual or psychic state.

Venus is a symbol of what is termed The Fall, which should be thought of as a psychic experience rather than a historical event. It is the subliminal awareness of something perfect, some ideal way of life, that has been lost; the awareness that everyday existence is but a shadow of this. Venus symbolises the state of grace, or what some call God's love, that transforms the experience of the world as a base and fallen place into the experience of it as a place of harmony and beauty.

Taurus at an abstract level relates to the idea of Eden. That is, to the loss of innocence, the need to accept the existence of evil and a harsh world. It represents the need to relinquish the world of being and accept existence in the world of becoming. But then to work to regain what has been lost, to wrest something meaningful from the world of existence. Taurus symbolises, at the abstract level, the first stages of the life force seeking to manifest in individualised form. It has some relation to what Freud termed libido, the instinctive drive of an organism to grow and become itself.

Libra relates to collective values, to what are commonly called the mores, those beliefs-held-in-common that cement a society and constitute its morality, its sense of what is right and wrong, and good and proper. Venus and both its signs relate to things like ethics, attitudes and standards, the more transient and local aspects of morality. Life is dynamic; values need to change accordingly to reflect this, and some Librans find their lives' work in reinvesting society with new values.

Libra symbolises the desire to come together with others in some kind of greater harmony. It represents the transition from the individual to the social world, so there can be an almost exaggerated awareness of others, and of the consequences of individual action. Hence we have the concern with the 'right' way to live, that one's actions are in accord with propriety.

World of Senses: When Venus or either of its signs are strong in a chart we generally find charm, agreeableness and affability. Venus is associated with a kind of charisma, an attractive power that inspires liking (in contrast to Mars magnetism that inspires fear and respect rather than love). Venus equates to warmth and kindness (particularly the Taurus side), and with a mannered, refined, genteel quality. Libra particularly can be rather 'ivory tower', placing a high value on culture and aestheticism.

When Venus or either of its signs are marked there tends to be a streak of laziness, a tendency to procrastinate and, more in Libra, indecisiveness. There is often a difficulty in being firm. There is often a dislike of ugliness or unpleasantness — of disharmony — although Taurus is possessed of a stoic fortitude that enables the bearing of hard circumstances; chronic rather than acute courage. Taurus is a survivor.

Both signs can be moralistic, concerned with standards and attitudes. Venus, particularly in Libra, is a diplomatic influence, tactful and capable of finding the common ground amongst conflicting parties. It inclines to compromise and co-operation. Libra is an Air sign. It tends to tolerance, level-headedness, and calmness. It is detached and capable of appreciating another's point of view.

There is a sensual side to Venus, most evident in Taurus. There is sometimes indulgence here, but sometimes an urge to refine the desire nature. Taurus needs to learn the lessons of non-attachment, and to distinguish between lust and love. Guilt, sex and religion can sometimes run concurrent in Venus and its signs and the urge is felt to move along the spectrum of love from the carnal to the divine. Guilt can also arise in Libra from putting oneself first, or doing what one wants to do rather than what one ought to. Libra has a self-conscious side, and a marked awareness of how others react to its actions.

Taurus often has an affinity with the young and a capacity for educating. Sometimes, particularly with Taurean men, it is as if the child within remains alive, so we have a sort of boyish quality, an innocence, a reluctance to grow up, particularly at the emotional level; an unwillingness to face the challenge and responsibility of the adult world. Idealisation is often marked in the Venus signs, the yearning for, or belief in something perfect. Sometimes there is nostalgia. There is often good memory with Taurus, and in both the signs a facility with image. As far as any one planet relates to productive art, it is Venus.

Gemini Mercury Virgo

World of Thought: The Mercury principle relates to multiplicity. To the actualisation of some idea or abstract entity through myriad form (and thus to the biblical creation myth). Mercury symbolises what Eastern philosophy terms *maya*, the illusory surface of life with its ever-shifting, ever-changing forms, the visible manifestation of a more fundamental and timeless reality. Mercury stands for being transformed to becoming through interaction with space and time. It relates to the idea of development of potential in the sense of attainment of appropriate fate or destiny through the interaction of individual and life.

Mercury and both its signs relate to the visible, tangible forms of nature. They represent the divorce between life and mind, the reasoning mind that wins victories over nature and circumstances. They represent the capacity to adapt creatively to change. Virgo relates to the urge to control nature and life circumstance. It symbolises the Primitive's fear of smallness and insignificance, the sense of self surrounded by hostile and arbitrary forces over which it has no control. Virgo particularly symbolises fear of the unknown, and the related urge to reduce the unfamiliar to familiar terms. It is that part of human nature that seeks to make life predictable (through things like routine and habit). The unexpected can often throw the Mercury person, although it is just such circumstance that can provide the potential for growth. Virgo crises can often revolve about humility, to facing up to the fact that the small self's will is not paramount in the universe. Mercury must often learn to trust life.

Mercury and its signs symbolise the reductionist side of the human mind. It represents the discriminating capacity, the power to understand through the discernment of fine distinction between things. Mercury stands for the real over the ideal; fact rather than myth; pragmatism rather than dogmatism; the secular as opposed to the religious; the contemporary as opposed to the traditional; individualism rather than collectivism.

World of Senses: Both Mercury signs are flexible and adaptable, although it is Gemini that more naturally and obviously delights in change, variety and novelty. In Virgo there tends to be an instinctive aversion to the unfamiliar that needs to be overcome. Certainly those strong in Virgo can react strongly to interruptions to their routine.

Gemini is an extrovert influence, with an interest in people and the objects of the real world. It is an intellectual influence, one that holds great store by education. Both Mercury signs learn quickly and easily — provided the interest is aroused and sustained. Both can be bookish, with a tendency to parade knowledge. Reasonableness, common sense, level-headedness, tolerance and open-mindedness are qualities associated with Mercury and its signs. With Gemini there is often the spontaneous vitality we call sparkle. Mercury has its own sort of charm, perhaps more evident in Gemini. Gemini is friendly but cool, and can appear aloof and arrogant. In the creative sphere it is a very fertile sign.

Virgo is generally a shy, diffident, modest influence, and sometimes plagued by feelings of insignificance. It is a hard-working, diligent, behind-the-scenes sort of influence. Virgo by nature is abstemious and moderate. There is a need for order and regularity, sometimes an obsession with detail and trivia. Gemini's greatest failings are superficiality, fickleness and deviousness. Boredom is the bane of both Mercury signs; the struggle to fill the vacancies of attention. Movement is one way of lessening the burden of time, and Gemini particularly has a restless nature.

Both signs can be rather sceptical and not given to looking beyond the obvious. Gemini is sometimes troubled by a sense of existential emptiness, there being an inability to perceive meaning in the confusing complexity of the world. The more conscious Gemini seeks to establish some underlying principle that will unify the disparate parts. Gemini must also learn commitment to experience and a definite course of action, and that it can not keep options open for ever. It must learn also to connect with the moment rather than leap ahead to the next. Virgo, if it is not to suffer a sense of ennui must seek meaning beyond some material vein. It must also come to terms with the urge to rigidly control life.

In both Mercury-ruled signs the urge to communicate in some way is strong, and in Gemini we have a very voluble influence.

Cancer
Moon

World of Thought: At a fundamental level the Moon stands for what is commonly called personality, that essential quality that distinguishes one individual from the next. The Moon represents that part of us where images are formed. Our Lunar faculty gathers in information and data and focuses it into readable images. It creates a picture of the world unique for an individual. It symbolises the associative faculty. The Moon represents the self in a more immediate, more tangible sense than the Sun. It symbolises the instinctive processes that constitute biological life. It represents a fluid self, one that is shaped and modified by interaction with the environment. It's that self which changes from day to day, and situation to situation. It is a vehicle for the Solar impulse, an interface between the spirit and the matter principles.

Cancer at a fundamental level relates to that urge in an individual to find a place, something that will give a fluid nature identity and definition. It is to do with outgrowing the past, rather than attachment to it. It relates to enlarging or upgrading the self so that the purposeful Solar impulse may express through it more fully (and we are reminded that the Moon is a very ancient symbol of rebirth or regeneration).

World of Senses: When Cancer or the Moon are strong influences in a chart there is often a marked subjective nature, a tendency to relate everything to one's own experience, with a corresponding difficulty in obtaining a detached, objective view. There is often a marked maternal/paternalism, a warm, caring, kind, sympathetic nature, although this is often hidden behind a tough, or dour exterior. For the human qualities to emerge there needs to be familiar and congenial surrounds, and a sense of trust in the company. In other words, Cancer people must feel relaxed and secure before they can really be themselves. There can be a marked sensitivity to atmosphere. Cancer people like their own space. The urge for privacy can be strong, with a need for time to adjust mood to outsiders.

When Cancer is strong there is often hypersensitivity, particularly to any sort of criticism or rejection. There is often a defensive prickliness about those strong in Lunar influences. There is a tendency to remember wounds and harbour grudges. There can be a marked shyness and reticence, a tendency indeed to withdraw into a shell, if an individual does not feel safe in his or her surrounds. Equally, it seems, there can be an aggressive response to insecurity. Cancer is a very responsive influence. It's the child in us that never really dies, though finds more subtle ways to express. It responds to friendliness or affection. It's the insecurity that needs to be fed by reassurance and attention. Cancer can be a selfish and self-centred influence. It can get rather huffy if things are not to its liking, withdrawing in fits of pique and resentfulness. Like a child, it can be very demanding with regard to its own needs.

Another manifestation of the impressionable nature is a strong memory. The past can remain very much alive within the Lunar person, so that, for example, current response can be rooted in precedent. The instinctive, often illogical response to a circumstance is a sort of after-taste of a past experience similar in essence which comes up uninvited in response to certain triggers.

The sense of loneliness, of being an outsider can be strong in Cancer. There is the urge to belong and to feel accepted. There is often patriotism. It can be quirky and individual, a 'character'. It likes to be as it is without external constraint. It likes to please itself. It is one of the more humorous influences of the zodiac. Cancer is a moody, changeable influence, although there can be persistence and tenacity in pursuing own ends.

Leo
Sun

World of Thought: Leo and Sun relate to purposeful as opposed to conditioned existence. They symbolise the recognition that one should not dissipate freedom in play ('amusements and pleasures') but rather use it to discover purpose and pursue it. Leo and Sun symbolise that pressure, felt by some, not by others, to find or make a meaning of life. They represent also the urge (rather than the ability) to create, to externalise a very basic sense of self, for it is such creative acts that give Life an awareness of itself. The Sun's connection with creativity extends to making a creative pattern of our life. The Sun sign meaning is very often apparent in the pattern of a life taken as a whole (although at the same time the Sun sign also equates to more immediate character traits).

Leo relates to the evolutionary urge, and to the idea of levels of being. The challenge in Leo is to grow in self-awareness, to accept the notion that there is no upward limit to consciousness. And to make conscious the unconscious (in the sense of the raw material of consciousness). Leo and Sun symbolise the pressure of life to spiritualise itself, and the idea of the individual as the spearhead of this evolutionary process.

Leo and Sun relate to what Jung called archetypes, timeless patterns that mould life, imbuing it with unique characteristics and potential. Particularly they seem to relate to racial archetypes, so that Solar individuals are often capable of embodying what is unique about a race, and that which represents its highest potential.

World of Senses: Like Cancer, Leo is a very individual sign, subjective and aware of its own uniqueness. It can be proud, self-centred, elitist, arrogant and autocratic. Solar types often succeed through force of personality, through who they are, rather than what they do. There is a high opinion of the self, although at the same time there is sensitivity to the adulation or criticism of the crowd. There is often a natural affinity with children. Like Cancer, Leo men can be paternalistic, though more father-teacher than father-protector.

Being a Fire sign, Leo has a noble, dignified, high-minded side. Those strong in Leo are often able to embody in their being all that seems admirable about human nature. Solar types are often generous in act and spirit, and appalled by baseness, meanness, and pettiness. There can be a marked *joie de vivre* about the sign, a sort of intoxication with life and with its own felicity. There is the tendency to see the good side in everyone, to be encouraging, and to work towards bringing out the best in others. This is the positive side of the sign and one that does indeed bring the love and admiration of the crowd. Often enough Leo types are lionised.

Leo is romantic in both the narrow and broad sense of the word. There can be a dramatic larger-than-life quality about the individual, or perhaps just a tendency to view life in this way. There is a gregarious, fun-loving, sociable side. The Sun and Leo generally represent a wilful, determined, single-minded nature. With age there sometimes comes what is called gravitas, a very visible impression of dignity and authority. Leo more than Cancer seems to be in love with the past. There can be chauvinism in the original sense of the word — an unreasoning and fervid nationalism — but also in the more common sense of the word. Because the Sun has a relation to what might be called archetypal maleness, there is often in Leo men the ingrained assumption that the female of the species is inferior (particularly with regard to quality of mind). Perhaps this is faintly reflected in the fact that we never see a lioness as a symbol of this sign; always the maned male.

Sagittarius Jupiter Pisces

World of Thought: Jupiter relates to the principle of expansion. It represents the capacity to perceive the possibilities inherent in anything and to express these to the full (Mercury providing the forms that allow the possibility to be realised). Jupiter symbolises the ideational spirit, where the ultimate reality is perceived as something beyond appearances. Cultures that embody this spirit, such as those of the East, are characterised by stasis, quiescence, certitude, obscurantism and dogma. Linked to this is Jupiter's relation to absolutism.

Jupiter is a social planet, relating to collectivism and to phenomena created by this. It symbolises syncretism, the merging of separate cultures and identities. It stands for universalism, particularly the creation of one law or one belief system. Jupiter symbolises faith in the broad sense, and religion as a collective phenomenon. The Jupiter principle does not, as is commonly supposed, relate to freedom, but to obedience and subservience to what is perceived as a higher authority — some religious, political or moral principle. However, it can be argued that this surrender in itself represents a type of freedom, albeit different from the contemporary Western concept of freedom. In the same way, it can be argued that the Western (Mercurial) concept of freedom, of thought and speech, the freedom to be different, is itself illusory and irrelevant.

Sagittarius is a dual sign, relating to the human-animal dichotomy in human nature. In this sign the awareness is strong that man is a mixture of the base and the sublime. The lesson associated with Sagittarius is that one must not be prey to passion, but must put trust in Reason, that is in man's higher, moral or spiritual nature. Pisces is the last sign of the zodiac and its essential meaning centres on the idea of coming to terms with one cycle in preparation for another. It is a sign that may be understood in terms of a seeding process. A meaning must be condensed from the past to be carried forward to the future (something of the twin-fish symbolism here). Pisces is a sign that must learn to find its own moral centre in a universe of flux; make itself stronger than the cultural forces of one sort or another that bear upon it.

World of Senses: There can be breadth of thought or vision in both signs. Equally, both are poor on discrimination, not able to readily adjust to individual differences and circumstances. Sagittarius particularly can be uncompromising and inflexible. Jupiter and its signs are intuitive in that they can see the potential in an idea before it has unfolded, and have faith enough to bring it to reality. Though equally, people with these influences accented are full of impractical big ideas and grandiose schemes.

Both signs are given to mood swings, and Pisces in particular has a tendency to emotional extreme. Pisces can be self-deprecating, self-pitying, or a self-denying martyr. But it is also compassionate, with an instinctive empathy with outcasts and underdogs. It is a sign that invariably forgives. There can be a shy, passive, retiring nature. It values solitude more than any other sign. There can be torpor, lethargy, sometimes a sort of paralysis of the will.

Sagittarius is probably the most forthright influence of the zodiac, and the most dogmatic and didactic. It can be moralistic and self-righteous. There is a very upright, high-minded side to the sign, and a striving to be above baseness and to live according to the dictates of a conscience. In both signs there is a need for something other than the mundane working world, something more exciting, elevated, heroic, adventurous, glamorous, or refined, and so an attraction to those spheres that embody these things (or, more generally, to where the boundary between reality and fantasy is blurred).

The escapist tendency is strong in Pisces. It will often look ahead to a brighter future and condition life by the hope of this. Jupiter and both its signs stand for optimism, or equally just wishful thinking. Deception is one facet of the Jupiter principle and it is more evident in Pisces. There is the tendency and capacity to confuse and dissemble. Sagittarius is an essentially honest influence although the tendency here is to self-deception and delusions of grandeur. There can be a tendency to inflate the ego and imagine oneself greater or more glamorous than one really is.

Jupiter and its signs have a flair for language. They are stimulated by travel and foreign places, although this aspect has been somewhat over-stated in the past. A strong Jupiter influence usually imparts spirit or enthusiasm in manner, or what is sometimes called a passionate nature. There can be a jovial, buoyant side. Sagittarius makes for a good raconteur, knowing what to keep as fact and what to exaggerate and embroider. Extravagance can be marked in both signs, with a tendency to live beyond the means. Both can be generous and philanthropic. There can be a tendency to take on too much, and not be aware of limitations. Jupiter and its signs can expect too much of others, and the world of them.

Capricorn
Saturn
Aquarius

World of Thought: Saturn as a principle stands for the difference between inner and outer form; between public and private. It stands for the principle of organisation at whatever level. Saturn relates to state power and collectivism in its positive and negative aspects. To the order that comes through trammelling wilderness and instinctual savagery with laws, roads and civilisation in general. It symbolises the cosmopolitan benefits that result from civilisation. On the negative side Saturn stands for the despoiling of the natural world by the advance of civilisation. It relates to uniformity, conformity, and the diminution of the individual to nothing in the face of vast systems (state or cosmic). Saturn symbolises a fear of vastness, and of the untamed. It is a symbol of Impersonality.

Saturn, and particularly Earthy Capricorn stands for instinct held in check. But it also stands for the momentary release of this as a kind of safety valve. This can be on a vast and horrific scale such as occurred following the lifting of British rule from India, or on a more trivial level such as regularly occurs on Saturday (*Saturn's Day*) night the civilised world over, when the discipline and duty of the working week are relaxed and vent given to the lusty, exuberant, and sometimes violent side of human nature. Saturn relates to those nature forces that are symbolised by deities such as Pan and Dionysos.

Saturn relates to all processes of culmination and to the idea of turnabout. It relates to law and limitation in the Taoistic sense: that point where a given development can go no further without beginning to change into its opposite.

Aquarius relates to the idea of the evolution of the mass, that is, to the lessening of the burden of material demands so that on a collective level human potential can be expressed more fully. Aquarius must effect a balance between force and form. At the fundamental level the function of Aquarius is to vitalise society with new creative impulse. Revolution is sometimes essential to effect this, but more usually an equilibrium between individual and collective is established, and new vision infused through the processes of gradual improvement.

World of Senses: Strong Saturn in a chart often concurs with a down-to-earth, hard-headed shrewdness. With Saturn and both its signs there is often the capacity to organise and administer; to think big and sacrifice the personal and immediate for long-term goals. Saturn is a dutiful influence and Capricorn particularly is willing and able to shoulder responsibility.

With Saturn and Capricorn there is usually patience and

perseverance. There is a tendency toward slow development. People with strong Capricorn often come into their own as they age. Aquarius, on the other hand, inclines to precocity, likely through the influence of co-ruling Uranus. There is often a self-conscious and suspicious nature where Saturn is concerned, and a certain sober quality also. But often Capricorn will develop a polished social mask and a capacity to be at ease in the public world. Aquarius is decidedly gregarious, with a marked sociable and clubable nature. Yet Saturn also imparts coolness; neither of its signs is particularly at home in the world of feeling. Aquarius is a notably friendly sign, but it tends toward aloof detachment at the same time, as if it is more into the idea of friendship, rather than individual friends. In both signs there is a great loyalty when it comes to friends. Aquarius is humane, universal and democratic by nature. It is an intellectual influence, and there can be a strong urge to teach and enlighten others.

The impersonality of Saturn, particularly when Capricorn is strong, can lead to callousness or even ruthlessness. It is cold-hearted in this sense. Ambition is generally very marked with Saturn and Capricorn. There can be the determination to achieve, to be someone or something. Integrity is often a marked characteristic of Saturn and both its signs. Capricorn is not the conservative influence it is often made out to be, nor Aquarius the radical. A common manifestation of Aquarius is differentness within a peer group — a need to embrace both individuality and conformity. The radical does, however, seem to be more marked among women.

References:
1. Calvin Hall and Gardner Lindzey, *Theories of Personality*, John Willey & Sons.
2. *Dictionary of Business Biography* vol 1, Butterworth & Co.
3. *Dictionary of National Biography 1941-50*, Oxford Univ Press.
4. See, for example, Dane Rudhyar, *The Lunation Cycle*, Shambhala.

Part 2

Astrology in action at the individual level

53 astrological profiles

There is no general agreement as to the best way of presenting a chart. I feel clarity is of major importance, and so adopt a minimalist approach. In my view, too many lines, circles, glyphs and characters tend to detract from the important features of the chart.

For a number of reasons I have not drawn in house divisions. In the first place this means opting for one particular system, and to do this offends at least one half of the astrological fraternity. It makes sense to present a chart in a way that reflects one's own emphasis in interpretation. For those who attach most importance to house positions it is perfectly in order to draw charts that show these at a glance. However, as I noted in the introduction, I put more emphasis on aspects, angularity and signs than on houses and prefer a chart that highlights these. The angles of the chart are very important and these are always included. Readers can themselves, if they wish, draw in the divisions of the house system they personally favour.

Woody Allen

Comedian, film actor/writer/director.

Born: Allen Stewart Konigsberg, 1 December 1935, 22.55 EST, New
York 40N51 73W54.

Source: Birth certificate (from AA/Lois Rodden 'Data News No 11')

Something like 90% of the population have a sense of humour. Most
people like to consider themselves amusing, but when it comes to it
relatively few people have the ability to intentionally and consistently
make people laugh. Woody Allen, however, is one who does.

I don't believe we can identify a comedian from a birth-chart.
However, I think certain astrological factors are more related to
humour than others. Jupiter, Moon, and their signs are very
commonly accented in those regarded as humorous. Gemini also has
its humour, characteristically quick, sparkling and punning. Indeed,
the whole phenomenon of humour can be fruitfully explored using
the astrological vocabulary. Suffice to say here that what often
underlies Jupiterian wit is the capacity to focus beyond the obvious
and immediate. Jupiterians tell good stories because they know how to
exaggerate, when to invent, and when to be factual. Some Jupiterians
make their life a story, and the result isn't necessarily funny. Events
very often didn't happen in the way a Jupiterian recounts them, to the
extent that we are sometimes left wondering if they are talking about
the same event that we witnessed. To extract the humour from life it is
often necessary to fictionalise, hypothesise, elaborate, and so long as
the result makes us laugh we excuse the deception.

What also often characterises Sagittarian humour is its mocking
quality. They are society's jesters, lampooning the absurdities of the
times and (particularly) deflating its pretensions. Mark Twain was one
Sagittarian who did this, Woody Allen is another. We note a strong
Jupiterian overtone to the chart, with Sun, Mercury and Jupiter all
conjunct in Sagittarius. We note also a Virgo ascendant, and this
symbolises a second side of his comic persona: the insignificant,
anxious, hypochondriac, ill-at-ease and at odds with the complexity of
the modern world (a common enough figment in Virgoan literature).
In his early roles he consciously cast himself as the inept fool-figure,
and audiences were pleased to project their own foibles and anxieties
on to him.

Woody Allen is a somewhat reclusive and private individual. He has
the retiring, modest nature associated with Virgo, and some of the
fastidiousness also. One biography talks of 'anhedonia', an inability to
enjoy pleasure, but with Virgo strong it is likely the case that he finds
more pleasure in productive work than in conventional leisure
activities. He is self-disciplined and hard working. His films mark an
ongoing process of improvement, and he is regarded as a self-taught

master of his medium (again, very Virgoan). He is often labelled 'cerebral' or 'intellectual', and seems to be a man looking for a philosophy to live by. He is selective regarding friends, but very loyal to those so counted. Neptune is strong in the chart, in the first house, and this is a planet often accented in the charts of those drawn to the world of films (for reasons we will discuss in a later chapter).

He does not fit in with the traditional view of Sagittarius as a great traveller. On the contrary, there is nowhere he would rather be than his home town of New York. With Moon in Aquarius he is comfortable in a cosmopolitan environment, and indeed, seems to have something of a phobia regarding the countryside. Nor does he demonstrate the ebullient nature of Jupiter. Once more, just the opposite: in television interviews he is seen to be a rather timid, cautious, serious, even melancholic individual. Plainly the Saturn overtone of the chart (the planet conjunct the descendant, and Moon in Aquarius), and the Virgo ascendant hold the balance here. At the same time, these also constitute a stabilising element, a necessary counterweight to the strong Fire of the chart. He has achieved results and not fallen prey to the Jupiterian failings of extravagance and over-ambition. He works on a very modest scale and with realistic aims.

Despite no obvious physical advantages, he has proved attractive to women. Venus in Libra closely trine the Moon suggests an appeal to the opposite sex that goes beyond fame. He seems to have an affinity for Saturnian mates. Two women he has enjoyed serious relationships with are Mia Farrow and Diane Keaton. The charts of both are given in *The Gauquelin Book of American Charts*. The first shows Sun in Aquarius, Mars in Capricorn, and Moon in Capricorn opposing Saturn; the second shows Sun in Capricorn opposite Saturn, and Moon in Aquarius. His taste in women is perhaps a reflection of Saturn conjunct his 7th house cusp, and his own Aquarian Moon.

The film he regards as his best is *The Purple Rose of Cairo*. It is a film which doesn't deal with narrow autobiographical aims, or consciously strive for laughs. Rather, it is one that explores the interplay between reality and fantasy — a common Sagittarian theme in literature.

Polite and mild-mannered.[1]

Woody is very private, very reserved, excruciatingly — at times maddeningly — controlled.[2]

His insatiable appetite for work.[3]

The thought of vanishing into a disembodied presence, free to roam at will without interference or the need to communicate appeals to him enormously ... tendency to ethereal remoteness.[3]

Sources/references:
I. Myles Palmer, *Woody Allen,* Proteus.
2. Ralph Rosenblum, cited in above.
3. Gerald McKnight, *Woody Allen: Joking Aside*, W.H. Allen.
4. Robert Benayoun, *Woody Allen*, Pavilion Books.

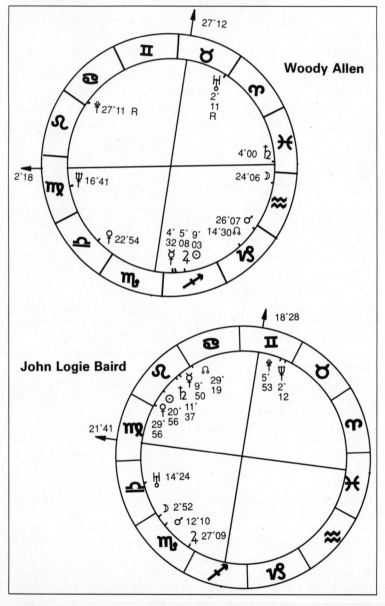

John Logie Baird

Co-inventor of television.

Born:13 August 1888, 08.00 GMT, Helensburgh 56N00 4W44.

Source: Birth certificate.

Like many modern inventions, television came into existence as the result of the work of a number of people. However, most agree that it was Baird who on 2 October 1925 gave the first demonstration of television by electrically transmitting moving pictures in half-tones. Also to his credit are a number of other notable firsts in this field: the first transatlantic transmission; the first colour transmission; the first demonstration of ultrashort wave transmission. So it is with some justification that he is sometimes regarded as the father of television. Baird's achievement becomes the more impressive when one appreciates the conditions under which he laboured. He had no financial and technical backing from university or large corporations. Instead he worked alone in an attic in considerable poverty and discomfort. His apparatus was makeshift, consisting in part of bicycle bits and a hat-box. What he did have was ingenuity, patience and dedication.

There is not a great deal of description available regarding his immediate character. Such as there is emphasises his energetic, hardworking side, poor health, and a certain modesty and phlegmatic calm. This seems to relate to the Virgo ascendant more than anything, with Moon conjunct Mars in Scorpio adding to his energy and single-mindedness. Broadly speaking his life was one of penury, hardship and frustration. This is suggestive of the strong Saturn (conjunct Sun and Mercury, and square Mars). He had many ideas but his inventiveness was not matched by acumen. He remained poor for much of his life, despite the importance of his invention. Perhaps, on a straightforward level of interpretation, his penury is a reflection of an 'afflicted' 2nd house Moon. The Leo Sun mirrors the fact that he demonstrated the value and worth of the individual in an area dominated by organisations (and in this regard he is similar to other Leos whose charts appear later in this section). A strong 11th house and a first house Uranus are also traditional indicators of inventiveness.

His first demonstration of television was marked by a progressed full Moon (with the Sun sextile Jupiter). Transiting Neptune conjuncted his natal Sun in the summer of 1925, when his work was coming to fruition. This is a planet that seems to have a connection with the phenomenon of television (see later chapter). About August 1922 he had a complete mental and nervous breakdown. This traumatic event was marked by the progressed Moon opposed to Saturn, and progressed Venus and Mercury sextile Saturn. The symbolism is apt here for this breakdown altered his life's path, putting an end to his trivial business pursuits and forcing him to concentrate on a greater and more fulfilling destiny.

A spare but agile frame full of nervous energy. His head was crowned with a most amazing shock of tangled light-brown hair.[1]

The frankness, the modesty (of his character).[2]

Amazing capacity for hard work.[1]

His activities in the commercial world form an amazing record of persistent enterprise and tenacity of will in the face of the vital handicap of ill-health ... Time and time again his unquenched pioneering spirit plunged him whole-heartedly into some new line of business ... Time and time again fate intervened in the form of recurrent illness and swung back the pendulum of his career to the starting point once more.[1]

Sources/references:
1. Ronald F. Tiltman, *Baird of Television: the Life Story of John Logie Baird*, Seeley Service.
2. Ian Gordon, *Famous Scottish Lives*, Odhams Books.

J.M. Barrie.

Dramatist. Inventor of Peter Pan.

Born: 9 May 1860, 06.30 LT, Kirriemuir 56N42, 3W0.
Source: Birth certificate.

J.M. Barrie was a successful dramatist in his day, and was duly honoured and remunerated by his peers. Much of his writing has proved ephemeral, but in the character Peter Pan he created one of those rare imaginative figments that lodge in the collective consciousness. It continues to captivate, particularly children.

Peter Pan is a boy who refuses to grow up, that is, to relinquish childhood. There are other Barrie characters in the same mould, notably Mary Rose in the play of the same name (his second most popular work, still performed today). Both characters are able to move back and forth with seeming ease between normal reality and a fantasy world, and this facility is commonly focused upon by Taurean writers. It reflects the idea of Venus as a bridge between the ideal and the reality, and as a symbol of that borderline where the invisible is made fleetingly and tantalisingly visible. What these characters yearn for is the *state of* childhood, to be as little children, as it were. Part of this state is security, the presence of a mother, who protects from a hostile and unfamiliar world, and who reassures when doubts, worries and sensitive moods arise — an essentially Lunar facet. The other major quality of the state of childhood is the innocent and untarnished view that doesn't know sin or evil, and which still countenances fantasy and magic (a Venus/Taurean facet).

Barrie's characters are simply a reflection of his own inner nature, and it is simple enough to draw parallels between his life and his art. And also to see the astrological mirrors of it: this is a strongly Venusian chart, with the Sun in Taurus and Venus conjunct the ascendant, and a strongly Lunar chart, with Cancer rising and Moon conjunct the descendant. In some sense Barrie was a person who didn't put childish things behind him. He had a powerful mother fixation, and one consequence of this was that his own capacity to deal confidently with immediate surroundings remained underdeveloped. His Lunar nature was, as it were, still projected onto his mother. He was a very shy person, almost a hermit in later life. Even amongst friends, in private, he tended to withdraw into his own inner world, and sit wrapped in a sad sort of silence. Yet he was very confident and adequate to the situation in some ways. The sign position of the Moon provides a clue here. It is placed in Capricorn. Although this is traditionally regarded as the sign of its detriment, this doesn't mean that the Moon is weak and inoperative. As we will see in other cases, it means that the Lunar energy is going to function best in a public or impersonal sphere. So it was with Barrie; he was successful in his career. When it came to pursuing his vocation, there was a good deal of energy and initiative (and we note that Mars is also placed in Capricorn). He started life as a journalist, and moved to London to further his ambitions. He worked very hard, producing some 800 articles in two years. He earned a lot of money from writing of one sort or another, and when he died was able to leave £173,000 in his will.

Another consequence of his mother fixation was an inability to relate to women in a mature way. He married, but it seems that the marriage was not consummated. Venus and Taurus relate to the idea of sublimation. We can see this expressed through the artist or craftsman who transmutes formless raw material into something beautiful, meaningful, or useful. We also see it expressed in the natural world in the way a plant transmutes the base matter of soil into a flower, according to a specific seed pattern. In the same way, Venus and its signs relate to sublimation, the urge to transform carnal passion into a more refined form of love. It seems that for Barrie sex came to be associated with guilt and shame. For him women were not flesh and blood, but something to be worshipped and idealised. His image of women is embodied in characters like Mary Rose, and Wendy in *Peter Pan* — naive, sexless innocents.

The idea for *Peter Pan* came sometime at the end of 1901, early 1902. We note a progressed new Moon at this time, conjunct Venus. The play was first produced 27 December 1904 (transiting Saturn on MC). He was married 9 July 1894. His mother died 3 September 1895. In July 1909 he discovered his wife's infidelity, and the Neptune transits of the time seem apt here: transiting Neptune sextile Sun; transiting Mars conjunct Neptune. Saturn by transit squared Mars, while Uranus conjuncted it. They were divorced 13 October 1909. He was awarded The Order of Merit 1 January 1922, a rare honour for a writer. He died 19 June 1937.

... his personality was a fruitful blend of ruthlessness and vulnerability.[2]

(Regarding his mother). Consciously as his mother, unconsciously as the source of inspiration, she moulded his life and his work. From the time he was a small boy he idealised and all but worshipped her. She was the centre of his universe.[1]

There is no evidence that any woman had ever excited him in the way other men were excited by attractive women. His worship of them did not go deeper than admiration for their beauty.[3]

It is not difficult to understand why he still flinched away from any full-blooded approach to women. Margaret Ogilvy (his mother) had put her thumb mark on him in his most impressionable years, and subconsciously he still accepted her appalling puritanical attitude to a man's relations with his wife ... It is probable that the only way he could resolve the complexes which this attitude set up was by sublimating his natural desires — turning them into a kind of romantic worship.[3]

Sources/references:
1. W.A. Darlington, *J.M. Barrie*, Blackie & Son.
2. Clifford Hanley, *The Scots*, David & Charles.
3. Janet Dunbar, *J.M. Barrie, the Man Behind the Image*, Collins.

Charles Baudelaire.
Poet.
Born: 9 April 1821, 15.00 LT, Paris, 48N50 2E21.
Source: Birth records (Gauquelin).

Baudelaire's contradictory and complex character is described with great perceptiveness and considerable detail in the biography cited below. It is likewise an unusual chart, with seven planets contained within twenty-two degrees of zodiacal longitude in the 7th and 8th houses. This gives rise to a number of conjunctions which, translated, give us an insight into the man's nature. It is the case also that some of these can be interpreted along straightforward and traditional lines.

For example, the Sun/Saturn conjunction in the 8th house applied with keyword simplicity: delays and frustration in matters of wills or legacies. Baudelaire was left a considerable sum of money in his father's will, which he set about spending, extravagantly, once it was in his possession. Alarmed by this, his stepfather instigated legal

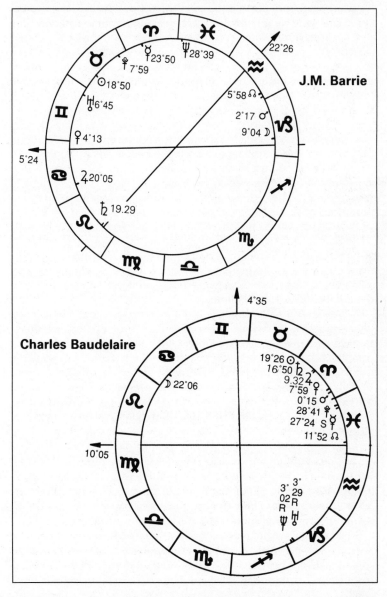

J.M. Barrie

Charles Baudelaire

proceedings. The court judged that Baudelaire was not capable of running his own affairs. The legacy was put into the hands of a lawyer, who fed it out in small regular amounts. This took place in July 1844, and marked the turning point in Baudelaire's life, as the significant transits and progressions leading up to the event suggest — transiting Pluto conjunct Sun, and a progressed new Moon (in the latter part of 1843). The court judgement meant in effect that for the rest of his life debt and poverty were a constant burden (and his art suffered accordingly). Similarly, a marked change in his character can be traced to this development. There grew in him a deep sense of humiliation, resentment and bitterness at having his independence restricted in this way by his elders. He could do nothing about the situation, save boil in impotent rage. Self-sufficiency and self-determination are generally very important for Aries' development and wellbeing, so it must have been particularly galling for Baudelaire to be frustrated in this manner. The Pluto/Mars conjunction seems an apt mirror of it. There was a Scorpionic quality to it: the means to his independence and freedom to create was so close at hand, and yet forever out of reach. Being the time of a major Pluto transit, a planet that moves in mysterious ways, we can only opine that in some way the frustration of will was necessary for his development as a poet.

The Sun-Saturn conjunction also manifested as a strong ambition. He pursued literary fame. It was important to him, not only to succeed, but to be seen to (particularly by his mother). Baudelaire is now accounted one of the greatest of poets, and yet he received little recognition in his own lifetime.

The Jupiter/Mars/Venus suggests his extravagant nature, which was fuelled by a love of luxury. It also mirrors part of a complex attitude towards women. On the one hand they were for him objects of worship and inspiration. On the other hand, for much of his adult life he had an intermittent relationship with an 'unrespectable' mulatto woman, Jeanne Duval. It was a Scorpionic sort of affair, likely reflected in the Mars/Pluto/Venus conjunction. Through her he experienced great heights and great depths; disgust and shame, yet great emotional intensity. It seems that she was the only person capable of generating the intense passion from which sprang his best poetry. The Venus/Mars conjunction is also suggestive of the perverse habit he had of antagonising those he most wanted to please. His was the general Aries failing of not being able to gauge accurately the impact he had on those about him. At times he was offensive and provocative, and then surprised and hurt when ostracised for this.

As a boy and young man he embodied much of the overt Fiery nature of Aries; he was spirited, impatient, impetuous and volatile. As he aged, however, he became disillusioned, bitter, and melancholy. Despite a Virgo ascendant his Earth nature was not strong. His ideas and aspirations always ran ahead of his ability to realise them. He struggled to meet the demands of everyday, and otherwise had difficulty coming to terms with the demands of the body. His Virgo ascendant did emerge in other ways, however, such as a marked fastidiousness with his appearance, and also with regard to his work. He was very self-critical, ever refining his writing, even on the compositor's slab.

Despite his Martial qualities, his hot temper, his provocative nature, he was accounted by most a timid, shy person, and very gentle, particularly with women. This is in keeping with a Virgo ascendant, Cancer Moon combination. He was very close to his mother, and often turned to her for help. He was a sensitive person, and one who was poignantly aware of the solitariness of the human condition. All in all he was a man made to suffer for the mistakes of youth. But above all he was a man who nurtured his spirit. His Fire burns brightly today, a century and more after his death.

Temperamentally he was incapable of living without the society of women ... He found it necessary for his spiritual wellbeing. Merely by their presence they inspired him.

To hide his distress he built up amongst his friends the reputation of a man who hated love and despised women, who was sufficient to himself. This personality, which he deliberately forged for himself, became a steel armour riveted to his body, a mask clamped to his face ... he was solitary and alone, a shrinking figure inside his glorious shining armour.

(For Baudelaire) Beauty was the flame of the fire, the radiance of the energy, generated by the spiritual shock which the artist received when he was moved.

... a man of great vulnerability. Few have been as hypersensitive as he ... this sensitive shyness was hidden beneath a sophisticated and polished manner and few people guessed its existence.

Except in the days of his rebellious youth, the most constant of Baudelaire's preoccupations was a quest for spiritual values, a hunger and thirst for spiritual food.

Baudelaire had been accustomed , whenever he was in trouble, to turn to his mother for help ... even in his pride of independence, he sought her out ... like a child in search of protection against a harsh world.

Source/reference:
1. Enid Starkie, *Baudelaire*, Penguin.

Chay Blyth.

Adventurer. Rowed Atlantic. Lone, round-the-world yachtsman.

Born: 14 May 1940, 04.30 BST, Hawick 55N25 2W48.
Source: Birth certificate.

Chay Blyth first came to public attention when, along with another, he rowed the Atlantic in an open boat. Since then he has continued to pit himself against the sea, most notably during his solo, non-stop voyage around the world the 'wrong way', that is, sailing against prevailing winds and currents.

Blyth admits to a strong restlessness, to a thirst for challenge and adventure, and to a 'morbid fear of settling down.[2]' This is all most obviously reflected in a strong Jupiter, conjunct the ascendant. Taurus, at a basic level, is a sign that relates to the idea of the human being alone in life, having to face up to the challenge of a harsh world, and eventually wrest something meaningful from it. Perhaps more than anything Blyth has demonstrated the ability of the individual human being to triumph over the most difficult of circumstances, not through mind and technology, but through personal resource, very Taurean qualities like stoicism, fortitude, and dogged determination. There is a strong first house, containing Sun, Mercury, Saturn and Uranus, which suggests he is a man attempting to prove himself to himself, and also trying to generate a sense of aliveness by pitting himself against the challenges of the environment (the first house, we are reminded, has an 'Aries' quality to it).

Jupiter may dream dreams, but it is Earth that makes them reality. This is a strong Earthy chart, with Sun, ascendant and two planets in Taurus. It suggests his self-discipline (and the strong Saturn contributes here also), and his capacity to endure physical hardship. Taureans often make good fund raisers, and this has been necessary in his case, to finance his adventures. What also helps here is Jupiterian enthusiasm, as the following suggests:

> It is one thing to have an idea, even to be prepared to undertake a formidable task; to fire other men's imaginations with the peculiar rightness, the necessity of such a task is something quite other. Chay has this quality.[1]

This ability to treat as real and concrete something that is only potential relates to Jupiter and its signs, and indeed is at the root of its optimism. In Chay Blyth's case, the strong Earth, and Saturn conjuncting both Jupiter and ascendant provide a good counterweight, and prevent the optimism and enthusiasm from degenerating into mere wishful thinking, or rash adventurism, as can so often be the case with Jupiter.

The Moon in Leo and Sun conjunct Uranus suggest an autocratic and independent individual. He classes himself a moody man, 'depressed when things are going wrong and elated by the slightest upturn in fortune.'[2] In a similar vein he notes:

> I know that my emotions go in peaks and troughs — one of the most dangerous aspects of my character — but even that knowledge cannot abate the enthusiasm, or cure the depression.[2]

Moodiness is a Lunar trait, but mood swings also relate to Jupiter (particularly the more extreme sort).

Sources/references:
1. Chay Blyth *The Impossible Voyage*, Hodder & Stoughton.
2. Chay Blyth, *Theirs is the Glory*, Hodder & Stoughton.

Henry Bowers

Polar explorer. Member of Captain Scott's party who perished on the return from the South Pole in early 1912.

Born: 29 July 1883, 05.00 LT, Greenock 55N56 4W45.
Source: Birth certificate.

Most who knew Bowers spoke in glowing terms of his fine human qualities, a reflection of the strong Leo side of the chart. They praised particularly his optimism and *joie de vivre*. Much biographical description, however, seems to relate to the Gemini side of the chart — Moon, Saturn and Mars in this sign, and Mercury closely conjunct the Sun. He was very restless. When not doing something or moving somewhere, then he was planning to do these things. He had a methodical mind and took responsibility for the daily scientific measurements on the polar expeditions. He had a great interest in natural history, reflecting Gemini's interest in the myriad forms of the real world.

He was an ambitious man with a strong urge to rise within the navy, a side of him symbolised by the accented (equal) tenth house, and particularly Saturn here. He was healthy, strongly constituted, and had a passion for physical fitness. He seemed impervious to cold and harsh conditions. His taste for ascetic self-discipline and capacity to endure is perhaps most obviously mirrored in the chart by the Saturn/Mars/Moon stellium. The one chink in the armour of an otherwise intrepid man was an obsessive fear of spiders.

He had a strong, though inner and personal religious nature. He recorded an event in his diary for 20 April 1902: 'one night on deck when things were at their blackest, it seemed to me that Christ came to me and showed me why we are here, and what the purpose of life really is.' He goes on to describe how from this time onward he was aware of an inner spiritual core. This revelation is very Leonine in its quality. Both this, and the other significant period of his life, his final assault on the Pole are rather devoid of the major transits and progressions we might hope for. However, transiting Jupiter was active at both times, being conjunct the descendant in the first case and opposed to natal Moon in the second.

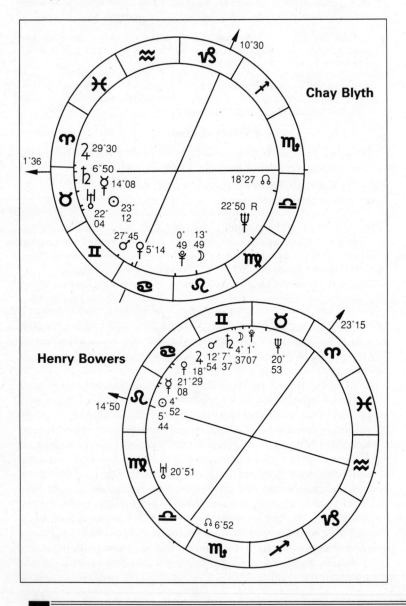

Naturally intelligent and wide-awake, he had also that power of application and attention to detail which is moral rather than mental in origin.

If his brother officers ... had been asked to name the characteristics in Bowers that most struck them, they would probably have replied — his incurable optimism, his happy unconventionality, and his perfectly preposterous good luck.

Socially he was hail-fellow-well-met with everyone, and yet continued to steer his own course by his own star. His gay zest for life, varied interests and restless activity ...

(His) natural exuberance of a soul in love with life. His high spirits were irrepressible ... no one ever saw him depressed; his incurable optimism was the expression of an inner joy.

Genuinely interested in his studies ... for their own sake as gateways to knowledge.

Source/reference:
George Seaver, *'Birdie' Bowers of the Antarctic*, John Murray .

Marlon Brando.

Actor, director.
Born: 3 April 1924, 23.00 CST, 41N17 96W1.
Source: Birth records (*The Gauquelin Book of American Charts*.)

This is a chart strong in Aries with Sun, Moon, and Mercury placed here. And this sign is apparent in both his character and his creative roles. His first important film, the one that made his reputation, was *A Streetcar Named Desire*. This was based on the play by Tennessee Williams, an Aries Sun, and the central male, Kowalski, played by Brando, is very Arien. He is a selfish, brutish character, but a virile one. He is ruled by instinct and primitive urges, experiences life raw and responds emotionally and directly. Being strong himself in Aries Brando could quite naturally play a character like Kowalski (and I think there is something to be said for directors matching parts and players in this astrological manner.) The Mars signs are noted for conferring intensity and magnetism and these are qualities Brando has brought to some of his screen roles. It allows him to excel in those parts that require a great presence, characters like Don Corleone and Kurtz (in *Apocalypse Now*), for example, who must dominate a film even though they are not on the screen for much of the time.

From an early age Brando was competitive, disruptive, independent, nonconformist and undisciplined. There is wide agreement that he is a difficult man to work with, due to a wilful, arrogant, headstrong nature (again, very Martial). He is noted for testing his will against that of his directors, seemingly needing this tension to bring out the best in himself. He is noted for his perfectionism.

As he has aged, so politics and social concerns have become more important to Brando, a likely reflection of the Sagittarian ascendant, a

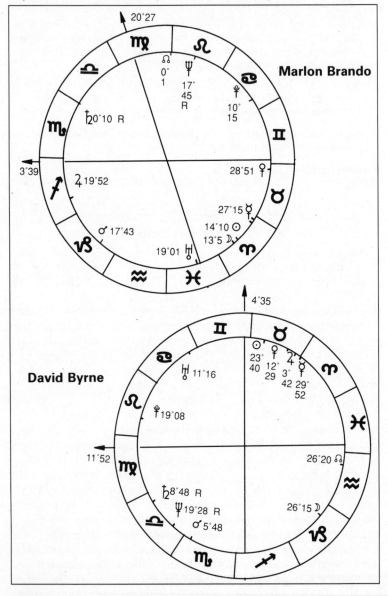

sign that often concerns itself with broader social issues. Jupiter likes to get beyond the surface and it became increasingly important that his films should have a meaning or a message. The strong Jupiter in the chart also concurs with an extravagant, wasteful nature. There is a marked Lunar side to his character, which might be attributed to the Sun/Moon conjunction. He can be withdrawn, moody, over-sensitive, and shy with strangers. He has a strong need for privacy. The same conjunction suggests something of his early parental experience. He was drawn more to his liberal, artistic mother (herself an actress) than to his father, which must have been confusing to an adolescent Aries male looking for suitable models of maleness.

The fierce independence Brando has carried with him through life.[1]

Noted for his energy, his competitiveness, his general refusal to conform and his intuitive feeling for the underdog.[2]

He gets bored easily. He gets bored with women, and he leaves them or neglects them after the initial conquest. He gets bored with conversations, and he daydreams or walks away. He gets bored with movies, and he tries to change his characterisation, or he simply walks through his scenes. Any kind of discipline bores him. (Quoted in reference 3)

When his spirits were low, he revealed himself as a withdrawn, introverted boy, intensely shy, and sensitive to slights real or imagined ... In addition to this hypersensitivity, Marlon was also plagued by a serious inferiority complex.[4]

Sources/references:
1. David Shipman, *Brando*, Macmillan.
2. David Downing, *Marlon Brando*, W.H. Allen.
3. Bob Thomas, *Brando: Portrait of the Rebel as an Artist*, W.H. Allen.
4. Gary Carey, *Marlon Brando, the Only Contender*, Hodder & Stoughton.

David Byrne

Singer, musician, composer; creative force behind rock band *Talking Heads*.

Born: 14 May 1952, 14.00 BST, Dumbarton, 55N58 4W35.
Source: Birth certificate.

Rock music is essentially pagan — and here lies its power and appeal. It utilises the most biological aspects of music, rhythm and beat. The advent of rock music marked a turning point. An influx of crude but vital energy, which immediately distinguished it from the dry and abstracted 'serious' music of the twentieth century. The power of (authentic) rock music lies, not in turning our minds skyward, as the music of earlier centuries did, but in transporting, often in conjunction with dance or drugs to a state of Dionysian ecstasy. This communing with biological force relates in astrology to the element Earth and so it is not surprising that a strong Earth nature is the most common distinguishing feature of the charts of successful rock musicians. David Byrne is a good example, with Sun, Moon, ascendant, Jupiter and Venus all in Earth signs.

Although there is a marked pagan side to his music, particularly his use of complex overlapping rhythms, there is also a sophisticated and intellectual quality. Critics have dubbed him a thinking-person's musician. They have remarked also on his eccentricity, and it seems likely that Byrne has sedulously cultivated a persona of strangeness. He is plainly respected by other musicians and he has collaborated with a number of other avant-garde artists in a variety of fields. He has managed to walk a fine line between artistic integrity and popularity, having a strong and substantial following.

Eccentricity and the striving to be different are most often related to Uranian influences. This planet is not strongly placed in his chart. However, it is closely sextile Venus and ascendant, falling almost exactly on their midpoint, and perhaps this is an apt mirror of the particular quality of his artistic nature.

Byrne's early home life seems to have been contented. His parents were Quakers, liberal, tolerant, progressive and encouraging the same attitudes in him. He was a good but lazy scholar demonstrating

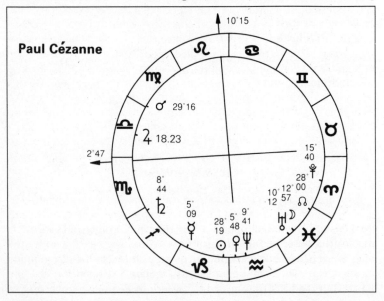

Paul Cézanne

an early talent in painting. He exemplifies the more refined side of Taurus, being arty and intellectual rather than sensual and stolid. Like the other members of *Talking Heads* he has a good business sense, as Earthy types often do, and the band has fared better than most in the jungle of rock contracts.

The Capricorn Moon reflects in an ambitious nature, a determination to succeed and a tendency to put his art and career before friends and personal life. It suggests also the need to develop a well-defined social persona. There is an analytical and sceptical side to his nature. In interview the diffident side of Virgo shows through, along with some Capricornian self-consciousness. But on stage we witness Venusian charisma, and the energy and magnetism of a Scorpio Mars.

Source:
Jerome Davis, *Talking Heads*, Omnibus Press.

Paul Cézanne.

Artist.

Born: 19 January 1839, 01.00 LT, Aix en Provence 43N32 5E27.
Source: Birth records (Gauquelin).

Cézanne's life was one of labour and self-sacrifice, a long lonely path to which he became increasingly resigned. He seemed to tolerate the solitariness of his labours well enough. What depressed him was the awareness of the time and effort that was going to be necessary to achieve his self-set artistic goals. It is acknowledged that he achieved a great deal, although he was middle-aged before he received any recognition. Like many strong in Capricorn his talents took time to develop, and he found great reserves of strength in his old age. He was a great influence on succeeding generations of artists, and he became known as the father of modern painting. His great patience and dutiful steadfastness in working towards a distant goal suggests Capricorn; his single-minded intensity — he had no interests outside his work — reflects the Fixed Scorpio ascendant. He also possessed the great integrity that often goes with Capricorn, the determination to be true to one's own truth.

If we are not able to articulate precisely what Cézanne attempted to achieve then there is at least general agreement regarding the salient qualities of his work (and again these suggest Capricorn). His work is most often described in terms of density, massiveness, solidity. His early work had Martial passion, but as he matured so it became much more deliberate and organised. In contradistinction to the Impressionists his art attempted to capture some permanent aspect of the sensual world, something of the enduring cosmic architecture that underpins it.

This is a Watery chart, with a Scorpio ascendant and Moon in Pisces, and the characteristics of this element figured strongly in his character. He possessed both the vital intensity of Scorpio, and the fluid and extreme emotional range associated with Pisces. At best he was inconsistent, at worst unstable, with a violent temper. There was little equanimity or capacity for cool reason. He instinctively distrusted intellectuals and those he deemed his betters. He reacted particularly strongly against people he suspected of attempting to influence him with their own ideas. He couldn't argue his point of view and attempts to draw him usually met with hostile rage. He was his own judge and teacher and learned slowly from his own mistakes. The only man whose advice he accepted was the kindly, fatherly Cancerian Pissarro.

Cézanne was a shy, hesitant, suspicious, antisocial type. He could be offensive and brusque, and had a coarse, earthy side. His mother is suggested by the Moon-Venus conjunction in Pisces — 'a sensitive, tender, lively woman' who encouraged him to paint; his father, 'a hard-headed realist' who wanted him to be a banker by the Capricorn. Cézanne and his father were often at odds, but the son was provided with an allowance, which gave him the freedom to paint and escape from the common artistic predicament of having to couple a creative bent with the need to make a living. There was a kindly, compassionate side to him, which came out in his dealings with those less fortunate than himself. This is suggestive of the Pisces Moon. Likewise is the restlessness that beset him for much of his life, and the dreamy torpor that characterised him as a young man. For most of his life he was at odds with his peers and the conservative art establishment, which is not unusual when there is a Moon-Uranus conjunction. In the end he achieved recognition, not by conforming, but by being true to himself and so infusing new and lasting ideas into the world of art.

He was a simple man in spite of his good education, self taught through a need for independence, and suspicious to the point of distrusting the experiences of others. He was headstrong, bad-tempered, obstinate, refusing to recognise his mistakes, claiming always to be in the right. But these very faults helped him, for, by relying on his own abilities, it was up to him to make a success of his career.[1]

If genius is great patience, Cézanne was undoubtedly a genius.[1]

Nothing came easy to Cézanne. His art emerged from a constant struggle to reach an almost unattainable profundity. He would set every goal a little beyond his means and, unlike other artists, would never rest upon a facility he had gained.[2]

The depth and violence of his nature, the tremendous vigour with which he experienced life and which shook his whole being.[3]

Sources/references:
1. Frank Elgar, *Cézanne*, Thames & Hudson.
2. James Ackerman, *Brief Lives, a Biographical Guide to the Arts,* Allen Lane/ Penguin.
3. Karl Badt, *The Art of Cézanne,* Faber & Faber.

Charles 1.

King of England, Scotland and Ireland, 1625-1649.

Born: 29 November 1600 ns, 23.00 LT, Dunfermline 56N5 3W28.
Source: A letter from the English Ambassador to his Secretary of State: 'On Monday last the King rode to the Queen to Dunfermline and returned yesternight. They never loved better. This night at 11 of the clock the Queen was delivered of a son and word thereof this night at about 3 hours brought to the King' (cited in ref 2, below).

Charles's childhood and youth were not happy ones. He was weak, sickly, timid, and otherwise lacking in self-confidence. His speech was stammered. He was meek and inoffensive, eager to be liked and to please others, to the point of obsequiousness. He lacked a close relationship with his mother and was ill at ease with his father. For a number of years he lived in the shadow of a brilliant elder brother, Henry, the Prince of Wales. But Henry died in his teens, so Charles had to be king. The diffident and deferential nature reflect Neptune conjunct the Virgo ascendant and the Libran Moon. Biography talks of a 'rigorous self-discipline', of 'the clockwork regularity of his habits', and of the 'neatness, order, decorum, moderation (that) were and remained the notes of his personal life.'[3] Again, these traits relate to the Virgo ascendant.

This chart is strong in Sagittarius, with Sun, Mercury, Venus and Mars placed here. However, he didn't seem to enjoy any of the good fortune traditionally associated with this Jupiter-ruled sign (and a seventeenth century astrologer might have put this down to Jupiter itself being in the sign of its detriment, badly aspected, and the Sun being conjunct an 'evil' fixed star). On the contrary, he exhibited many of the negative traits that go with it. He was extravagant and wasteful; he had poor judgement and little practical sense, with the result that his reign has become associated with ill-conceived foreign policy that invariably ended in disaster and humiliation. With Sagittarius there is often a reluctance to let detail stand in the way of vision or hallowed principle. He saw his role as a formulator of broad policy; it was up to Parliament to find the means and money to carry out the policy. The day to day details of running a country bored Charles. The more boisterous side of this sign seemed only to emerge in his love of hunting. He was a good horseman, and headstrong and reckless in the chase.

There was about Charles a refined, genteel, decorous quality, which suggests once again the accented Neptune and the Libran Moon. Sagittarius also can be moral and virtuous, and there is every evidence to suggest that he reflected this side of the sign. He was temperate in his food and drink, and, unusually for the times, took no mistress. Apparently, he was not a vigorous man sexually. His relationship to his queen, Henrietta Maria, expressed itself best in the formalised arena of the Court, the couple, in very Libran fashion, functioning as exemplars of a rather romantic, troubadour ideal of love. It was all very different from the lewd excesses of his father, whose Jacobean Court has become a byword in bawdiness, and from his son, Charles II, who sired many bastards. Another aspect of Charles's refinement was a passion for art. He was an outstanding connoisseur and collector, acquiring some 2000 paintings, sculptures and other *objets d'art*. He patronised many craftsmen and artists (Rubens most notably).

Charles is most remembered as the king who precipitated the English Civil War and who subsequently lost his crown and his head. The close Saturn-Uranus opposition seems an apt description of the struggle that formed the focal point of his life. We note that for much of the Civil War Neptune transited Sun and Mercury. His defeat and imprisonment coincided with transiting Uranus conjunct his natal Sun, and at his execution, in February 1649 (ns), Saturn and Pluto opposed natal Sun.

We talk about the background history to this period in a later chapter. Suffice to say here that Charles was at odds with the spirit of his times. He tried to swim against the tide. He was fundamentally Medievalist in his convictions. He wanted to be an absolute monarch at a time when constitutional monarchy was called for. He wanted to rule without a parliament, and he wanted and expected to be obeyed. This all relates to his Sagittarian nature, a sign that has much in common with the medieval spirit. It was this stubborn belief in absolutism, his divine right to rule as he saw fit, that was his downfall.

We can opine that what complicated the issue was Sagittarian self-aggrandisement. There is a self-deceptive side to this sign. Those strong in Sagittarius can view themselves as something more romantic, glamorous, or important than they really are. It's the Madame Bovary syndrome: a difficulty distinguishing between the real, and some ideal, conception of the self. In Charles's case there seems to have been a problem in discriminating between himself as king and himself as individual. His father, James, seemed to get the balance right. He took kingship seriously, but not himself as a man. He had a more realistic view of the flawed individual he was. But Charles perhaps needed the role of king to inflate a weak ego sense, to compensate for the low self-esteem of his youth.

Had Charles been more down-to-earth he would have kept his head and his crown. In the end, and appropriately for a Sagittarian, he was damned by his principles. His death had a Neptunian quality to it, for

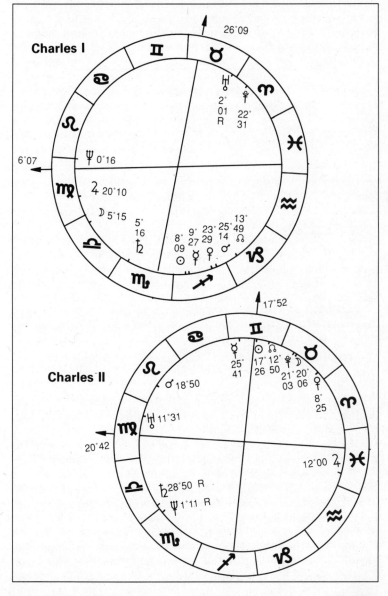

as one historian notes: 'In martyrdom he won by losing ... his death gave his life a tragic dignity.'[1]

Sources/references:
1. Charles Carlton, *Charles I The Personal Monarch*, Routledge & Kegan Paul.
2. Pauline Gregg, *King Charles I*, J.M. Dent.
3. Richard Ollard, *The Image of the King: Charles I and Charles II*, Hodder & Stoughton.

King Charles II

Monarch. King of Great Britain 1661-85

Born: 8 June 1630 (ns), 12.00 LT, London.
Source: Contemporary accounts - see reference 3.

Much of the recorded description of Charles can be reduced to three major themes in the birth-chart: a strong 'Mercury' overtone (particularly the Gemini side); a 'Venusian' side, with Moon and Venus in Taurus; and a 'Scorpionic' overtone (a Moon/Pluto conjunction squared by Mars).

The image of Charles II's court that has come down to us is one of frivolity and licentious idleness, and undoubtedly he was in his way both lazy and superficial. His idleness was not of a physical cast, however. He had a love of the outdoor life; he was a good sportsman and enjoyed exercise in general. Indeed, he seemed possessed of that restless, speedy quality often evident when Mercury is strong in a chart. His laziness was on other levels. He put pleasure before business and preferred others to do his thinking for him, so that too often decisions were based on what was the least trouble rather than what was the most prudent. This is most obviously a reflection of his 'Venusian' side.

Charles was affable, easy-going, sociable, diplomatic, tolerant, flexible and friendly (if cool). He was a vigorous man sexually, with many mistresses and illegitimate children (though no legitimate ones). He was fond of women in a platonic sense too, and they of him, and he was notably non-sexist. In all this we see the 'Venusian' and 'Scorpionic' overtones, and perhaps also the Venus/Uranus trine, and strong Earth. He had the Mercurial love of learning and need for mental stimulation. He had a strong interest in science, patronising the Royal Society and performing experiments himself. He had a love of gadgets. He was noted for his wit and conversation. He had the common touch. He was the most democratic of monarchs, encouraging his subjects to approach him on his daily perambulations. He was a man of the world, interested in it and his people, though not for long in any one thing or person. In all this we see Gemini, as we do in his major failings — he was fickle and unreliable, on occasion plain devious and shifty.

The most significant character-forming period in his life was his period of exile during the Civil War, and the Commonwealth that followed. This commenced in the summer of 1646 (transiting Saturn conjunct Moon/Pluto) and ended with the Restoration in May 1660. His coronation in April 1661 was marked by a progressed New Moon, and by transiting Saturn opposed to Moon/Pluto. The years of exile were marked by extreme penury, intense frustration, and uncertainty. But, for better and worse, they matured him. They brought out qualities of fortitude, courage, resourcefulness and self-reliance, but also made him more cynical and melancholy. Commentators note that following this period he developed the wariness of the man who has had the carpet pulled from under him, and who has experienced life at the level of raw survival (as Charles for a time was forced to). Charles lost much of the gaiety and good-natured warmth of his youth and developed what has been described as 'an indifferent agreeableness'.

In retrospect Charles's reign can be seen as positive and prosperous, one which laid the foundations for a modern Britain. That it was so is due in part to the fact that as an essentially Mercurial person he was in harmony with the secular, rational, scientific nature of the changing times.

An everlasting talker.[1]

It would be wrong to assume that Charles's interests were limitless, but they do seem to have covered a remarkable range of activities.[1]

He wished above all to appear a well-bred man, avoiding unpleasantness, smoothing and civilizing the rough and the harsh.[2]

The cool-hearted monarch.[3]

Perhaps the most fundamental weakness of Charles's kingship was a dislike of hard work.[4]

Although he read little he had a quick mind and retentive memory and could talk intelligently on many subjects. He was often highly amusing and was an excellent story-teller ... His intellectual curiosity led him to dabble in 'natural philosophy' and made him interested in all sorts of people ... (he) was incapable of sustained application. He could show great intelligence and perception if a subject really interested him ... but it was hard to hold his attention for long.[4]

Sources/References.

1. Tony Palmer, *Charles II, Portrait of an Age,* Cassell.

2. Richard Ollard, *The Image of the King: Charles I and Charles II*, Hodder and Stoughton.
3. Antonia Fraser, *King Charles II*, Weidenfeld and Nicolson.
4. John Miller, *James II A Study in Kingship*, Wayland.

Prince Charles.

Prince of Wales (heir to the British Throne).

Born: 14 November 1948, 21.14 GMT, London 51N32 0W0.
Source: Public announcement.

The cosmos is democratic. It does not distinguish between royalty and commoner. Prince or pauper, the signs and planets are the same in each case. However, the specific way in which the birth map manifests is dependent upon social standing. For example, it is well-established that Charles feels a need for danger, and for circumstances that will challenge him at a very basic level, thereby creating a sense of both aliveness and self-worth. This is a common enough experience when Scorpio is strong in a chart (as it is here, with Sun and Mercury in this sign). One way he has sought to live out this urge is the pursuit of tough, even dangerous sports like polo. The deprived inner-city youth, for whom Charles feels such an empathy, has scope to express it in a different way, such as fighting at football matches.

A chart, whether of commoner or royalty, generally contains its contradictory strands which must somehow be resolved. A basic divide appears in Charles's chart: the Taurus Moon, Leo ascendant on the one hand, and the Scorpio Sun, strong Neptune on the other. The Scorpio/Neptune elements constitute a Watery overtone and a strong feeling nature. The feeling function is undervalued in our culture, and this side of him is the one that the Establishment and the Press find incomprehensible. However, it is descriptive of his compassionate nature, and his sincere desire to alleviate hardship. Characteristically Scorpionic, he wants to *do* something about the social ills he sees about him. He is very much a man of action. The Leo/Taurus side describes his enjoyment of the luxury and privilege of his position. Being someone special, and the pomp of regal ceremony seem very much to his taste. He is a great traditionalist, with a firm conviction about the importance of the monarchy. I think the basic divide is also mirrored by the exact opposition of Jupiter to Uranus (a combination that also suggests his outspokenness). Jupiter is an essentially traditional, regal influence, and one that concurs with the idea of elevated and superior individuals. Uranus, on the other hand, is democratic, more tuned to the ordinariness and commonness of human beings.

There is a duality inherent in the meaning of Scorpio itself (as was noted in the introductory chapter). It is a sign that focuses on the difference between a detached, abstract, intellectual way of being, and existence at a more 'real', vital level of feeling. This duality is plainly experienced by the Prince. Many have commented on his boredom with the polite, refined, conventional world in which he performs as a functionary, and we are witness to his fascination with a different level of existence altogether, the nether world of the poor, criminal, and disadvantaged. Related to this duality is his passion for the countryside. His deep empathy for nature accords with what some have called 'participation mystique', a phenomenon associated with this sign more than any other, and whose meaning is encapsulated in the lines of Dylan Thomas, himself a Scorpio Sun:

> The force that through the green fuse drives the flower
> Drives my green age; that blasts the roots of trees
> Is my destroyer.

It is an awareness of a common level of being, that the same organic force pulses cyclically through all life, human, animal and vegetal.

The work of another Scorpio writer, Albert Camus, reveals much about the meaning of this complex sign. He once summarised his life's purpose in the following words: 'I have such a strong desire to help reduce the sum of unhappiness and of bitterness which empoisons mankind.' We can speculate that these same sentiments apply to the Prince of Wales. Despite the additional problem of how to effect such a task within the straitjacket of his regal destiny, he has been able to express his Scorpio nature. He has focused on some of the less palatable aspects of contemporary society and held them up to the light. And he has developed the ability to listen to others. He is willing and able to listen to the pariah or reprobate without condemnation or judgement, so drawing out the 'poison' of their frustration, hate and anger.

Many who do not count themselves royalists profess an admiration for Charles as an individual. Many in tune with New Age ideals sense that the same vision permeates his thinking, at least to some extent. His speeches on ecological matters and alternative medicine tend to be sneered at by a cynical Press. Yet he should take heart that many share his vision. It is he who senses the profundity of reality, and his critics who live in a dream world.

The quotations below highlight the importance of both Scorpio and the strong Neptune (conjunct the IC) of the chart.

Impressionable, receptive, even gullible.[1]

Instinctively shy and retiring, yet overcoming it with a deliberate effort of will.[1]

A pitifully low opinion of himself and a debilitating lack of confidence in his own worth.[2]

The Prince is clearly deeply distressed by the problems that he sees around him, the living conditions, the drug abuse, the racial tensions, the unemployment, the disintegration of the family and the despoliation of the environment. Some friends fear that he feels it all too deeply and too personally for his own good, that he will make himself ill.[2]

It is this demonstration to people who feel that no one gives a damn about them — the black community, the unemployed, the no-hopers festering in the decaying inner cities — that has perhaps been his most valuable contribution to society so far.He is seen to be championing the underdog, the most oppressed and dangerous section of society.[2]

Sources/references:
1. Anthony Holden, *Charles Prince of Wales*, Weidenfeld & Nicolson.
2. Penny Junor, *Charles*, Pan Books.

Sean Connery.

Actor (born Thomas Connery).

Born: 25 August 1930, 18.05 BST, Edinburgh 55N57 3W11.
Source: Birth certificate.

Neptune relates, among other things, to the phenomenon of mania, those waves of fanatic, mass adulation which periodically sweep the country, or the Western world. At the root of any mania is the irrational elevation of the mundane to a wondrous, mysterious, exciting or holy level, and it can perhaps be understood as a distorted manifestation of the religious urge in an over-secularised world. The capacity to stir the public imagination in this way seems to be a facet of Neptune, and Connery with his close Sun-Neptune conjunction expresses this Neptunian principle in his ability to create the compelling and glamorous, though essentially false figment that is secret agent James Bond. 'Bondmania' swept the world through 1964-5, a time when Neptune was transiting back and forth over his midheaven.

Bond is superhuman, a hero-figure living out the fantasies of the common person (as was once compulsory for screen stars). He was perhaps more credible twenty years ago when people were prepared to think of the Secret Service as a dedicated body of individuals waging a constant and thankless war against foreign powers and demented criminal minds. In recent years the reality has become more obtrusive, with revelations of far less glamorous and altogether more insidious pursuits directed against fellow-citizens. Bond is very much a product of Connery. Other actors have not been anything like as successful in the role, and the screen figure bears little resemblance to Fleming's fictive character. Fleming has said that Bond was never intended as a hero, but simply as a peg on which to hang a story. He has also commented that Connery's Bond was 'not quite what I had in mind

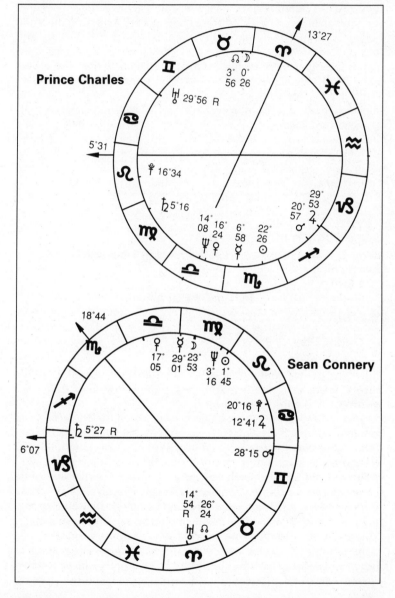

Prince Charles

Sean Connery

...but he would be if I wrote the books again.'

Connery is a private person and available biography is not too revealing about his deeper nature. As a youth and young man he was something of a loner, directing most of his energy to two jobs of work. He was in the navy for a time but was given a medical discharge (because of a duodenal ulcer). He was into body building and entered for 'Mr Universe' contests. Although he is plainly at home in the world of fantasy his feet are firmly on the ground (mirroring the strong Earth of the chart). Success has never gone to his head and he has been highly successful in translating his talent into hard cash. He has always maintained a strong sense of the value of money and has eschewed extravagance. The strong Capricorn overtone of the chart reflects his rags-to-riches rise from poor working-class background to the summits of wealth and fame. One suspects that Saturnian ambition — the desire to succeed, and to be seen to — is the motivating force here. Evident to most who meet him is a great integrity and self-honesty, again traits associated with Capricorn. Other qualities that emerge from media interviews are a certain dourness, a pawky sense of humour, and a tough-minded individuality.

Source:
Kenneth Passingham, *Sean Connery*, Sidgwick & Jackson.

John DeLorean

Automotive engineer, businessman.
Born: 6 January 1925, 12.00 EST, Detroit 42N20 83W3.
Source: Birth certificate (*The Gauquelin Book of American Charts*)

John DeLorean found fame as an ambitious and idealistic businessman, then notoriety for milking an extraordinary amount of money from the British taxpayer.

He started working life an engineer and his considerable talent in this area brought him success. He joined General Motors (September 1956) and worked his way up to Chief Engineer (11 November 1961) and then to Divisional Manager (1 July 1967). However, he was forced to resign in April 1973, generally because he would not conform to the Company way, but more particularly because of dishonesty and abuse of his authority. So began a new career and a new life phase — the start of his attempt to build a 'dream' car and a vast business empire. Appropriately this time is marked by a progressed new Moon.

His ambition and career success is suggested in his chart by a 10th house Capricorn Sun and by the strong Aries. These factors also show up in certain of his character traits. Charm and courtesy are not strong points. Indeed, he was often blunt and uncivil in his dealings with others. The brazenness of the man is astonishing. He was unsociable, and lacking in small talk and social arts. Many describe him as 'over-serious'. He was vindictive and unscrupulous with those who opposed his will. He was very aware of the image he wished to project to the world, as those strong in Capricorn often are. He has a great deal of energy, as we would expect with such a strong Mars set-up, and he was always able to fire others with his schemes.

This latter is suggestive of strong Jupiter (conjunct the MC), and indeed a significant part of what is John DeLorean is described by this planet. It suggests his grandiose schemes to build a huge business complex that would rival General Motors. It describes his over- and often empty optimism. It describes his *over*-ambition. While he had the ingenuity and practicality of an engineer, he was impractical in the sense of an inability to put his big ideas into effect. He had no time or facility for day-to-day organisation and administration. He was, it seems, more into the idea of a thing than the thing itself. Jupiter, Gemini, and a strong Aries is about the most potent combination for boredom, and this was certainly a problem for DeLorean. He lost interest easily, and was always looking ahead to the next great project. Also characteristic of Jupiter was his great extravagance and wastefulness.

Jupiter on the Midheaven imparts a 'Piscean' overtone. He was able to propagate a false and rather romantic image to the world at large. For a long while he was held up in the Press as a caring, courageous, admirable man who was out to shake up the car industry for the benefit of the consumer. Pisces and Gemini are the influences that relate more than any other to dishonesty, and without doubt DeLorean was a slippery customer who inhabited an ambiguous shadowland between crime and business.

For a long while he enjoyed the good luck traditionally associated with Jupiter. Events seemed to conspire to work well for him. That his dream car materialised at all was due to the political situation in Northern Ireland. That the mantle of saviour was cast on a man like him is more a measure of the desperateness of the situation in that province rather than the gullibility of civil servants.

John DeLorean had considerable personal resource and talent, and the capacity to contribute to his society in a powerful way. However, the selfishness of Mars prevailed, and he chose to use his talents wholly for the enrichment and aggrandisement of John DeLorean.

There are two themes that characterize John DeLorean's childhood: his disappointment in and lack of respect for his father's perceived weakness, and his own embarrassment at coming from a factory-class background.

(As a young man) he developed the patterns of diligent, hard work that brought him advancement and promotion throughout his career.

(His) notorious contempt for almost everyone else.

His remarkable capacity for self-delusion and his ability to convince himself that he was always right ... remained with him to the end of the project. John DeLorean had believed that only he at General Motors had glimpsed the truth, only to him had Divine Providence shown where the American auto industry was going wrong.

An inexhaustible supply of energy and ambition.

Source/reference:
Ivan Fallon and James Strodes, *DeLorean: The Rise and Fall of a Dream Maker,* Hamish Hamilton.

Sir Arthur Conan Doyle.

Writer. Creator of Sherlock Holmes.

Born: 22 May 1859, 04.55 LT, Edinburgh 55N57 3W11.
Source: Birth certificate.

Love is an emotional thing, and whatever is emotional is opposed to that true, cold reason which I place above all things.

Sherlock Holmes, *The Sign of the Four*

Sir Arthur Conan Doyle is remembered primarily for the invention of Sherlock Holmes, probably *the* best known character in literature. Holmes was first conceived in the early months of 1886 (although he didn't appear in print until Christmas 1887) and we can note significant activity in Doyle's chart at this time. His progressed Sun stood at 26.09 of Gemini, conjunct Jupiter and square Neptune, while Pluto was transiting the natal Sun-Uranus conjunction. The progressed Moon was at 25 Capricorn, thus also contacting natal Jupiter and Neptune.

As the quotation above suggests, Holmes is a personification of the rational, inductive mind and this seems an obvious reflection of the strong Gemini (or more broadly the strong Air) of the chart. One critic has noted of Holmes that he is 'the embodiment of man's deeply held conceit that he is a reasoning animal.'[1] Another, Rex Stout, a contemporary crime writer, has noted: 'Our aspiration to put our reason in control of our instincts and emotions is so deep and intense that we constantly pretend we are doing so. We almost never are, but Sherlock Holmes always is.' This is suggestive of the deeper meaning of Gemini, a sign where a degree of detachment is required from life so that it can be understood and (eventually) utilised for our own ends.

Much of Doyle's science fiction writing reflects this side of Gemini. In line with Victorian rationalism, he asserts again and again the supremacy of modern scientific man.

Doyle wrote quickly and easily, but at the same time carelessly. He earned a great deal and was probably the highest paid writer of his day

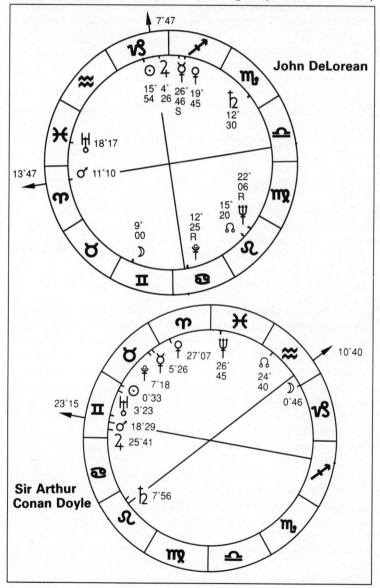

John DeLorean

Sir Arthur
Conan Doyle

(one American publisher offered him $5000 for a single Holmes story). There is a strong Aquarian overtone in the chart, with Moon in this sign on the MC, and Uranus closely conjunct the Sun. With writers this often seems to concur with the power to universalise and penetrate the popular consciousness, and to appeal equally to all types, all classes and all ages of people.

Mars is conjunct the ascendant in this chart and this reflected significantly in Doyle's character. He was energetic and possessed of a certain pugnacity. He had a Hemingwayesque interest in manly pursuits. He enjoyed boxing and excelled at cricket, representing the MCC and once bowling out W.G. Grace. There is something of the St George about Mars and its signs and this was quite evident in Doyle. He was a defender of the weak, specifically those who were victims of legal injustice. He was quick to take up arms on behalf of those who suffered through the impersonal monolith of the Law, and championed a number of notable cases. But in other ways he was conformist and reactionary.

The early part of Doyle's life was hard and he exhibited considerable stoicism in establishing a position for himself. He qualified as a doctor of medicine but was unable to make a living in this profession. He travelled a great deal. His later years were taken up with propagating the cause of spiritualism (1920, and Neptune transiting natal Saturn mark the watershed here.) His enthusiasm here is perhaps a reflection of the strong 12th house, and of an inferior Water function (the chart being overwhelmingly Air). He channelled a lot of his royalties into this crusade — as much as a quarter of a million pounds — and he lost many of his friends through it. It shows up a gullible side, and he was duped on more than one occasion.

Sources/references:

1. Ronald Pearsall, *Conan Doyle, a Biographical Solution.*, Weidenfeld & Nicolson.
2. Ivor Brown, *Conan Doyle, a biography*, Hamish Hamilton.
3. Sherlock Holmes Society of London.

Bob Dylan

(Robert Zimmerman) Singer, songwriter, hero of a generation.
Born: 24 May 1941, 21.05 CST, Duluth 46N47 92W07.
Source: Birth certificate (*The Gauquelin Book of American Charts*)

We can isolate three major overtones in Bob Dylan's chart:
1. A strong 'Jupiterian' side, with Sagittarius rising, and Jupiter conjunct Sun and Moon.

2. A strong 'Mercurial' side, with Sun, Mercury, and Venus in Gemini, and Mercury conjunct the descendant.

3. A strong Uranus, conjunct Sun and Moon.

The Uranian side reflects his independent spirit and a marked nonconformity, both evident from an early age. He was 'different' from his peers, dissatisfied with his society, and was determined to be free of its norms and to seek his own creative course.

The strong Mercurial side reflects a nervous, restless, changeable nature, an active mind and vocal cords, and great creative fertility. It reflects his imitative and eclectic musical style. It describes his role as a communicator. He was very much a spokesman of his generation. He articulated the Uranian spirit of the 60s. Songs like *Blowin' in the Wind* and *The Times They Are A-Changin'* spoke directly to millions of people. That his songs have proved universal in their power once more reflects the strong Uranus. Sensitivity to the times also suggests Gemini, a very contemporary influence, seeking expressive forms pertinent to time and place.

All sorts of exaggerated claims have been made about Bob Dylan. He has been spoken of as prophet, mystic and messiah. Many things have been read into his lyrics which are not there. The 60s generation, as much as any other, wanted its heroes, and upon Dylan this mantle fell. Not that he has ever encouraged these romantic projections, and, indeed, he seems ill-fitted to carry them. This phenomenon is a product of the Jupiter principle, and it is sometimes the burden of the Jupiterian to have to live up to the unrealistic expectations of others. There is that of the preacher and pamphleteer about Dylan, with his honest and open protest about social ills, and this too is typically Sagittarian.

His first album appeared at the end of February 1962. He wrote *Blowin' in the Wind* in April 1962, and it was soon adopted as an anthem by the Civil Rights Movement. On 9 August 1962 Bob Dylan became his legal name. A high point in his career was The Newport Folk Festival at the end of July 1963. In the words of one biographer[1] this marked the 'transformation of Bob Dylan-hobo minstrel into Bob Dylan-the eclectic poet visionary hero who was orchestrating a youth revolution.' He married 22 November 1965. On 30 July 1966 he suffered a serious motorcycle accident and almost died.

The first two quotes below reflect his Taurus Moon, the rest the major overtones isolated above.

He had a little boy appeal that made women of all ages want to mother him.[1]

Bob Dylan was totally possessive about his women.[1]

That boyish enthusiasm that many would find so infectious.[1]

The mythic representative of a generation and a culture.[2]

As a child he was quiet and secretive, a loner. Growing to adolescence he was an inveterate story teller, fabricating myths about himself so vividly that he hardly knew whether he spoke truth or falsehood.[2]

He is one of those outlaws who intuitively reject a standardized society, whose consciousness has not been frozen in the immediate and confining present.[3]

Sources/references:
1. Anthony Scaduto, *Bob Dylan*, Abacus.
2. Wilfred Mellers, *A Darker Shade of Pale. A Backdrop to Bob Dylan*, Faber & Faber.
3. Pearce Marchbank (ed), *Bob Dylan in his Own Words*, Omnibus Press.

Elizabeth I.

Queen of England 1558-1603.

Born: 17 September 1533 (ns), 15.00 LT, London 51N29 0W0.

Source: A letter from Eustace Chapuys, Imperial Ambassador at the Court of Henry VIII, to Emperor Charles V (preserved in *Calendar of Spanish State Papers*): 'On Sunday last, on the eve of Lady Day, about 3 o'clock in the afternoon, the king's mistress was delivered of a girl, to the great disappointment and sorrow of the king and the lady herself.' (cited in *The Girlhood of Queen Elizabeth*, Frank Mumby, Constable & Co.)

Elizabeth is remembered as 'The Virgin Queen'. She didn't marry or bear children, and it is quite possible she remained physically chaste. Elizabeth was also a very dutiful woman, as we might expect with Capricorn rising, so it must have gone greatly against the grain not to discharge what was considered a major responsibility for any monarch — the production of an heir. Plainly there were strong reasons for her not to do so, and we can examine the testimony of the chart to see what they might be.

There are obvious, as well as not so obvious, aspects of the chart that seem to describe the situation. On a straightforward level of interpretation, Saturn, the ruler of the chart, is in Cancer in the 7th house, and traditional astrology would take this as a clear indication of a denial of marriage (7th house) and motherhood (Cancer). Saturn conjuncts her father's natal Sun, and the more psychologically oriented astrologer might suggest that a negative image of men-as-husbands was formed within her because of Henry VIII's example, and that this constituted the substance of her revulsion of marriage. This is quite plausible, but there seems more to it than this.

Elizabeth's Sun is in Virgo, and this is a sign that has a traditional association with virginity, though in a broad sense, as an attitude

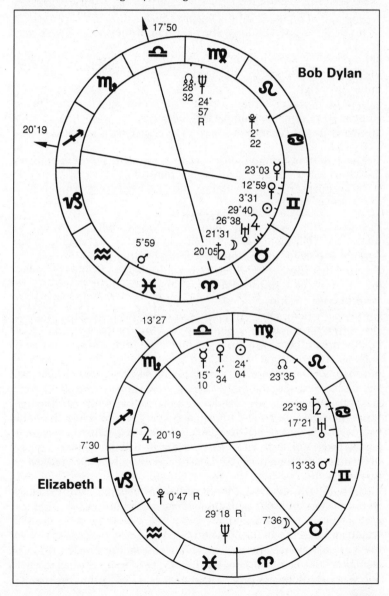

rather than a physical state. This deeper concept of virginity has been described, among others, by M. Esther Harding. Talking of the mythical figure of the virgin goddess, she notes:

> She is essentially one in herself. She is not merely the feminine counterpart of a male god ... and thus her actions are not dependent on the need to conciliate such a one, or to accord with his qualities and attitudes. She bears her divinity in her own right.[1]

Elizabeth, then, was virgin in this sense of one in herself, not prepared to compromise herself to a husband's wishes, but to rule as she saw fit, in her own right.

Harding identifies another aspect of the term virgin. It applied to the woman who remained unmarried because she was pledged to a greater being or cause. Writing of the Vestal Virgins she notes:

> They could not unite themselves to a husband, for their woman's nature was dedicated to a higher purpose, that of bringing the fertilizing power of the Goddess into effective contact with the lives of human beings.[2]

We have the connection here virgin-Virgo-service, and further relevance to Elizabeth, for it is often said that she was wedded to her people, and lived not for herself but to serve her nation. I think it is also true that Elizabeth's 'virgin' state allowed her to be the vehicle for the larger forces of history. We can see her as a midwife facilitating the birth of a new world. She was entirely humanist, and thus in accord with the changing times. A number of historians have remarked that she formed a surrogate Virgin Mary for the common people, thus helping wean them away from the Roman Church and medievalism.

This is a chart strong in Earth, and she succeeded through and lived out many of the qualities of this element. She was shrewd, patient, self-disciplined, and dutiful (reflecting the Capricorn ascendant). She was very pragmatic, and possessed of a sharp mind and much common sense. She was healthy and robust, and took a motherly interest in the health of those around her. She was cultured. She was strongly pacifist, with a distaste for violence (suggestive of the 'Venus' element of the chart, Venus and Mercury in Libra, Moon in Taurus). Despite her reverence for chastity, she was coquettish. In the words of one biographer, she enjoyed 'purely verbal lovemaking'[3] with her male favourites (symbolised, perhaps, by Mars in Gemini).

Her faults were mainly minor. There was a foolish vanity, and she would go to great lengths to maintain a favourable image of herself in the eyes of others. She was notably inconstant and fickle, forever changing her mind (suggestive of the strong Moon, conjunct the IC). She was irresolute and procrastinating (again, the 'Venus' element).

... deep conservatism, a passion for order and hierarchy, and a respect for the established procedures and institutions.[3]

If Elizabeth had an enduring passion, it was the assertion of her dominion over men by the power of her position and the force of her intellect.[3]

Elizabeth was a practical realist through and through; her knowledge of what was feasible amounted almost to genius. She won her victories by way of a shrewd utilisation of thoughts she had long digested in her mind.[4]

Her power resided not in venturesome plans and decisions, but, rather in a tough and circumspect persistence for obtaining the utmost that was compatible with security ... and in the cultivation of such virtues as are habitually ascribed to burgesses and housewives... Her very faults — timidity, excess of caution — bore fruit in the political field.[4]

She was wise with this world's wisdom — resourceful, self-reliant, cautious, and morally courageous in moments of stress ... suspicion was a second nature to her.[5]

Sources/references:
1. M. Esther Harding, *Woman's Mysteries*, p.125, Rider.
2. *Ibid*, p.132.
3. Paul Johnson, *Elizabeth A Study in Power and Intellect*, Weidenfeld & Nicolson.
4. Stefan Zweig, *The Queen of Scots*, Cassell.
5. J.B. Black, *The Reign of Elizabeth 1558-1603*, Oxford Univ Press.

Sir Alexander Fleming.

Medical Scientist. Awarded Nobel Prize for his work on penicillin.
Born: 6 August 1881, 02.00 LT, Ayrshire 55N37 4W16.
Source: Birth certificate.

Be prepared to accept such good fortune as the Gods offer.

(Sir Alexander Fleming.)

It is generally recognised that by his work he has saved more lives and relieved more suffering than any other living man, perhaps more than any man who has ever lived.[1]

In terms of human wellbeing, of the alleviation of pain, suffering and untimely death, penicillin represents one of the most important advances of all time. In the public mind it has come to be associated with one man more than any other, Alexander Fleming, and this despite the fact that others played equally important roles in the drug's development. The medicinal value of certain moulds had long been established. Fleming's part was the discovery of the exceptional lytic action (that is, power to inhibit bacterial growth) of a particular mould, *penicillium notatum*. To others fell the formidable practical problems of developing this mould into an effective and widely available therapeutic agent.

It is generally the case with discoveries that we remember the developer rather than the discoverer. But the reverse is true for penicillin. Fleming has indeed received a lion's share of the adulation. Over the period 1942-45, through a concerted propaganda campaign, Fleming became a famous world-figure. More than that, he became a legend, with the facts of the situation being exaggerated and distorted to accord with the romantic mould in which he had been cast. The public loves a hero. At that time the authorities needed one, to boost sagging War morale, and Fleming fitted the part.

Outwardly he seemed an inappropriate choice. He was shy, modest, unassuming, unambitious, an unimposing figure and an unimpressive speaker. But plainly there was that in him that formed a suitable hook for the world's hero-worship. The obvious reflection in his birth-chart is the strong Fiery nature, with the Sun in Leo and the Moon in Sagittarius. It is the Fire signs more than any others that are capable of projecting a larger-than-life image. Leo specifically relates to the power to constellate archetypes — in Fleming's case a Promethean, or Hero archetype.

Not that Fleming had to wrest Fire from the gods. He was given it freely. The discovery came about through a highly unlikely series of coincidences. This added to the romance of the story, the idea of a benign providence intervening directly in the affairs of man. A modern miracle in fact. Fleming is reputed to have said: 'I can only suppose that God wanted penicillin, and that was why he created Alexander Fleming.' So saying, and likely without knowing it, he expresses a fundamental side of Leo. For it is a sign that relates to the notion of the outstanding individual, to the self-conscious individual who is capable of being a vehicle for evolution, both in the sense of improving existence and, more abstractly, of giving life a greater knowledge of itself. Leo is to do with purpose, and plainly penicillin was Fleming's life purpose. He also expressed the essence of Leo in the fact that he demonstrated the importance of the individual in the creative process (c.f. Baird). It seems that the intuitive or inventive germ must be planted in an individual consciousness (which is always more advanced than the collective).

The discovery of penicillin is dated at 3 September 1928. On this day the Sun was closely conjunct Fleming's natal Uranus. Transiting

Jupiter conjuncted his natal Saturn, and Pluto the ascendant. The time was also marked by the approach of a progressed new Moon. The progressed Moon stood at 14 degrees of Virgo, once more, conjunct natal Uranus, the progressed Sun at 29 of Virgo. The time of the progressed new Moon, according to Rudhyar, marks a kind of seeding

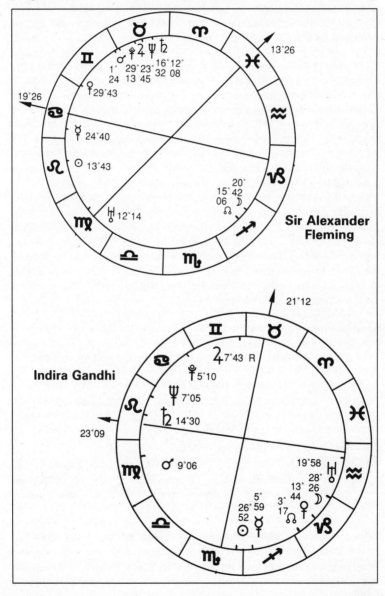

Sir Alexander Fleming

Indira Gandhi

and the start of a significant new departure in the life. The progressed full Moon, on the other hand symbolises a blossoming (and a culmination) of what happened at the seeding. In Fleming's case the full Moon phase of 1942-3 corresponded to the wide release of the news of a new 'wonder' drug and Fleming's rapid rise to the status of what today would be called a megastar. In May 1944 Fleming received his knighthood and appeared on the cover of *Time*, events aptly mirrored by transiting Jupiter conjunct natal Sun.

His scientific skills are likely a combination of a strong Mercury (conjunct the ascendant) and a strong Uranus (conjunct the IC), compounded, as they were, of 'ingenuity and originality ... innate curiosity and perceptiveness regarding natural phenomena ... a high degree of technical inventiveness and skill.'[3] He was basically an exemplary craftsman scientist who could translate theory into experiment and apparatus. He learned very quickly and had a good memory, as often seems to be the case with Cancer/Mercury combinations for there is the retentive capacity of the Lunar nature coupled with the ease and swiftness of retrieval of Mercury.

Fleming was a gregarious, clubable sort of man, reflecting his Leo Sun and an accented 11th house. At the same time he was very introverted. He was remarkably taciturn and reticent, given to silent staring with 'large, observant, penetrating eyes.' This sort of silent, essentially protective introversion is a reflection of the Cancer side of the chart. Yet he enjoyed being lionised by the world. He opened out in response and otherwise carried his greatness well. He died of a massive coronary on 11 March 1955.

Sources/references:
1. Funeral address by Prof C. Pannett.
2. Gwyn MacFarlane, *Alexander Fleming The Man and Myth,* Chatto & Windus.
3. *Dictionary of National Biography 1951-60*, Oxford Univ Press.

Indira Gandhi.

Politician; Prime Minister of India.

Born: 19 November 1917, 23.25 (IST Zone 5.5), Allahabad 24N27 81E50.
Source: In Lois Rodden's *Profiles of Women* two times are noted, not greatly differing. Both sources seem credible so I have taken an average of the two.

When on 24 January 1966 Indira Gandhi was sworn in as India's 3rd prime minister she became only the second woman in recent history to head a government. I'm not convinced there is such a thing as a well-defined politician's chart, although in the case of the outstanding statesperson Saturn factors are very often present. However, this is not the information we should be asking of a birth-chart. What it is better suited for is describing the essential quality of an individual. Also, in the case of Mrs Gandhi, it will tell us the *type* of politician she was. In broad terms this is well described by the element balance of the chart, which is well represented in Fire, Water and Earth, but weak in Air. She was a politician of the heart rather than the head. She succeeded through force of personality and through an intuitive capacity to relate to crowds and the broad mass of the people. Her achievement in dominating Indian politics for the best part of twenty years is rooted in her demotic appeal (suggested by Uranus on the descendant) but also in her Earthy pragmatism. She was a shrewd and capable politician, with no illusions about people or politics. With the Air element weak, however, she was no intellectual, and lacked coherent and consistent political ideas. She could move a crowd with oratory but was a poor debater, resorting to vagueness or emotion when faced with reasoned argument.

Indira Gandhi had a singular childhood, one that marked her for better and worse. The Sun conjunct the IC suggests the importance of her past, while the Moon sign of Capricorn describes in a broad way the nature of it. There was a very public and political atmosphere about her early home life. Her father, Nehru, and other of her relatives were political activists and a focus for the struggle for independence. It was a stimulating, but hardly an intimate or secure atmosphere, with its gatherings of famous and fascinating people, the domination of family life by momentous but distant events beyond the home, the regular arrival of police to arrest her parents and confiscate family possessions. She was alternately pampered and ignored, a focus of attention, then dwarfed by the importance of world-moving outside events. And, significantly, she was pampered for *what* she was, the daughter of a famous man, rather than *who* she was as an individual. This generated, among other things, a suspicion of people and their motives, which remained with her throughout her life. Overall her childhood seemed to be one of loneliness and unhappiness. She was introverted and moody, with little of the frivolity and spontaneity usual in children. She developed a formidable reserve and reticence, although at the same time a great self-reliance (and these traits are quite characteristic of Scorpio).

Like many with a strong Capricorn side she matured slowly and was past forty before making any real impact politically, or before the assertive Scorpio/Leo side of her nature developed. Her Scorpio nature is quite evident in her public personality. We detect the aloof dignified severity that often goes with this sign. She could be high-handed, strong-willed, impatient and authoritarian. At the same time there was genuine concern for the poor and suffering. There were great reserves of energy and courage, and the capacity to act, particularly in a crisis. She was very intuitive in the sense of being able instantly to size up a person. She was cosmopolitan and cultured.

She married in March 1942. Among other things transiting Uranus opposed her natal Sun, which is significant because the match ran against her father's wishes, and transgressed conventions of class and culture. In effect it was an assertion of independence. On some level it represented a break with her father (a powerful influence in her life). At this time she became more of a person and more of a political entity in her own right. Significantly the time also corresponded to a progressed new Moon. The year 1959 marked an important milestone in her career. In February she was elected president of the Congress Party and in June she was given a post in the government. This period was marked by the progressed Moon conjunct Saturn (exact in August) and, in February, by transiting Jupiter conjunct natal Sun. Her father's death, on 28 May 1964, was reflected in her chart by transiting Uranus and Pluto conjunct Mars, and transiting Mars on the MC. She was assassinated on the morning of 31 October 1984 (progressed Moon quincunx Uranus).

She generally conveys to the average observer, a mood of melancholy and loneliness.[1]

She had always been shy, but her shyness was to harden into an aloofness and remoteness of manner which often prevented her from showing warmth to others.[2]

(In her childhood) what she did lack, and what these extremes of indulgence and neglect only served to emphasise, was the even tempo and discipline of a stable and secure home, in which she could be truly a child, free from the anxiety and tension of a world which she was too young to comprehend.

Like so many other children who grow up in a disturbed environment and of whom much is expected, Indira seems to have felt threatened and vulnerable. And like other children, she sought compensation, partly through defence mechanisms which insulated her from intimacy with people other than the very few she felt she could trust, and partly through fantasies ... The result was an obsessive desire to excel and prove her mettle, coupled with a painful shyness and diffidence which, for many years, would cramp her personality.[3]

Climbing hills and mountains, then and later, seems to have fulfilled for her both a psychological and a physical need.[3]

The fierce emotions and ambitions that smouldered beneath her calm and reserved manner.[3]

She never really lets her defences fall, and there are large areas of feeling and experience which she refuses to discuss or glosses over with generalisations.[3]

She herself is no intellectual. She has neither the capacity nor the inclination for theoretical speculation and analysis. Her pragmatism and intuition enable her to respond magnificently to political events ... but these very assets are a handicap when it comes to coherent planning and long-term perspectives.[3]

Sources/references:
1. *Current Biography* 1966, H.W. Wilson & Co.
2. Dom Moraes, *Mrs Gandhi*, Jonathan Cape.
3. Zareer Masani, *Indira Gandhi: a Biography*, Hamish Hamilton.

Paul Gauguin.

Painter.

Born: 7 June 1848, 10.00 LT, Paris 48N35, 2E20.
Source: Birth records (Gauquelin).

It is widely held by art critics that Gauguin made a significant, if not major contribution to modern art. But he is more widely remembered for the romance and drama of his life events. He enacted an escapist dream, one still very much alive today: that of abandoning a routine existence in an over-urbanised world and returning to a simple life in some idyllic retreat.

Gauguin was essentially an unconventional and restless wanderer, although up to his 35th year he embraced normality, marrying, producing five children, and working successfully as a stockbroker. At the same time, he developed his interest in painting. By October 1883, however, he no longer had the energy or inclination to pursue two careers. He gave up stockbroking and pursued painting full-time. This was plainly a major turning point in his life, and particularly it was a time of great sacrifice. He renounced money, position, security and, in effect, his family, for what, at the time, were just tenuous dreams of becoming an artist. The transits and progressions at the time are suggestive of this renunciation, and also of a great restlessness, the desire to shake off the shackles of convention and follow his own path. The progressed Sun had moved to conjunct Jupiter and square Uranus; transiting Neptune was conjunct the MC (we note the sacrifice of his status); transiting Uranus opposed natal Saturn, and transiting Pluto squared natal Moon.

A strong feature of the chart is the Moon-Neptune opposition across the ascendant axis. In his life this reflected in a number of ways: in his need to embody sacrifice in some way; in a strong streak of self-delusion; in the sedulous cultivation of an idealised, glamorous image; in his need to be a martyr to his art; in the fact that he was the stuff of which legends are made and was a vehicle for a collective dream; and also in the fact that through his art he brought to the West something of the legends, myths and mystery of an ancient culture. This all suggests Neptune, and in the last we note the 'go-between' function of Gemini, his Sun sign (cf Thomas Hardy).

Gauguin's odyssey to Tahiti in April 1891 was as much as anything a quest for renewal, a cleansing and rejuvenation of his over-civilised soul through contact with a primitive culture. These, we note, are the prevailing themes of his work. In modern astrology this idea of regeneration is generally linked to Scorpionic factors. In Gauguin's case we note that the Sun falls on the midpoint of Mars and Pluto, but on the whole it is not a Scorpionic chart. However, we must not overlook the fact that other astrological factors can legitimately be related to regeneration. The Moon, for example, is a very ancient symbol of rebirth, and there is a strong Moon in this chart.

The Leo ascendant of this chart figured strongly in Gauguin's character for better and worse. He was self-centred, conceited, proud, condescending, and with a flair for self-publicity and gaining attention. He was very individual and independent. He couldn't work with others and was not popular amongst his peers. He liked to surround himself with admirers and exhibit his work amongst lesser artists so he would not be outshone. On the positive side, he had great confidence in his own abilities and this carried him through difficult times. The Solar urge burned strong in him. There was a single-minded desire to follow his own artistic course, whatever the cost to himself and those around him. In the end this self-confidence was justified.

Few men have worked harder at creating an image than Gauguin did. His consummate self-invention in Tahiti was the final stage of a long process of evolution.[1]

Gauguin's concept of his divinity, of his power as an artist and as a man apart from other men, resided in his capacity to capitalise on his dreams. As time went on, the earth made less and less of a claim on him, and he came to accept his fantasies as his true substance.[1]

Paul Gauguin made it his business to achieve a high public profile.[2]

Gauguin had an extravagant capacity for self-delusion, for fixing his sights on illusory goals.[2]

Sources/references:
1. Wayne Andersen, *Gauguin's Paradise Lost,* Viking Press.
2. Belinda Thomson, *Gauguin*, Thames & Hudson.

Kenneth Grahame.

Writer, most famously of *The Wind in the Willows*.
Born: 8 March 1859, 10.15 LT, Edinburgh 55N57 3W11.
Source: Birth certificate.

I think there must remain some doubt about the Gemini ascendant. Although the time is recorded to the quarter-hour, it would take only another three minutes or so to move the ascendant on to Cancer, a sign that accords more with biographical description. He was a quiet, shy man, more interested in his own company and his own inner world, which is not typical of Gemini. It is true that there was a marked dualism to his life, but this is more of a Piscean dualism, as we will see shortly. At any rate, in view of the uncertainty, we will focus on the other parts of the chart.

Grahame was a placid, courteous, charming sort of man. He had a passion for solitude, a state often cherished by Pisces. In his writing, his characters or narrators seem most often content when they are wholly alone.

There is a fearsome T-square in the chart involving Moon, Pluto, Saturn, Mars and Venus. In the broadest terms this suggests a complex and difficult emotional nature. A little more specifically, it tells us something about his attitude to women and relating, for Venus and Moon in a man's chart are the indicators of the women in his life, while Venus and Mars are the most immediate symbols of the emotional life. This complex suggests that, at least subconsciously, he had rather a jaundiced view of women. With Pluto and Mars involved it is likely that he feared domination. Grahame did marry, but it was not a happy marriage. In most respects it was arid. There was one son, who committed suicide after a short, unhappy life. His wife's chart, with a Capricorn Sun and an Aquarian Moon, suggests a strongly Saturnian character, and in many ways this is what the marriage was: long-lasting, but a union in name only, and not in spirit.

The Mars/Moon/Pluto complex is also a planetary mirror of the fact that Grahame's mother died when he was very young. He was sent to live with relatives. He was treated well enough, but it was all rather cool and formal. And perhaps because he never knew a real mother, he never learned to relate to the opposite sex on the feeling level. This side of him remained stunted and childlike. On the positive side, through his writing, this allowed him to speak directly to millions of children, and to awaken the child in millions of adults. But on the negative side it precluded mature, emotional relationship. This sort of emotional pattern in men is indicative of Taurus — the Moon's sign in this chart — and we noted it earlier with Barrie (and will note it again in the case of A.S. Neill).

Grahame led something of a double life. For 30 years he was employed at The Bank of England, working his way up to the senior position of Bank Secretary. When he was a young man he flirted for a while with bohemianism, but the traditional, chaotic artist's life didn't work for him. There was a need for stability and financial security

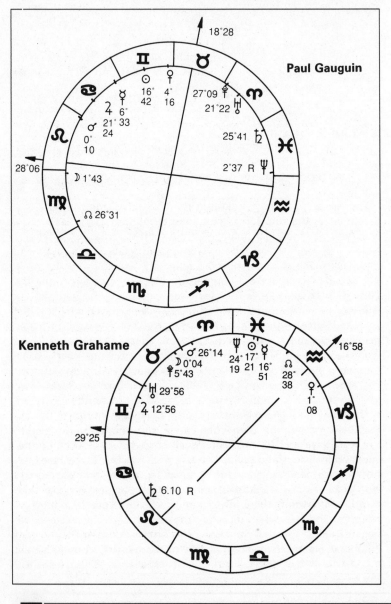

Paul Gauguin

Kenneth Grahame

(perhaps his Taurus Moon). It wasn't particularly congenial work, and he responded as Pisceans are sometimes wont to in such circumstances, through escapism. He retreated to some inner world of his own imagining, and it was on this imaginative level that his life was really lived at this time. It was a very Piscean duality he lived: outer bondage to conformity and routine, but an inner freedom. It seems sometimes as if the tension of this duality is necessary to the Piscean creative process. It was certainly the case with Grahame, for once he retired from the Bank, upped anchor as it were, he wrote very little. He seemed to drift away and surrender more and more to the torpid indolence that is the bane of Pisces.

His period of outer bondage is well marked astrologically. As a young man he wanted to study at Oxford, but was prevented from doing so by his guardian, who refused to pay the fees. Grahame was forced into menial clerical work to earn a living. It was a period of denial, disappointment and frustration in his life, and it was signalled by Saturn transiting his Sun and Neptune (mid-1877). It was about 30 years later, the same transit, that he was released from his bondage. He had earned enough from his writing to retire from the Bank.

His major work, the one for which he is remembered, is *The Wind in the Willows*. It is a work that was, astonishingly, rejected by one publisher and accepted only with reservations by Methuen. It has since run to over a hundred editions and sold some five million copies. On one level the work is a charming fantasy, but there are other levels to it. Literary characters often reflect their creator's Sun sign, and Toad particularly brings to mind a certain type of Piscean, with his emotional extremes, his irresponsibility, and tendency to fantasise. It is a work compounded of Piscean escapism and Taurean nostalgia. Grahame was a backward looking person. What he created in his writing, in response to the social currents of the time, was some idealised golden age, the rural idyll of his childhood transmogrified to some Eden. Historians widely acknowledge that the latter half of the nineteenth century marked the death of a way of life. It was the onset of modernism, and the collapse of the old order founded on an essentially rural world. Industrial centres were sprouting the length and breadth of the land; roads and railways were swallowing up the countryside. There was social ferment, and anarchic forces seemed further to threaten the old order. There was a pervasive unease among the upper and professional classes, and the subjective sense that things had changed irrevocably. A cycle had come to an end, another was beginning. It was a very Piscean time, one that saw the discovery of the planet Neptune (and we discuss this further in a later chapter). In *The Wind in the Willows*, what Grahame captured, consciously or unconsciously, was the essence of that old, stable rural world. He preserved it in a sort of seed before it was finally dissolved.

Grahame's obsessional, almost mystical passion for solitude.

... one suspects of Grahame's art ... that it throve best on deprivation, nostalgia, the ideal never quite attained.

... later in life ... he quite consciously urged the use of 'the countries of the mind', of daydreaming and fantasy as a psychological therapeutic.

We only learn by our losses: it is the theme that recurs again and again in Grahame's work.

He had a charming sense of humour ... He never spoke much, only when he had something to say; he never said anything unkind about anybody, or to anybody, except through inability to say something sincere.

Source/reference:
1. Peter Green, *Kenneth Grahame, A Biography*, John Murray.

Earl Haig
Field Marshal. Commander-in-Chief British Army First World War.
Born: 19 June 1861, 21.45 LT, Edinburgh, 55N57 3W11.
Source: Birth certificate.

'Don't be vague, blame Haig' (line from 60s protest poem).

There was a time in the pacific 60s when Field Marshal Haig became something of a focus of opprobrium. The carnage of Vietnam seemed to invoke his memory and for some he became the epitome of militarism, and a scapegoat for the senseless slaughter of the Great War. But given the course of history, the First World War was inevitable, a culmination of centuries of unconsciousness, and the eruption of unredeemed stupidity and greed in a fearful crudescence. The individuals on the stage at the time were simply pawns who had to accept their fate and play their part. Given the extraordinary conditions it can be said that Haig acted his part well, as a cog in the machinery of country and empire, and a cog in the greater workings of history. And when we are dealing with these vistas of time, parochial human concepts such as right and wrong and the apportioning of blame tend to dim into insignificance. This meeting of fate, of doing what had to be done within some larger context of history is indicative of the strong Capricorn nature of the chart. We note that at the start of the Great War, August 1914, Haig's progressed Moon opposed natal Pluto, and transiting Saturn conjuncted natal Sun. The time had come to meet his fate. We might also note the cross-contacts between his chart and the UK (1801) chart. Haig's Mars and ascendant/descendant axis conjoin the UK Moon, while Haig's Pluto conjoins the UK Mars. These contacts seem very apt given the nature of the relationship (and we'll note later   similarly apt cross-contacts in the case of another military man, Lord Dowding).

Biographical descriptions of Haig tend to reflect the Capricorn (his ascendant) and Martial (Moon in Scorpio, Mars conjunct descendant) sides of the chart. He was reticent, aloof and taciturn. He was industrious and self-disciplined. In thought he was swift, decisive, vigorous and alert. He had great powers of concentration and an unbending determination to win. His was the organisational capability to manage what was (at the time) the largest army ever put in the field by Britain. His was also the capacity to shoulder the enormous responsibility of command. The superhuman detachment required to send millions of young men to certain death is suggestive of Capricorn (and perhaps also his Airy Gemini Sun).

Surprisingly, considering the Gemini emphasis of the chart, he was a notably inarticulate man, inept at public speaking and with little capacity for small talk and easy communication. Plainly the reticence of Scorpio and the self-consciousness of Capricorn held the balance here. However, he could communicate well in writing and he paid much attention to the clear formulation of orders.

Historians rank him a good commander, if a little rigid and unimaginative. He was respected by his troops, who seemed inspired by his spirit of determination to win. It seems he had something of the Scorpio magnetism, able to compel attention simply by his presence. He was a fine horseman. John Buchan talks of Haig's 'sobriety, balance of temper', and 'unshakable fortitude'.[2]

… the strong faith, the religious conviction and the strict sense of duty that were so essential a part of him throughout his life.[1]

Except for his profession of soldiering, and later his family, he had no real interests of any kind, and little knowledge; nor had he any desire for knowledge, unless it bore on his own special subject. Very quick of temper in his youth, he had so disciplined his mind and body to serve his fixed purpose that he seldom showed anger or impatience.[3]

Immense professional expertise … a man of rock.[4]

Preeminently he was a man of action; but … also … the calm, concentrated and logical thinker, and the look in his eye suggested unplumbed depths of feeling and understanding.[4]

Undemonstrative, and always remained in a measure aloof. [4]

His coolness and detachment of mind under all forms of provocation.[4]

Haig was steadfast, deliberate, true and loyal, always limiting himself to his own personal duty and responsibility.[1]

Sources/references:
1. E. Sixsmith, *Douglas Haig*, Weidenfeld & Nicolson.
2. John Buchan, *Memory Hold the Door*, Hodder & Stoughton.
3. Lord Wavell, cited in source (1) above.
4. G.S. Duncan, *Douglas Haig as I Knew Him*, Allen & Unwin.

Keir Hardie

Politician. Founding father of the British Labour Party.

**Born: James Kerr, 15 August 1856, 16.15 LT, Legbrannock 55N54 4W15.
Source: Birth certificate.**

Hardie reflected the strong Fire of his chart. In the eyes of working class people he was a hero, a promethean figure who could help them escape their mean and squalid conditions and who could express their needs and aspirations. But like many Fiery politicians he was unsuited to the more pragmatic and humdrum aspects of political life. The patience and practicality of the successful career politician are Earth qualities and Hardie's chart is notably weak in this element (and Saturn is also weak by traditional tenets). He was too independent to be an organisational man, chafing at the restrictions of high office. He was agitator and prophet rather than statesman; inspirational and idealistic rather than intellectual. He provided an essential energetic input (and perhaps Mars on the MC is important here), but it was left to others to construct a theoretical framework and an organisational structure for the Labour Party. He was very much a father figure of the Party cherishing it throughout his life as a sort of offspring, insisting he knew what was best for it, resenting and resisting others' attempts to make their mark on it. This sort of paternalism is not uncommon when Leo is strong.

Hardie stood out from the crowd in both superficial and fundamental ways. He was the first working-class politician to enter the House of Commons, wearing working tweeds when frock-coat and top-hat were the order of the day. This differentness within a peer group is the mark of Aquarius (his Moon sign). Leo's individuality is of a different nature. It is a sign that relates to individuation in the Jungian sense, to the way of consciousness, and a self-directed purposeful existence. That this applied to Hardie is confirmed by at least one biographer who writes:

The energy and spiritual force that might have been expended in sport or religion, or dissipated in excesses, were expended first in developing his mind, and then, when he discovered his life's

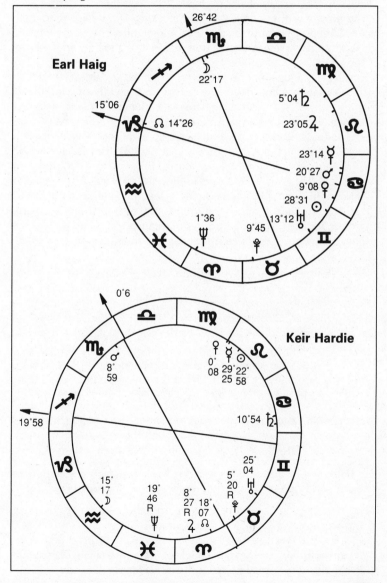

purpose, in furthering that purpose ... that purpose came to him with all the power and force with which a religious conversion affected men of his time. When he saw clearly what life called on him to do he went at it with every fibre of his being, and continued unflinchingly throughout his life.[1]

That purpose was basically to move the working class masses to self-improvement, to convince them that they should aspire to a life more in keeping with human potential and dignity. This single-minded sense of purpose seems a reflection of the strong Mars and the Fixity of the chart, particularly the Leo Sun.

Hardie was illegitimate and never knew his father, a fact which haunted him to some degree. It was a hard childhood working in coalmines. He had a strong charismatic personality and a strong presence. He wrote a lot, particularly political journalism. He was open, honest and direct. Like many of the early socialists he abjured alcohol. He was at times stubborn, vain and self-righteous. He became a Christian sometime in 1878 (Saturn conjunct natal Neptune in February of that year). He married in June 1879. He was first elected to Parliament in August 1892. It is widely agreed that the winter of 1886-7 marked a significant time in his emergence as a political figure, reflected, perhaps, by the Saturn return of mid-1886. A number of the quotes below are suggestive of the Sagittarian ascendant.

He had the power of standing alone for ideas that he believed right.[1]

He was guided by religious, or perhaps I should say, moral convictions.[2]

For Hardie the boundary was too vague between rightness and righteousness, and between righteousness and self-righteousness. He was too ready to let fly with his tongue at political opponents while stubbornly confident of the rightness of his own views.[3]

His appeal necessarily depended on sheer force of personality.[3]

But, first, last and always, he had staying power. This was his greatest strength ... once convinced that he was right, nothing would deflect him from his path. He could brush off any amount of failure and ridicule that would deter almost anybody else.[3]

His extreme individualism, his tendency to take refuge in a romantic, quasi-spiritualist milieu of his own.[4]

Hardie's vanity, his extremely high opinion of himself, was one of the things which made him a difficult colleague.[3]

Sources/References:
1. James Maxton, *Keir Hardie Prophet and Pioneer*, Francis Johnson.
2. J. Bruce Glasier, *Keir Hardie The Man and His Message*, ILP.
3. Iain McLean, *Keir Hardie*, Allen Lane.
4. Kenneth Morgan, *Keir Hardie Radical and Socialist,* Weidenfeld & Nicolson.

Thomas Hardy

Poet and novelist whose works include *Far From the Madding Crowd, Tess of the d'Urbervilles,* and *The Mayor of Casterbridge.*

Born: 2 June 1840, 08.00 LT, nr Dorchester 50N42 2W26.

Source: *The Early Life of Thomas Hardy.* A biography by his wife though ghosted to a large extent by Hardy himself.

Hardy was a major writer in his day, winning both popular and critical acclaim. The appeal of his work lies not so much in narrative or character as in the vivid rendition of a fictional world, which he called Wessex. The specific nature of his creative talent is well described by the Gemini and Cancer mix of the chart. He had the Mercurial interest in things and people, and in the forms of nature. He was keenly observant, and kept detailed records of the things he had seen and the factual incidents garnered from historical researches. These formed the building blocks of his Wessex world. What makes it so memorable, however, is the way in which these facts are transfigured into fiction through Hardy's Lunar consciousness. It is the Lunar faculty in an individual that synthesises in this way, infusing an otherwise dry and lifeless assortment of facts with a unique human and personal quality. Hardy was very impressionable and from an early age absorbed and stored the very atmosphere of the environment of his birth and ancestors; in the traditions, customs and values of his region, here lay his creative source. In effect what Hardy succeeded in doing was preserving a moment in space and time (Cancer). This was half of his achievement. The other half was to communicate (Gemini) to an urban audience this impressionable account of a dying English rural past.

Like many strong in Gemini he held great store by education. He regretted the denial (because of his background) of a university education but took great pains to educate himself. He was very diligent and bookish, and given somewhat to parading his knowledge. This side of his nature, his concern with learning, is given expression in Jude Fawley in *Jude the Obscure.*

For the most part, however, his immediate character is described by his Cancer Moon in the 12th house. He describes his approach to life as instinctive rather than intellectual. He had a marked reclusive side, taking great pains to preserve his privacy. He was on balance introspective with an uneventful outer life. He was rather shy and silent in public, although far more communicative in private, when he felt secure in the surrounds of his own home. At the same time, there was a gregarious side, suggested by the cosmopolitan areas of the chart — the strong 11th house (by quadrant systems), and the Leo ascendant. He would emerge periodically from his rural retreat to conduct business and socialise with the famous of the day. He was hypersensitive to criticism, often over-reacting in a defensive way (a mark of his ascending sign Leo, as well as Cancer). When *Jude the Obscure* was heavily criticised, on moral rather than literary grounds, he went into a sort of huff. He gave up writing novels, that is writing for an audience, and concentrated instead on writing poetry for himself. This marked transition in his creative life came at the end of 1895 and was marked, among other things, by Pluto transiting natal Sun.

He was very influenced by his mother. She was the spur to his own ambitions but also, on Hardy's own admission, hindered his emotional development through her clannishness and domineering maternalism. It is plain that the bond with his mother impinged heavily upon his relations with women. His own marriage was not a success.

> Hardy was an intensely, almost morbidly reserved man who clung tenaciously to an inviolable privacy even when he was world famous and persistently lionized. This is not to say that he was a recluse or a misanthrope, for one of the many paradoxes of his character is that his deep reticence did not prevent him from going into society and enjoying the friendship or acquaintance of many men and women.[1]

> (A) deeply sensitive nature, capable of being wounded by even moderate criticism.[1]

> Too prone to almost instinctive shifts in direction rather than of calculated action, intellectually conceived and deliberately undertaken.[2]

> Best able to define and refine his own ideas in response — which often meant in opposition — to the advice he received from those around him.[2]

> That extreme vulnerability to hostile criticism which was to recur again and again, even in the days of his greatest success.[2]

> Drawn by instinct and upbringing towards habits of rootedness and retirement, the values of the hearth and the continuities of family tradition.[2]

Sources/references:
1. Norman Page, *Thomas Hardy*, Routledge & Kegan Paul.
2. Michael Millgate, *Thomas Hardy, a Biography*, Oxford Univ. Press.

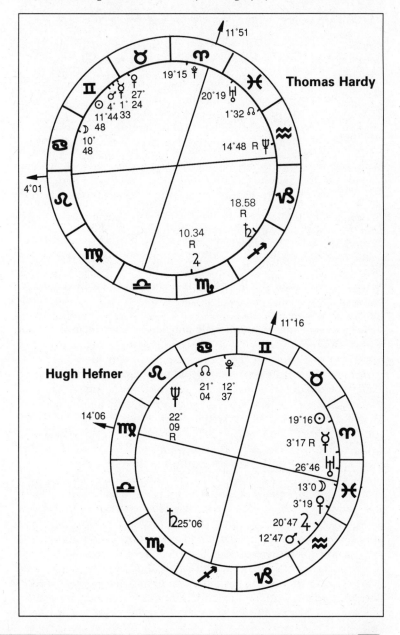

Hugh Hefner.

Self-made man, founder/publisher *Playboy*, **hedonist.**

Born: 9 April 1926, 16.20 CDT, Chicago 41N52 87W39.

Source: Birth records (*The Gauquelin Book of American Charts*).

Hefner wrote prodigiously from an early age and was driven by an ambition to own a magazine, an ambition fulfilled in October 1953 with the launch of *Playboy*. Aries, here the Sun sign, is noted for a capacity to initiate and there was evident in Hefner as a young man much go-getting energy, drive, and self-belief. Courage also, for he staked everything and risked the wrath of the establishment with what was at the time a bold venture.

Hefner somewhat romanticised his role as publisher. Aries needs dragons to fight and he believed that with his magazine he was striking a blow for the freedom of the individual against the hidebound constraints of the prevailing puritan morality. There may be some truth here, but it is probably more accurate to say that his venture coincided with a broader loosening of attitudes. As with most successful business ventures, luck played its part (although we are reminded that it generally favours the bold). Through the 50s and 60s *Playboy* moved from strength to strength, establishing itself as something of an American institution. Hefner diversified and expanded so by the end of the 60s he owned a vast business empire and was one of the richest self-made men in America.

Hefner's personality and lifestyle are clearly reflected in the major chart-factors. He has a Virgoan penchant for trivia, being 'obsessed with minutiae', and 'very detail oriented'. He is very fussy and every-thing in his immediate environment has to be ordered just the way he likes (with special attention to the way his food is prepared). Also evident, and typical of Virgo is an abstemious, shy, retiring nature.

He has the naive, boyish charm not uncommon in Aries. He is very autocratic, insisting on making all his own decisions. He is capable of energetic bursts of activity. He has a romantic, adolescent view of relating, once more characteristic of Aries. There is a plain need for sexual conquest, but with a waning of interest once a victory is won. Women are essentially a projection of his own needs, passive sex-slaves to fuel the flames of an exaggerated maleness, and this view is projected into his magazine. His vision of maleness as portrayed here seems to reflect his Aries Sun (domineering and masterful), and the Aquarius placement of Mars (urbane, cool and detached).

A good part of Hefner's character is described by the strong Piscean overtone of the chart. He has the Moon in this sign closely conjunct the descendant, and Jupiter and Neptune are strong by aspect, forming a T-square with Saturn, and both making close, major aspects with the Sun. There is a strong reclusive and escapist nature. For a good deal of his adult life he has cocooned himself in a dream-world of his own construction. For six years during the 60s he didn't leave his Chicago mansion, a garish Versailles furnished with many delights and entertainments for the delectation of himself and his celebrity guests. One commentator called it 'the strange, unreal, pampered womb of the Playboy mansion.' The *Saturday Evening Post* spoke of it as a 'love temple in the last days of ancient Rome.' There was about it something of the overblown, exotic, decadent flavour that often characterises civilisations in decline (a phenomenon symbolised in astrology by Pisces and its planets).

The Piscean overtone of the chart also manifests as a gross extravagance, and in the chaotic way he came to run his business empire. Fish decays from the head runs an old Portuguese proverb, and the blame for the decline of the Playboy empire through the 70s must ultimately be his. Part of the failing was too narrow a focus (again, his Virgo side). He did indeed fiddle while Rome burned, anguishing for hours over minor editorial and production decisions while the outposts of his empire ran to seed or afoul of the Law. He was reluctant or unable to address adequately the broader and complex issues of the business world. His Piscean nature also reflects the fact that he purveyed a glossy dream that for a time at least was believed in. Ultimately what he sowed, however, was disenchantment and disappointment as a generation of adolescent males learned that the beguiling siren centre-fold images of femininity had little to do with reality.

Sources/references.
1. Russell Miller, *Bunny, The Reality of Playboy*,
2. *Current Biography* 1968, H.W. Wilson & Co.

Glenda Jackson.

Actress.

Born: 9 May 1936, 08.00 BST, Birkenhead 53N24 3W02.
Source: Originated from subject (see *Profiles of Women*).

Glenda Jackson is universally admired for her acting talent. She remains one of a select band of actresses to have won two Oscars — for *Women in Love* and *A Touch of Class*. She has excelled in a variety of roles but made her reputation playing obsessed or sexually fraught characters. Her naked flesh was a common sight on the cinema screens of the late 60s.

A number of key areas of the birth chart contribute to the biographical picture:

1. A strong Sagittarian influence, with Moon conjunct Jupiter in this sign.
2. A strong Taurus side, with Sun, Venus and Mars placed here.
3. A Cancer ascendant.
4. A strong 12th house (by quadrant systems).
5. A number of prominent aspect patterns, namely: Venus conjunct Uranus; Sun conjunct Mars, both sextile Saturn; a T-square involving Saturn, Neptune and Moon.

Saturn is strongly aspected, and in the tenth house (by quadrant systems), and its characteristic cast is evident in her career pattern. In the first instance the easy way to success was barred. Her looks were not 'right', and in other ways she didn't seem to accord with what directors wanted at the time. She resigned herself to this, and to the fact that 'I'd have to work, work, work if I wanted to amount to much.' Basically she was forced to develop her acting talent to a high degree. This is very much the mark of Saturn: some kind of outer denial that forces an individual to look inward and develop inner resource to compensate. She had to struggle to achieve. Following drama school there were eight lean years when parts were scarce and it was necessary to take on menial jobs simply to live. No doubt Taurean stoicism helped her survive this dispiriting apprenticeship. Her first real break came through The Royal Shakespeare Company, in January 1964, as transiting Saturn approached the MC. Her reputation developed swiftly over the next few years, as Saturn transited the tenth house and returned to its own place.

Many in the profession have found it uncomfortable working with Glenda Jackson. Her character has been described variously as formidable, dour, severe, domineering, flinty and aggressive. Such traits are not uncommon when there is a Sun-Mars conjunction, but they also suggest the prickly defensive barrier that often accompanies a Cancer ascendant. Cancer is often wary about showing its true feelings, or letting its own feelings be touched by others. There is often a very private side when Cancer is strong, and this is the case with Glenda Jackson. A number of directors have remarked on her impenetrable reserve. She owns to being anti-social, and has eschewed the high-flying social life that is available to film stars.

She has the blunt, forthright nature associated with Sagittarius and not one of its most endearing qualities. This is also a sign that sometimes divides the world into gods and mortals, and this kind of elitism seems to mark Glenda Jackson's character. She has very high standards. Being very talented herself, she expects others in the profession to be so, and can be scornful of those who are not. The philanthropic urges of this sign have made themselves felt. She has involved herself with a number of charitable organisations, and there is a desire to be involved in good works; a growing conviction that entertainment is not enough and personal energies might be better directed to the serious business of improving the world (cf Marlon Brando and Jane Fonda, other actors with marked Sagittarian natures).

With Taurus strong there is a very pragmatic, no-nonsense approach to acting and life in general. The glamour of show-business has held little attraction. A common observation is of a marked ordinariness that is only transcended on the stage. Despite considerable wealth she has maintained the frugal habits of childhood and the struggling apprenticeship. Like many Taureans, she maintains a strong sense of the value of things.

However, it is possible to detect something of a conflict between the down-to-earth nature of Taurus, and a Fiery restlessness, the need for the extraordinary, that is symbolised by Sagittarius. With the Sagittarian Moon in a T-square with Saturn and Neptune (and with a strong 12th house) there has been the tendency to imprison the Jupiter nature in ordinariness and domesticity, as well as a reluctance to trust life, or give vent to the ebullient Jupiter energy in the normal course of things. Perhaps because it is denied (save on the stage) this Jupiter energy has tended to manifest as a feeling of restriction. School was experienced in this way. Until her thirteenth year she was an ideal pupil, but there came a sudden and marked change and she began to loathe it. Her academic performance declined and she became a trouble maker. We note in her chart at the time, transiting Uranus on the ascendant, and progressed Moon opposite natal Jupiter. What seems to have been the root of the problem is a sense of confinement, and a characteristic Sagittarian dissatisfaction, rooted in the conviction that there must be something more and something better to life than the daily round. In short, she had outgrown her environment. When she left school in the summer of 1952 transiting Jupiter was conjunct natal Sun, which accurately describes the great sense of release she experienced.

She married on 2 August 1958, at which time transiting Moon conjuncted Saturn, transiting Saturn conjuncted Moon, and transiting Mars conjuncted Venus and Uranus. Like most marriages it had its ups and downs, but was essentially stable, lasting seventeen years. However, it did become another prison for her. She was divorced in January 1976, when transiting Mars opposed natal Moon, transiting Uranus opposed natal Venus, and progressed Venus opposed natal Jupiter. There was also an approaching progressed new Moon, opposite natal Jupiter. This time was experienced as a great release. She became notably more buoyant and carefree. More Jupiterian in short. She informed all her friends that she felt reborn. Her biographer notes that following her divorce, 'she was conducting herself like a woman released into the world after years of incarceration. She behaved like a liberated eagle.'

She was always sharp as razors under the cosy mateyness: articulate, opinionated and a bare-knuckle fighter with anybody who presumed to argue the toss.

Regards her private life as being sacrosanct.

She is reluctant to reveal any chinks in her armour.

All her life, despite the tough 'I can cope' exterior which she presents to the world, Glenda Jackson has been a chronic worrier. She is a born pessimist.

Always a clever girl, but stubborn — very stubborn. (Her mother, cited in reference below).

Source/reference:
Ian Woodward, *Glenda Jackson, A study in Fire and Ice*, Weidenfeld & Nicolson.

James VI/I.
King of Scotland (1567-1625); King of England and Ireland (1603-1625).

Born: 29 June 1566 ns, 09.30 LT, Edinburgh 55N57 3W11.

Source: There is some variance regarding the time of birth, although there is agreement that it took place between 9 and 11 in the morning. I have used a time of 9.30, taken from Lord Herries' *Historical Memoirs* which states 'betwixt nine and ten o' clock in the morning.' However, we should bear in mind the uncertainty.

When Cancer, Moon, or 4th house are strong in a chart it is often the case that the early life experiences are highly significant in the shaping of character. This seemed to be so with James, with his Sun and Mercury in Cancer. He lived in turbulent, lawless times, and as he was the focus of plot and power struggle, he went in constant fear of his life. For his own safety much of his childhood and youth was spent locked up behind castle walls. From this hostile and insecure background developed a phobia about violence, particularly as this might be directed against his own person. He has come down to us as the most cowardly of British kings. We note that Mars is not happily placed in this chart, in the 12th house conjunct Saturn. The courage that comes with Mars was denied, or held in check. However, and perhaps the obverse of this, James was a great peacemaker, and his reign was characterised by stability and harmony (symbolised by the strong Venus).

The early life atmosphere left its imprint in other ways. James didn't know his father or his mother. He was raised by austere scholars in a climate rigorous, formal, and devoid of warmth and emotional sustenance. The sensitive Cancerian James had no one to comfort or reassure him in a motherly fashion; no one to treat him affectionately for what he was as a person. Lonely and insecure, he remained for

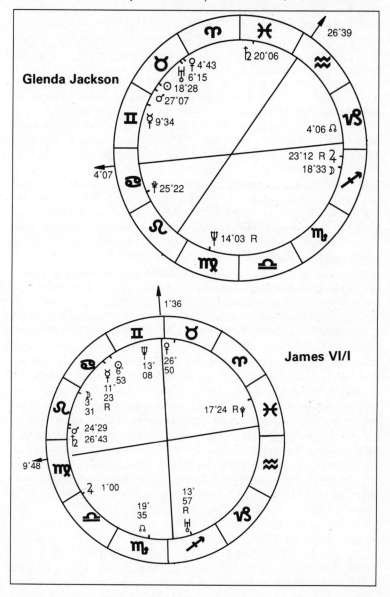

much of his life easy prey to anyone who showed him the least warmth and friendship. The first to do so were young men, and James has come down to us as the most overtly homosexual king.

The most striking aspect pattern in this chart is the close Mars-Saturn conjunction squared by Venus. Other writers[1] have pointed out that Mars-Saturn combinations in a man's chart sometimes concur with homosexuality. And Charles Carter's analysis of Venus-Mars squares[2] applies very well to James. 'Venus', he writes, 'is (the) significatrix of those from whom affection may normally be expected ... and the action of Mars tends to make these persons either harsh and non-understanding, or it may remove them.' He goes on to say that 'Venus weakens the courage and hardihood of Mars ... if Venus predominates, then there is such sensitiveness that the least roughness has a prostrating effect.' He adds that this aspect does not necessarily manifest in the married life, but most often in the early domestic sphere: 'it is rare to find a person ... who has not lost, or suffered through or at the hands of, one of the parents.'

As was required of a monarch, James did marry. His union with Anne of Denmark produced three children, one of whom died young, and another (Charles I) who almost did. His wife's noon chart shows the Sun in Capricorn, and Moon, Venus, and Saturn in conjunction. This suggests a loyal and dutiful wife, but a cool one, ill-suited to meeting emotional demands.

James has also come down to us as the most scholarly of British kings. His childhood was a gruelling regimen of learning, and before his tenth year he had mastered Greek, Latin, French and a number of other subjects. His work was accounted good, and one of his books, *Counterblaste to Tobacco*, was reprinted as late as 1954. He comes across as a strong individual, in the sense of being strongly characterised, very much himself and no one else. This is often the case when Cancer and Leo are strong in a chart, as they are here. He seems to have been modest, mild, unostentatious, extravagant and witty. He seemed as he aged to become more lewd and offensive in his personal habits. He had a love of hunting, and this likewise brought out a vital, earthy side. He was strongly paternalistic, again a reflection of the strong Cancer and Leo of the chart. The major event of an essentially uneventful life was his leaving Scotland to succeed to the English Throne, in April 1603. It was a major break in his life. He had little love for Scotland, and returned only once. We note in his chart at this time progressed Moon conjunct natal Uranus.

So long as his favourites continued to love their 'Dear Dad' — which was how James described himself — his generosity rewarded them and their kin. He delighted in their marriage, since their wives were no threat and their children a source of pleasure to the ageing man who called himself their 'grandfather'. In short, his favourites were the king's Peter Pans; they could be naughty, then contrite, spoilt but still loving brats, in fact almost anything so long as they never grew up, and became independent. He was determined that his fledglings would never completely leave the nest.[3]

... a deep and canny reserve, the ability to keep his own counsel and form his own judgements.[5]

...his chronic inability to resist the importunity of suitors.[6]

... had as many witty jests as any man living, at which he would not smile himself, but deliver them in a grave and serious manner.[6]

He apprehends and understands everything. He judges reasonably. He carries much in his memory and for a long time.[6]

James grew up with a passionate desire to love and be loved, in the Romantic sense, to worship something beyond himself, something fairer, more physically perfect.[5]

Sources/references:
1. Liz Greene, *Saturn*, Samuel Weiser.
2. Charles Carter, *The Astrological Aspects*, Fowler.
3. Charles Carlton, *Charles I The Personal Monarch*, Routledge & Kegan Paul.
4. Caroline Bingham, *James I of England*, Weidenfeld & Nicolson.
5. Antonia Fraser, *James I*, Weidenfeld & Nicolson.
6. Robert Ashton (ed), *James I by his Contemporaries*, Hutchinson.

Samuel Johnson.

Dr Johnson. Lexicographer, novelist, poet, journalist. Second most quoted writer in English language (after Shakespeare).

Born: 18 September 1709 ns, 16.00 LT, Lichfield 52N40 1W50.

Source: A hand-written note in a volume of Johnson's works given by Johnson to his housekeeper. Stated as 'about four o'clock in the afternoon'. (I'm grateful to the curator of the Samuel Johnson Birthplace Museum for this information.)

'When I took the first survey of my undertaking, I found our speech copious without order, and energetic without rules; wherever I turned my view, there was complexity to be disentangled and confusion to be regulated; choice was to be made out of boundless variety, without any established principle of selection.'

Johnson wrote the above lines in the introduction to his Dictionary, and his intention provides a good example of Virgo in action. This is a sign that seeks to impose order at whatever level, to break down what is vast, threatening, complex or confused, into something simple and manageable. In human affairs this principle manifests in a number of ways, perhaps the need to live a highly regulated life, or in the compulsion to impose intellectual constructs on an essentially disordered universe. With Sun and Mercury in this sign, what Johnson wanted to order was the English language. His two-volumed dictionary, which took nine years to produce, was the result.

Johnson's Moon is in Pisces opposite the Virgo Sun, and this opposition is descriptive of a good part of his life and character. Not least, the specific nature of his mind seems a fruitful compound of a Jupiter and a Mercury sign. He had both breadth and capacity for detail. He had an extraordinary range of knowledge, and a capacious memory, never forgetting anything he heard or read. The sheer scale of something like the Dictionary speaks Jupiter (and the Capricorn ascendant). We should remember that his was the first English language dictionary. There was nothing to build on; he started from scratch. He wrote definitions for some 40,000 words, whose meanings he illustrated with 114,000 example quotations drawn entirely from his own knowledge of English literature. He had the Virgoan ability to scan a work and digest the significant information from a mass of detail. Likewise Mercurial was his capacity to reduce his great store of knowledge into pointed or witty statements — he is remembered for his aphorisms. As well as lexicographer, he was poet, novelist, and prolific journalist. He was regarded as one of the greatest conversationalists of his day, able to discourse at length, and with wisdom and humour on a great range of subjects. He was factual and objective, a by-word in common sense. He had an immense curiosity. As Boswell noted, his supreme enjoyment was the 'exercise of the reason'. Again, all very Mercurial. Nor was this breadth at the expense of depth, for certainly his creative writing touches on universal truths.

His Piscean Moon was evident in a strong compassionate nature. He ran a strange and chaotic household, where he sheltered and supported an assortment of misfits, disabled, and down-and-outs. He was extravagant in his generosity, though frugal in his own habits. We note that the Piscean Moon is descriptive of his domestic circumstances. The Pisces and Virgo worked against, as well as with each other. He seemed to fear his chaotic, Watery inner world. The shifting sands of Pisces inspired in him a need to grasp, at times desperately, at the stability of external fact. So that, for example, when subjective fears threatened to swamp him, he would indulge in numeric exercises to provide the sense of order and clarity he craved. Although noted for his humour, it seems he was not himself a content man. He suffered a number of nervous tics and mannerisms, and the fretful, anxious nature that sometimes goes with Virgo. Boswell speaks of a morbid, melancholy nature.

Johnson's life-pattern is one of a swing between self-mastery and helplessness. There were protracted periods in his life when he was bogged down in a hopeless sort of paralysis. At such times his will and capacity to act were almost totally eroded. These periods provoked such a state of despair that Johnson's friends feared for his sanity. The Pisces side seemed to set up a protest against the Virgo pressure of self-demand. The subsequent torpor and paralysis of will then invoked guilt and an even greater determination to be the master of his own circumstances. This in its turn would invoke more of Pisces' incapacitating paralysis. And so on, in a destructive closed circuit.

Although such a pattern is suggested by the Sun-Moon opposition, we should also look to Mars, because at a basic level this planet symbolises the capacity to act. In Johnson's case Mars, traditionally judged, is 'weak'. It is placed in Libra, the sign of its detriment, conjunct Venus and opposed by Neptune, both of which, in their way, weaken the power of Mars to act; Venus saps the inclination, presents a barrier of indolent inertia, while Neptune defuses and defocalises.

> ... his imaginative speed in getting a point, his restless imagination and hunger for novelty ... his impatience and quick capacity for boredom.[1]

> The deepest single emotion Johnson was capable of feeling towards others — and he was a strongly emotional man in many ways — was that of gratitude.[1]

> ... fierce and exacting sense of self-demand ... The part of himself from which he needed to escape was the remorseless pressure of 'superego' demand, of constant self-criticism.[1]

> (His) habit of leaping ahead in imagination into the future and forestalling disappointment and hurt by anticipation.[1]

> His own lifelong compulsion to get all evils anticipated in advance, shrewdly, realistically, and digested into habitual response in order not to lose his ability as a 'free-agent' and become the helpless victim of chance, caprice, or malignity ... his massive attitude of distrust toward life generally.[1]

> (His) subconscious compulsion to 'order' subjective experience — to divide it up, round it off, or give it 'manageable pattern'.[1]

> Though indolence and procrastination were inherent in his constitution, whenever he made an exertion he did more than anyone else.[2]

Sources/references:
1. Walter Jackson Bate, *Samuel Johnson*, Chatto & Windus.
2. *Boswell's Life of Johnson vol 1*, Oxford Univ Press.

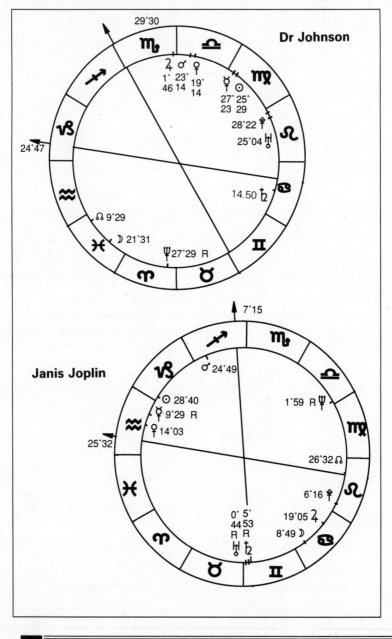

Janis Joplin

Singer. Rock legend.

Born: 19 January 1943, 09.45 CWT, Port Arthur 29N54 93W56.
Source: Birth certificate (Lois Rodden, *Profiles of Women*).

In her short life Janis Joplin became something of a 60s symbol, partly through the infectious power of music, and partly because of her spirit of rebellion. That phenomenon we call the Sixties has a mixed Uranian and Neptunian cast (of which more in later chapters). The fact that her chart shows a grand trine involving Uranus, Neptune, Sun and Saturn suggests that she became a channel for those outer planet energies that were in the air at the time and thus became a focus of generational interest. It is no easy matter to shoulder transpersonal energies, and the burden was one that broke her. She died an early death, aged 27.

The chart shows a strong Aquarian side, with the ascendant, Mercury and Venus in this sign, and with Uranus conjunct the IC. The Aquarian cast of her character is very evident from biography. From an early age she was obviously different, a free and independent spirit who wasn't to be bound by the standards and conventions of her community. She inspired fear, distrust, even hatred amongst her peers. She unhinged people with her 'unfeminine' and 'unAmerican' behaviour. This is characteristic of Aquarius, to run against the grain in this way. She seemed also to possess the frank, open, honest nature of this sign, and also the cultivated offensiveness that sets out to shock.

To understand her creative nature we must look to the Sun. It is placed in Capricorn, a sign not usually associated with the uninhibited abandon that was Janis Joplin in performance. Yet Capricorn is an Earth sign. On the deeper level it has a relationship to the exuberant life force that the ancients symbolised in figures like Pan and Dionysos. She was in essence a pagan high priestess giving vent to a flow of wild, crude and undifferentiated life-energy (and invoking the same abandon in her audience). Capricorn is a sign that equates not just to constraint and order, but to these punctuated by periods of licence. Thus, the meaning of Capricorn (and its ruling planet Saturn) is mirrored in things like the Roman Saturnalia, and in 'Satu(*rn's*)day-night syndrome', where the dutiful discipline of the working week is relaxed and the population as a whole more inclined to alcoholic and lusty abandon.

Without wishing to be glib, it seemed that every night was Saturday night to Janis Joplin. She had a problem with self-control and discipline. This is a chart strong in Saturn but individuals very often only begin to get in touch with the Saturn principle after their thirtieth year. The only way she could really exercise restraint and bring order into her life was to place herself in a constraining environment —

which she did from time to time. Wildness and chaos vitalised, but also frightened her. There were times when she yearned desperately for the anchors of normality. Her chart suggests that in a sense her life was a struggle between Saturn and Uranus; between a need for order and conformity, and a need for rebellion and freedom of the spirit. This is a struggle inherent in Aquarius itself, but is amplified in this case with the two planets themselves conjunct on the IC.

In more immediate terms the difficulty and discomfort she experienced in her life was the product of an over-sensitive and insecure Cancer Moon. She was by all accounts a very self-centred woman, concerned with her own needs. Cancer is the child in us and what she needed most was attention, affection and reassurance. Perhaps more than anything she wanted to be accepted by others, for what she was — a need denied in her childhood by the people around her. She was moody, volatile, sensitive to criticism, and often aggressively defensive to slights real or imagined. Capricorns often work hard at cultivating an image, a sort of social persona, but it seems likely that the coarse and tough image she developed was, in part at least, a carapace to protect what is often with a Cancer Moon a morbidly sensitive centre. Cancer must feel safe and secure before revealing its warm and sensitive side, and this seemed to be the case with her.

Her Moon is square Neptune, which suggests (along with the strong twelfth house) her drug dependence and a generally dissolute life-style. It mirrored also in a self-denying side; she seemed often to pull the carpet from beneath her own feet just as it seemed she might get what she most desired. What she did want most of all was to be close to another human being. She was a desperately lonely person. Her immature emotional nature and her Saturnian persona were two things which stood between her and sustaining partnership. Ways in which she tried to overcome her sense of isolation were indiscriminate sex, and drugs of oblivion like alcohol and heroin.

She craved acceptance by ... ordinary people, longed to believe what they believed.

Janis's emotional world was small, consisting almost entirely of her desires and needs.

Janis was consumed and driven by a need for love that was preposterous in its magnitude ... her excessive narcissism (was) the result of bitter frustrations and the very stuff of her insecurity ... She was in fanatical pursuit of affection while rendered incapable, by the self-direction of her feelings.

Her ambition — striving, nagging, persistent, screaming, ambition.

... defending herself before the attack that was sometimes not even coming. When she became aware of other people's feelings, she could be winningly sensitive, generous of heart, and touchingly sweet. Frequently, though, she was simply oblivious to the needs of others.

Source/reference:
Myra Friedman, *Buried Alive, a Biography of Janis Joplin*, W.H. Allen.

C.G. Jung.

Psychologist, sage.
Born: 26 July 1875, 19.32 LT, Kesswil 47N36 9E19.
Source: Gret Baumann, Jung's astrologer daughter, to Stephen Arroyo.

The psychology of Carl Jung embraces the spiritual and occult dimensions of reality, and perhaps because of this has found special favour amongst the astrological fraternity. For the most part psychologists and astrologers deal with the same subject — human nature, and the place of the individual in the world — and a number of writers have demonstrated how an understanding of Jungian ideas can augment astrological knowledge.

As with anyone who gives birth to creative ideas, Jung's thought reflects the meaning of his Sun sign. In *The Literary Zodiac* I discuss him in the chapter on Leo, and demonstrate that his work relates to the basic nature of the sign, and to the work of other Leo writers. Essentially Jung's is a self-centred psychology. It is not concerned primarily with the establishment of relationship between individuals, or between individuals and the world, but with integration within a single personality. It is to do with finding the self at the centre, the inner person. Jung himself has emphasised all this:

> My life has been permeated and held together by one idea and one goal: namely to penetrate into the secret of the personality. Everything can be explained from this central point, and all my works relate to this one theme.[1]

Jung reasserts the importance and dignity of the individual in a modern world that tends to dehumanise and collectivise, and this is characteristic of Leo.

Leo is a sign that relates to the idea of an evolution of consciousness, and particularly to the notion of self-conscious individuals as the spearhead of such growth. The unconscious (that is, the raw stuff of consciousness) has to be given expression through the creative lives of individuals. We get a clearer picture of this side of Leo (and the essence of Jung's psychology) through the Anthropos myth. The

Anthropos is a being of light, identical in essence to the godhead. It falls to earth and is scattered throughout matter, and there remains until liberated by a redeemer, either a Solar hero (like Christ), or through the lives of self-conscious individuals. This ties in with Jung's fascination with alchemy, for in one sense we can regard human beings as vessels for the conversion of base matter into the gold of consciousness. Nature gives us a body and an instinctive mind, and from this evolves intellect and, if all goes well, consciousness. Thus light is redeemed, through self-aware individuals who first discover and then live out the purpose and meaning of their lives. Each individual has his or her contribution to make in liberating some of the spirit. This idea of life as an ongoing process of evolution is a common one amongst Leo thinkers.

What about Jung the man? His Leo side was evident in the warm-hearted, outgoing *joie de vivre* of his maturity, and the roistering, fun-loving side of his student days. He was considered a good drinking companion, and generally dominated his peers through force of personality. At the same time there was a controlled side, which is what might be expected with a Saturn sign on the ascendant, and a strong Saturn in the first house. The photographs of him in his 30s (with Freud at Worcester College, for example) show a rather stiff, suspicious person, slightly austere with his cropped hair and wire-rimmed glasses. It seems also that there was the emotional reticence associated with a Moon/Pluto conjunction. People remarked that he could withdraw deeply within himself.

He had charm and charisma, which appealed to women particularly (often the way with men with Taurean Moons). There was a predom-inance of female disciples who jostled for favour and attention. The Moon in Taurus also reflects his love of the simple life, his pleasure in physical work, and the richness of his dream life. We note he was a traveller, a man who gained a good deal from his sojourns in primitive cultures. There was a rational, scientific side, suggested by the 'Saturn' overtone. His vocational choice was determined by the urge to marry his scientific and his religious/philosophical sides. It is a very Fixed chart, and this concurs with the single-minded determination with which he set about his quest for knowledge.

He had a love of solitude, and this is suggestive of Neptune, which forms an exact square with the Sun. Neptune also suggests his mediumistic sensitivity and a strong compassionate nature. He felt the pain of the world and hoped that his work might do something to assuage it. There was also the compassion of the Buddha (a more Aquarian variety), for having gained some sort of enlightenment himself through his own suffering and inner questing, he felt compelled to 'return' to instruct others.

The most critical period of his life was his break with Freud, at the end of 1913, followed by a period of intense introversion in which he came close to mental breakdown. This was marked by transiting Uranus conjunct the ascendant and opposite natal Sun. This is apt symbolism for a break with father-figure Freud, in order to search for

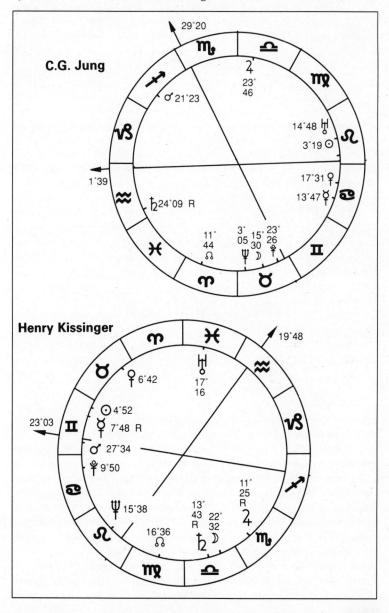

C.G. Jung

Henry Kissinger

his own 'father' within. It was a break he had to make if he was to become a mature, creative individual.

... an unusually large capacity for love, which both enlivened and burdened his existence. Jung had to an extraordinary degree the gift of empathy ... of sympathy and of human warmth for his family, his friends, his patients and, in the end, for all mankind.[2]

That which distinguished Jung's personality more than anything else, and which was especially conspicuous when face to face with him, was, in my opinion, his unqualified integrity and outspokenness.[2]

All his life Jung showed the generosity and the magnanimity which are typical of the strong.[2]

(The) habit of asking unorthodox questions characterized Jung's attitude all his life.[2]

Sources/references:
1. C.G. Jung, *Memories, Dreams, Reflections,* Collins.
2. Marie-Louise Von Franz, *C.G. Jung His Myth in Our Time,* C.G. Jung Foundation for Analytical Psychology.
3. Vincent Brome, *Jung Man and Myth*, Granada.
4. Anthony Storr, *Jung*, Fontana.

Henry Kissinger

Statesman, academic, diplomat, celebrity. Nobel Peace Prize recipient 1973.
Born: 27 May 1923, 05.30 MET, Fürth, Bavaria 49N29 11E00.
Source: Birth records (Gauquelin).

In the early 70s Henry Kissinger rose to fame as a global troubleshooter. A new term — shuttle diplomacy — came into being to describe his particular mode of operation. Essentially he was a go-between, always working to open avenues of communication and to build diplomatic relations. This is quite obviously reflected in two of the major influences in his chart: a strong Gemini side (Sun, ascendant, Mercury and Mars in this sign), and the 'Venusian' influence of Moon conjunct Saturn in Libra. It seems that most often it is a combination of Mercury and Venus factors that produce that amalgam of skills — charm, sociability, tact, sense of propriety, and objectivity — that we call diplomacy.

Neptune is also strong in this chart, conjunct the IC, and this is a mixed blessing for Kissinger. Neptune often imparts a chameleon quality, a capacity to be all things to all people and to defy categorisation, and this can certainly be an asset in the world of politics and diplomacy. But Neptune also tends to bring duplicity and a tendency to deceive. Gemini likewise has a devious double-talking side, and there are certainly those who have called him a con-man. But others have spoken highly of him. Moon conjunct Saturn in Libra suggests a foundation of honour and probity and it is likely this that has inspired the confidence of world leaders. Where Neptune undoubtedly shows is in his obsessive secrecy, and in the patina of glamour that has readily attached to him.

Kissinger often demonstrated the pragmatism, ready wit and banter associated with Gemini. He is a noted intellectual and achieved high office through brain power and through his wide knowledge of current affairs. This is a strong Air chart, with a corresponding weakness in Water. This suggests a very detached, objective person, one who is friendly but a little cool. There is likely a genuine interest in other people, but a tendency to tire quickly of them. The suggestions are of a person rather ill at ease in the world of feeling and more comfortable in structured, formalised relationship. The element balance of this chart lends weight to the comment that he has a very good brain but little heart.

Mars is strong in his chart, being closely conjunct the ascendant, and this reflects significantly in his character. He is a self-made man, achieving entirely on his own strength. He can be abrasive, hot-tempered, single-minded, and ruthless. In his work he was vigorous and energetic. Like many with strong Mars influences he enjoyed challenge and worked well under pressure. He had some of the special vanity of Mars, the egotism, which came to the fore when his will was opposed, or when he felt threatened. In face to face diplomacy however, the Venus/Mercury nature was to the fore. He used charm and humour to disarm hostility.

He is hawkish by nature, believing that peace is rooted in strength and in the tension of opposing armed camps. His broad objective was always order and he was prepared to sanction extreme means — including napalm — to achieve this end.

Kissinger achieved a good deal of fame and honour but future historians might well regard his achievements as more cosmetic and expedient than anything else. He extricated America from Vietnam, for example, but he brought no peace or order to that part of the world. Probably his most durable achievement is the husbanding of warmer relations between America and China and Russia.

Kissinger can be a connoisseur of nuance, with a talent for subtle explanations and, when necessary, for elegant double-talk.[1]

He has the remarkable ability to convince two people with

opposing viewpoints that he agrees with both of them — without in any way compromising his own position.[1]

Cautious, methodical, intense.[1]

A master of secrecy.[1]

Constant mentality in motion.[1]

When he catches a glimpse of a potential antagonist, Kissinger's instinct is to win him over with charm and humour.[1]

Sources/References:
1. Marvin and Bernard Kalb, *Kissinger*, Hutchinson.
2. *Current Biography*, June 1972 , H.W. Wilson and Co.

John Lennon.
Musician, songwriter. 'A catalyst and a dream-weaver for a generation's ideals.'[1]
Born: 9 October 1940, 18.30 BST, Liverpool 53N25 3W0.
Source: Pauline Stone, who knew John Lennon and his father, as recorded in *The Astrological Journal* (winter 1981-2): 'His father certainly believed his correct time of birth was 6.30 pm BST.'

On both the personal and transpersonal level John Lennon's life can be seen as a story of repolarisation, an equilibrating of the opposing principles of Mars and Venus. Such a story finds obvious symbolism in a chart where the signs ruled by the two planets are accented: Aries rises, and the Sun is in Libra.

For the first part of his life, Aries was to the fore and Libra in the background. He came over as tough, abrasive and cynical, with the exaggerated maleness that is characteristic of Aries. To many of the teachers at school and art college he was just a loud-mouthed trouble maker. There was a restless energy, and he gave the impression to many of a man in a hurry. There was a bullying nature, although this manifested verbally rather than physically. He had a caustic wit, and a cruel and sick sense of humour. The following biographical statements are indicative of Mars and Aries:

An outward veneer of ruggedness, which often manifested itself in raw aggression.

Lennon wanted his own way in most things and didn't relax his pressure until he got it.

The same principle applied throughout his life: first decide, then do it, then move on to the next situation — a new challenge.

In these younger days the Venusian side was occasionally evident in his music, but more consistently in his dealings with women. Many detected a warmer, softer side, and for his part he treated women with the romantic, slightly old-fashioned deference that is characteristic of Libra. He was also very traditional in his attitude to marriage.

The Moon is in Aquarius and this suggests his early rebelliousness and boredom with the orthodox. It reflects his honesty, lack of pretentiousness, and universal popularity. It suggests certain facets of his creativity, his fondness for Joycean stream-of-conscious wordplay, for example, and his desire for a new and more humane social order. The Moon in Aquarius tells us something about his taste in women. He was attracted to his first wife because she was 'supercool and different.' His second wife, Yoko Ono, was an Aquarian Sun who strongly manifested the unorthodox and avant-garde nature of the sign. The Moon is closely opposed by Pluto and trined by Mars, thus giving the chart a 'Scorpionic' overtone. He was from an early age made aware of death, through the loss of a number of people close to or important to him. This planetary pattern is also suggestive of the metamorphosis that was central to his life: the death of tough rocker and Beatle John Lennon, and the birth of John Lennon apostle of peace. This rebirth constituted the equilibrating of Mars and Venus.

From about 1968 onwards John Lennon became a conscious expression of the Venus principle. He became the focus for the Peace Movement, and he and Yoko Ono engaged in a series of stunts designed to capture world media attention and promote the cause of peace. However, his ultimate contribution to life goes beyond these. John Lennon once commented that he would like he and Yoko to be remembered as the Romeo and Juliet of the 1970s, and there was about this relationship an almost mythic quality. It may have fallen short of the perfection they sought, but in many ways it was exemplary. In it they created a single harmony, and if such a harmony were multiplied, there would be no strife in the world. War is not a natural state but comes about through the absence of love and the failure of relationship. Until we can learn to relate sanely to each other on the individual level there seems little hope of doing so on a global scale. Some would argue that we do not need to be shown how to relate, and yet we only have to look at the divorce rate, at the physical and mental cruelty that exists within some marriages and families, and at the number of marriages that are purely formal and void of content to realise that there is room for improvement. And there is plainly something askew in a world where governments consciously and con-sistently spend billions on armaments rather than on the alleviation of suffering. This is the politics of Mars not of Venus, and John Lennon vocalised the wishes of millions who want to balance the scales.

We might note some significant dates in his life. He first met Paul McCartney 6 July 1957. The year 1961 was critical for the Beatles, notably in early December when Brian Epstein took on the management. The first single in Britain was released 5 October 1962,

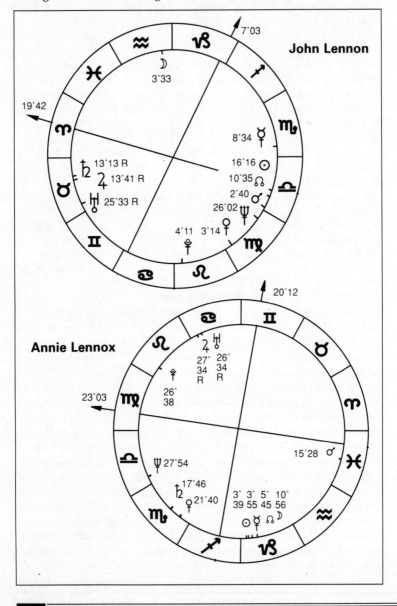

and the following year saw a rapid ascent to phenomenal success (John Lennon was a millionaire by mid-1964). His mother was killed in July 1958, his guardian uncle died 5 June 1955, his best friend 10 April 1962, and his manager 27 August 1967. He first met Yoko Ono 9 November 1966 and they began a relationship in May 1968 (and this marked the start of the death of The Beatles). They married 20 March 1969. On 22 April of the same year he changed his name formally to John Ono Lennon (to emphasise that he and his wife should be considered as one entity).

A powerful event occurred in his childhood, in July 1946. He was confronted with an 'impossible' decision, of choosing between his mother and father, who were splitting up after the failure of their marriage. A difficult decision for anyone, let alone a Libran. He chose his mother, but really what he wanted was to have them both. We can opine that the split was the 'irritant' that produced the pearl, the goad that, at a deep level, moved him to create a harmony of opposites within himself, and to strive for the creation of a perfect partnership in his own adulthood.

His murder appalled and saddened the world. Many, like me, who grew up with The Beatles felt they had lost a good friend.

Source/reference:
1. Ray Coleman, *John Lennon,* Fontana.

Annie Lennox

Singer, songwriter, musician. One half of *The Eurythmics*.
Born: 25 December 1954, 23.10 GMT, Aberdeen 57N10 2W08.
Source: Birth certificate.

The Eurythmics are one of the more talented and successful groups to emerge from the 1980s, and at least half the credit for this goes to Annie Lennox, with her fertile musical mind, and her accomplished and distinctive vocal style. Hers is a chart strong in Earth, particularly in Capricorn (Sun, Moon and Mercury conjunct here), and, as was noted earlier, this element has a strong connection with rock music. This is one expression of an overcivilised culture seeking the revitalising sustenance of pagan roots, and both Capricorn and Virgo at a deep level relate to this kind of turnabout. Elvis Presley, to the delight of the young and the consternation of the establishment, was the first white man to infuse popular music with a primitive element, and he was a Capricorn Sun. So also are Maggie Bell, Patti Smith, Marianne Faithful, and Janis Joplin, and we can detect in each of these ladies the crude but vital energy that is one facet of Earth.

Annie Lennox is a more sophisticated performer than any of these.

She comes across as altogether more cool, detached and refined, a difference which may relate to the Virgo ascendant. Virgo rising is generally a moderating influence. One *Rolling Stone* reviewer made the comment: 'Her stage persona, like David Bowie's, takes shape somewhere between control and abandon.' This is just what we might expect with a strong Capricorn nature, for the sign focuses (at one level) on just such an interplay. Interestingly, David Bowie is also a Capricorn Sun. The use of the word 'persona' is interesting too, for Capricorn has come to be related to this idea of a carefully crafted public face, one that reveals, not the real self, but a self one wishes to project, for reasons of approval or prestige. Capricorns can be very conscious of how they appear in the eyes of the world. With her Moon in Capricorn we can say that Ms Lennox's basic sense of security is connected to the recognition and approval she receives through her professional status.

There is also a strong 'Mercury' overtone in the chart, with Virgo rising and the planet closely conjunct the Sun, and conjunct the Moon. This suggests her fertile and creative mind, and also a chameleon nature; there is a delight in disguise, in dressing up, in constantly changing styles and images. It also suggests a favourite image, and the one that first caught the public eye: the elegant transvestite. Mercury is traditionally held to be androgynous, and this side of the symbol can translate in obvious as well as subtle ways. (We note that Boy George, who also rose to fame through an androgynous image, has Sun in Mercury-ruled Gemini, and Moon conjunct the Mercury/Sun midpoint. Sun and Moon are also widely conjunct in his chart, and Mercury stationary).

From biography we get the impression of a shy and essentially private person. There seems to be the sensitivity associated with the lunar new-Moon personality. She is prone to depression and pessimism, and she suffered for a time from agoraphobia. There is a serious, hard-working, professional approach to music. There seems to be the health and diet consciousness of Virgo.

She left home for London and The Royal Academy of Music in August 1972, when transiting Jupiter conjuncted natal Sun, and transiting Saturn was on her MC. The same two planets transited her ascendant through the latter part of 1980, the time *The Eurythmics* were being formed. For much of 1984 transiting Jupiter retrograded back and forth over her Sun and Moon, and Saturn about its own place. This coincided with superstardom.

She's a perfectionist (almost to the point of obsessiveness) who consequently can't stand people who are slow witted, who lack punctuality and who are untidy.[1]

Very precise and anxious to be appreciated fully, which is why — even now — she can appear cautious or restrained in interview.[1]

Sources/references:
1. J. Waller, *Eurythmics: Sweet Dreams The Definitive Biography,* Virgin Books.
2. *Current Biography*, May 1988, H.W. Wilson & Co.

David Livingstone

Missionary, and explorer of central Africa

Born: 19 March 1813, 22.30 LT, Blantyre, 55N50 4W10
Source: Warden of the David Livingstone Memorial in Blantyre: 'Family tradition puts the time as late (10-11pm) on a stormy night.'

Livingstone is a figure who has been somewhat idealised and it is only in more recent years with conscientious biography that a balanced picture has emerged. It is easier to detail his positive points first for these are fewer and more straightforward than the many failings of a complex and enigmatic man.

As an explorer he was as intrepid as they come, with great courage, determination and powers of endurance. Also laudable was his denunciation of the Arab slave trade that flourished in Africa in the 19th century. This reflects the strong 'Scorpio' in the chart (Moon and ascendant in this sign, Sun conjunct Pluto, Mars closely sextile the Moon and square the Sun) for this is a sign that at its best seeks to root out evil and oppression wherever it can be found.

There is also a strong 'Pisces' overtone to the chart and many of his more serious failings can be related to the self-deceptive nature of this influence. The Victorians wanted to believe in the image of a saintly man bringing God's light into the dark regions of the earth. They were willing, it seems, to subscribe generous amounts to the cause of such a man, and there were those willing to exploit Livingstone's fame along these lines. This capacity to propagate an essentially false but glossy image relates primarily to Pisces and its ruling planets. It is another case of the Victorians attempting to assuage their famed collective guilt. People like Livingstone, or rather the romantic image of him, provided a more ennobling reason for a European presence in Africa. In truth his concerns were more secular than religious; more self-centred than selfless. In his whole time in Africa Livingstone made only one convert, who later relapsed. As a missionary he was not a success. His interest lay in exploration and economic exploitation.

Livingstone had a remarkable capacity for self-delusion. This is not the harmless trait it sometimes seems, for it often lays the ground for future disillusion and disappointment and these can exact a heavy toll, particularly on the Jupiterian temperament. This was compounded in Livingstone's case because more than one expedition came to grief on the basis of false reports he filed regarding conditions in Africa. Indeed, Livingstone seemed to suffer many of the more negative traits associated with Jupiter. He was optimistic, but most usually this was

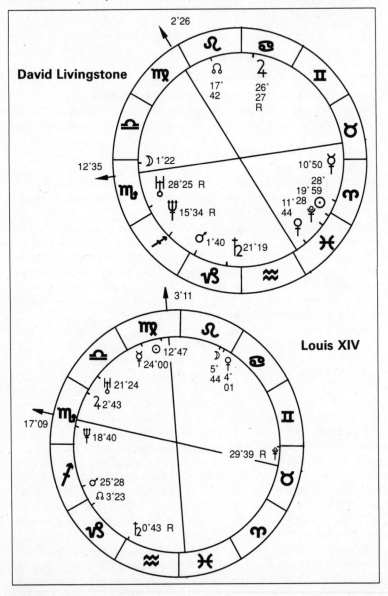

just wishful thinking. He was a dreamer full of impractical and grandiose schemes. He had a crusader zeal, and an inflated image of his own role in bringing about social and economic change in Africa. He was a vain and ambitious man (Mars and Saturn in Capricorn contribute here), determined to get a lion's share of the fame and glory.

His was a Jupiterian burden of having to live up to great public expectation. Haunted by fear of failure he would often lie, and malign others to cover his own shortcomings and errors of judgement. He had a Martial intolerance of weakness, both in himself and others. He carried a bout of malaria as if it were no more than a heavy cold, and expected others to do the same. He was basically an unsympathetic, selfish, isolated individual. He was unable to co-operate with others and displayed a marked ruthlessness when it came to sacrificing colleagues and family for the furtherance of his own ambitions. We learn also that he was brusque, taciturn, moody and given to holding grudges, traits related to Scorpio.

> Livingstone was intolerant, narrow and self-opinionated. He was also determined, courageous and resilient.

> His own Christian Faith was of supreme importance to him and he wanted others to be able to share it.

> ... a marked propensity for wishful thinking.

> Livingstone's notorious over-optimism and ambitious new schemes.

> Superhuman tenacity and endurance ... indestructible strength of will.

> By the end of 1870 the whole patchwork of Livingstone's thinking had become an impossibly intertwined web of fantasy and reality.

Source/Reference:
Tim Jeal, *Livingstone*, Heinemann, 1973.

Louis XIV.

Powerful French monarch. 'The Sun King'.
Born: 5 September 1638, 11.22 LT, Paris 48N50 2E20.
Source: Contemporary records.

This chart would seem to bear out those theories of Louis as an essentially timid and weak man who played — and played very well — at being king. Indeed, in some of the portraits we see what could be a petty official peering meekly out from a swathe of exquisite regal robes. It seems he did suffer from a Virgoan sense of inferiority and needed military conquest and dramatic display of the order of Versailles to convince not only others but also himself that he was the world's most powerful monarch.

His character is what we might expect from a blend of Scorpio, Virgo and Leo (Moon in this sign and Sun on the MC). He had a colossal vanity and pride and was given to frequent and ostentatious display of his own grandeur. He had great natural dignity. He was humourless, stiff and formal — though more at ease with women, reflecting the Moon/Venus conjunction. He was a heartless man who cared little for his subjects. There were a number of occasions when he was responsible for unleashing great cruelty and oppression, often to no greater end than the glorification of himself.

He was diligent, hard working and very regular in his day to day living. Like many Virgos, he valued the security of habit and Versailles, as well as being an extravagant projection of his majesty, was simply a regulated environment where he could live out his kingly role without interference from reality. He was shrewd, though not intelligent. He ruled through strength of character. And, whatever the real man, he was capable of maintaining an imperious and regal image. He was secretive and suspicious. He had a strong sexual appetite. He was strongly constituted, seemingly impervious to pain and discomfort.

He had persistent energy ... but his pride and egotism neutralised many of his best qualities.[1]

(An) icy, haughty, inaccessible automaton ... an almost superhuman self-control enabled him to play the king without faltering, every day, at every moment.[2]

...His self-assurance ... his adequacy to situations ... his poise and emotional stability.[3]

Every gesture, every movement, even the most trivial action of everyday was codified ... one sensed that the slightest hitch would bring disarray, if not collapse. But who would think of putting a single speck of dust in the workings of the King of France? And it was that inhuman, obsessive, smooth-running ballet that enabled him to impose his image on his century.[2]

Sources/references:
1. Joanna Richardson, *Louis XIV* Weidenfeld & Nicolson.
2. Prince Michael of Greece, *Louis XIV The Other Side of the Sun*, Orbis.
3. John B Wolf, *Louis XIV*, Gollancz.

Mary MacArthur

Trade union activist, social reformer

Born: 13 August 1880, 04.30 LT, Glasgow 55N51 4W16.
Source: Birth certificate.

Mary MacArthur's life work was fighting for the rights and welfare of working women, a task which started in earnest at the time of her first progressed new Moon. Her involvement with Unionism dates from 1901 but it was in the early summer of 1903 that she left a home too narrow to contain her energies and started work in London with the Women's Trade Union League.

The greatest gift she brought to her cause was a powerful personality. She had a dramatic, larger-than-life presence, which reflects in the strong Solar nature of the chart — Sun, Mercury, Venus and ascendant in Leo, and Sun closely conjunct the ascendant. Also indicative of Leo, and more broadly of the strong Fixed nature of the chart, was her undeviating sense of purpose; her determination to raise the status of working women and to combat the evils which infested the working world in the early decades of this century.

Hers was a volatile, enthusiastic, zealous nature. She was precocious, and lived her life in a sort of overdrive, dying young at the age of 41. She possessed a great deal of drive and energy, and what is more, the capacity to focus and utilise this. This likely reflects the Scorpio Moon, and the conjunction of Mars with Uranus suggests the focusing of her energy on wider social and humanitarian causes. As we will see in a later chapter Unionism, particularly the New Unionism that grew up in the 1880s is related to Neptune. We note an accented Neptune in this chart, for it forms a T-square with the Sun and Moon, and is close to the MC. Her reforming zeal is also likely rooted in her Scorpio nature, for this is an essentially compassionate sign, and one prepared to fight to alleviate misery and suffering. Both Mars signs can be powerfully struck by suffering because they perceive so immediately and intensely. Each time is as fresh as the last and habitualness brings no hardening.

Mary MacArthur did right wrongs and alleviate social ills, and her example is a reminder that at the end of the day change is often effected by strong individuals. Like other Leos, she demonstrated the worth and value of the individual soul in a modern, impersonal world.

The fixity and fervour, even the fury of her zeal.

In the throes of a strike she seemed in flame.

Her personality broke through by virtue of its natural right to dominate its circumstances.

Her sense of drama — of the human bigness of every such fight for the weak and suffering — gave a glow and splendour to the incidents of day to day.

She presented to all and sundry the vision of a person pulsating with energy, (and) full to the brim of joie de vivre.

She needs the stimulus of ... cheers. Praise to her is like wine. It lightens the weight of the day and clears her memory of all pains and stresses. Tasting applause all her powers deepen and expand.

Once started on her work, there are no deflections, no bypaths. Accident does nothing for her. Will and purpose do all.

Source/reference:
Mary Agnes Hamilton, *Mary MacArthur: a biographical sketch*, Leonard Parsons.

Ramsay MacDonald.

Politician. First ever Labour Prime Minister of Great Britain, for a short term in 1924, and again 1929-35.

Born: (James MacDonald Ramsay) 12 October 1866, 23.30 LT, Lossiemouth 57N43 3W18.

Source: Birth certificate.

Commentators agree that Ramsay MacDonald was an important figure in twentieth century British politics. His was a critical role in the establishment of the Labour Party as a major political force. He was very much a symbol, a figurehead around which condensed the inchoate forces of socialism and working-class idealism. One historian opined that MacDonald 'captured the imagination' of the Labour Party. Its hopes and future aspirations seemed to become embodied in him. At the height of his powers MacDonald was a charismatic figure. He constituted a powerful, heroic figurehead whose inspiring oratory swayed an electorate, and whose vision shaped the Party's ideology. All this suggests the strong Fire of the chart, the Leo ascendant and the Sagittarian Moon.

With Sun in Libra and Moon conjunct Venus, MacDonald was a harmoniser and a skilful negotiator. A major political achievement was his handling of the Reparations Crisis following WW1, a task requiring much Libran charm, tact and diplomacy to smooth the differences of nationalistically inflamed nations. It is part of Libra's gift to act as a bridge between potentially antagonistic factions, and it found further outlet in MacDonald in the early days of the Labour Party when a fusion was necessary between political and trade union wings, each with their own priorities. Libra finds the formula that maximises the greatest good for everyone. Libra is an Air sign, and part of his contribution was the construction of a theoretical framework in which such an alliance could exist.

The chart shows a strong Neptune, conjunct the MC and opposite

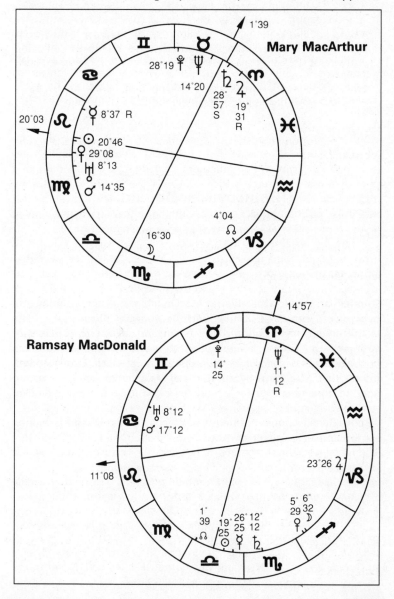

the Sun, and it is interesting to note how this manifested. The following biographical observation is pertinent in this regard:

> By temperament and conviction, MacDonald was better fitted than any of his potential rivals to become the focal point around which such a coalition could take shape. The ambiguity of his personality and philosophy were assets: the fact that no one knew exactly what class he belonged to, exactly what policies he would introduce, exactly what kind of person he was, made it possible for each section of the coalition to see in him what it wanted to see. His romanticism, his dislike of sharp outlines and his fondness for vague, elusive metaphors, all helped him to blur the differences between his heterogeneous and sometimes incompatible potential followers.[1]

This description is suggestive of Neptune (cf Dr Kissinger), a planet that mystifies, deceives (knowingly or otherwise), blurs distinctions and reduces to a common denominator. MacDonald was something of a symbol of the levelling of British society, of the further erosion of the traditional aristocratic power-structure. He was testament to the fact that those of humble background (like himself) could fill the seats of power and govern at least as well as upper-class individuals.

Biography establishes MacDonald as something of a loner, a brooding, vain, romantic figure. He was a great idealist. He was rather aloof, suspicious and hypersensitive. Although a good negotiator, as a leader he was autocratic. Physically he didn't seem suited to the stresses of high office and he died worn out from a lifetime of overwork, vicious calumnies, and the constant bickering of Party factions. There was a cultured side to him, and he developed a taste for antiques (and for the company of aristocrats — something which further alienated him from his socialist supporters). His happy, fruitful marriage was cut short by the death of his wife. Friends commented that he was never quite the same following this, and he never remarried.

John Buchan's impression was of 'courtesy' and 'old-fashioned elaboration'. He speaks of

> a queer romantic kink which made him see melodrama in perfectly humdrum affairs. He could not help picturing himself in dramatic parts. To the end there was an endearing innocence about him.[2]

He first left Scotland to seek his way in the world in the early summer of 1885. He first stood for Parliament in 1892, but was not elected until January 1906. He first met his wife in June 1895. On 3 February 1910 his son died, and eight days later his mother. His wife died later in the year, on 8 September. In the Spring of 1927 he contracted a mysterious throat infection which almost killed him. The late summer of 1931 represents the major political crisis of his career, with the formation of the National Government, and a subsequent split in the Labour Party. He died of heart failure, 9 November 1937.

He had an unusual capacity to see other people's points of view. If he had not, the Labour Party might never have come into existence.[1]

It was commonly said that he suffered from vanity, but that is not quite fair. It would be more accurate to say that he had in a high degree the Celt's sensitiveness to praise or blame. Adverse criticism of his conduct from however negligible a quarter distressed him acutely. On the other hand praise equally elated him. Like many sensitive people he was at his best when he found himself in a favourable atmosphere and he enjoyed the assurance of admiration.[3]

... a streak of moral and intellectual intolerance ... in the conflicts which had surrounded him throughout his political career, he had always been apt to give the impression that his opponents were wicked as well as mistaken.[1]

Indeed if I had to choose one epithet for him it would be 'endearing'. There was a sombre gentleness which fascinated me ... two things never failed him — courage and courtesy. The whole man was a romance, almost an anachronism.[2]

Sources/references:
1. David Marquand, *Ramsay MacDonald*, Jonathan Cape.
2. John Buchan, *Memory Hold the Door*, Hodder & Stoughton.
3. Hugh Pattison MacMillan, *A Man of Law's Tale,* Macmillan.

Charles Rennie Mackintosh.
Designer, painter, and regarded as one of the outstanding architects of the twentieth century.
Born: 7 June 1868, 11.15 LT, Glasgow 55N51 4W16.
Source: Birth certificate.

Mackintosh was very much a modern in that he aspired to a living architecture, to one rooted in the present day. In this he ran counter to the established practice in late nineteenth century Scotland, where the vogue was for buildings modelled on Greek temples and baronial castles. The Glasgow School of Art, designed by Mackintosh at the turn of the century, is regarded as the first truly twentieth century building in that it embodied a genuinely contemporary style. He hoped to convince his peers of the need for a modern architecture, but they remained unmoved. He eventually gave up the attempt and, somewhat embittered, sank into obscurity. Many of his decorative interiors were destroyed and when after his death the contents of his flat were auctioned they realised only £88. Today a single piece of Mackintosh furniture will fetch thousands of pounds. It is only in more recent years that he has been widely recognised as an outstanding architect and designer. He did gain some appreciation in his day from the Continental Art Nouveau movement, itself devoted to establishing a style independent of any tradition. But for the most part, in his own lifetime Mackintosh remained alone, isolated from the cultural mainstream.

His urge for recognition is suggested by a strong 10th house, and by Saturn conjunct the IC. But in a broader sense his life pattern is best described by the Gemini Sun and by the close Moon-Uranus opposition. This latter is most suggestive of his need to pit himself against the architectural establishment, a need strong enough for him to refuse lucrative offers of work in Europe, from where it would have been more difficult to influence his peers. Like that Uranian figment Miss Jean Brodie, Mackintosh saw himself as a 'leaven in the lump'. Aquarius and Uranus (strong in this chart) function to bring new vision to society. They vivify its structures through culture, consciousness and invention. There needs must be a balance lest the structural moulds be shattered or the light of vision extinguished through sheer inertia. In Mackintosh's case the balance was not effected. The lump was too dense and his Uranian vision was snuffed out.

Gemini, at root, is a sign of actualisation. It relates to the creation of new forms in the here-and-now world of space and time, thus allowing for the expression and development of some underlying 'idea' or symbol. We see this reflected in the physical world where a profusion of forms (or species) emanate from, and are the expression of, a single life-force. The production of different forms, as Darwin observed, depends at least in part upon environment, upon specific and particular circumstance. Hence the idea of Gemini as a contemporary sign, and something of the reason why Mackintosh as a Gemini Sun was not content to slavishly copy the forms of the past but sought instead to give novel expression to some underlying, twentieth century 'symbol' (or spirit of the age).

Mackintosh has Virgo rising, which reinforces his Mercurial side. He was a very observant man, particularly with regard to natural forms. He was aware that no two leaves on a tree, no two petals on a flower, were the same, and such subtle and minute variation often found its way into his designs. He was a fastidious man, paying the greatest attention to every last detail of an interior design. Mackintosh embodied the versatility of Mercury, being water-colourist, furniture designer, interior designer, graphic designer as well as architect. But most notably he was an embodiment of the great, inventive, creative vitality of Gemini.

On a personal level it seems that Mackintosh was of a highly strung, nervous disposition. There was a certain brooding, melancholic side (mirroring the strong Saturn side of the chart), but on balance he was accounted a strong and attractive personality. He was industrious and practical, and, although a modern, he had high regard for traditional materials and methods. This reflects the strong Earth of the chart — Virgo ascendant, Capricorn Moon, Mars in Taurus.

The years 1896-1906 marked a high plateau of industry and creativity. It was after 1906 — his Uranus opposition — that he gave up his attempts to influence the refractory architectural establishment. After this date his personality deteriorated to some extent. He became more taciturn and morose, and given to bouts of excessive drinking. He married 22 August 1900. In autumn 1927 he was being treated for tongue cancer, an affliction which finally robbed him of the power of speech. He died 10 December 1928.

> To his friends he was a warm-hearted, genial soul with simple tastes and pleased by simple things. With strangers he was reserved and aloof, especially if they were of the conventional sort ... but he warmed at once to the sympathetic mind. He was a tireless, voluble talker and he would spring immediately to the defence of any man, work or principle which he thought unfairly assailed — a characteristic which remained with him throughout his life.[2]

> His supreme self-confidence, his devil-may-care attitude and indefatigable industry, made him at once admired and respected by all who knew him.[2]

> ... his meticulous care of every detail both practical and aesthetic ... his minute attention to frequently overlooked incidentals.[2]

> ... a highly developed faculty for precise observation of detail.[2]

> A strong vein of brooding intensity.[1]

> The picture that emerges from the all too little evidence is of a tense and hypersensitive person — certainly of a man of forcible opinions and high idealism, capable of immense expenditure of energy and intense depression, warm-hearted and yet sensitive to criticism.[1]

Sources/references:
1. Robert Macleod, *Charles Rennie Mackintosh*, Hamlyn.

2. Thomas Howarth, *Charles Rennie Mackintosh and the Modern Movement*, Routledge & Kegan Paul.

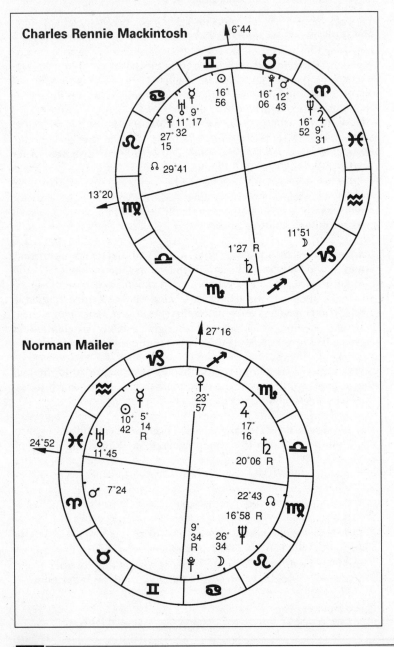

Charles Rennie Mackintosh

Norman Mailer

Norman Mailer.

Writer, journalist, radical, celebrity.

Born: 31 January 1923, 09.05 EST, New Jersey 40N18 74W0.
Source: Birth records (*The Gauquelin Book of American Charts*).

Norman Mailer's chart shows the Sun in Aquarius, and he is a good example of the Uranian side of this sign in action. Through the 50s and 60s he constituted a voice — and a loud one — for radicalism. He consistently inveighed against the American Establishment, and a number of those who emerged as leading lights in the late-60s period of youthful rebellion were inspired by Mailer's lectures and writing. A number of signs have rebellion as part of their nature. What characterises Aquarian (and Uranian) discontent is the awareness that a society has become an ossified form incapable of responding to new vision or ideas, and so consequently outlaws or stifles its more creative spirits. This forms the core of Mailer's radical stance.

As noted in the introduction, Aquarius is not essentially a sign of iconoclasm, for, in order to vivify society with creative spirit it is necessary to establish relationship with it. The sign relates as much to gradual and continuous improvement as to revolutions. This awareness seemed to come to Mailer. Many have commented on a change, a shift in perspective, that occurred around the middle of 1968. He took up a less extreme position, and there became evident an appreciation of some of the good points of his society. He adopted the view at this time that he could probably effect more good working from within the system than simply by beating on the walls from outside. This development was marked by a progressed new Moon (at the beginning of 1968). We also note Saturn transiting the first house of the chart at this time, and Uranus conjunct the descendant.

Mailer came to public awareness through his first novel, *The Naked and the Dead*. It won immediate acclaim as the first great novel to emerge from World War 2, and it went on to sell over three million copies. It was published in May 1948, when transiting Jupiter was conjunct his MC. Further novels met with little success, so he turned to a different form of writing, one better suited to his individual talents, and one that was to re-establish him as a major literary figure. This was his so-called New Journalism, a sort of subjective accounting of history as it is happening. Aquarius can be a very socially conscious sign, one attuned to the pulse of the times. Through his reportage Mailer became something of a chronicler, making people aware of the history that was being born and of which they were a part. Aquarius, we note, is tuned to the process of creativity (or life) rather than the products.

At the personal level his character is well defined and broadly described by a blend of Aquarian Sun, Cancer Moon, and the strongly placed Aries Mars. He exemplifies some of the galvanic nature of Aquarius. He likes to shock and provoke, and doesn't like those around him to feel too comfortable. This is Uranus the awakener who seeks to shake people out of their habitual response patterns. His frequent resort to obscenity is likely rooted here. He is noted for his enormous attention-seeking ego, and for his outwardly swaggering, macho displays. There is marked pugnacity, and combustibility. There have been regular eruptions of violence and conflict with the law, most notably on 19 November 1960, when he stabbed his wife (not fatally), and for which he later received a suspended prison sentence. At the time of the stabbing, transiting Mars was stationary on his Pluto/Moon midpoint, and transiting Pluto quincunxed natal Mars. These describe very well what was an essentially Scorpionic time. Mailer has spoken of it as a period of catharsis, when a lot of repressed bitterness came to the surface, and as a time when he was made starkly aware of the violence and darkness that lay within him.

Aggression is often rooted in personal insecurity, and with a Cancer Moon, there is the suggestion of this in Mailer's case. Cancer is a sign very sensitive to rejection. Following his initial success, there were ten years of failure during which he was consistently rejected by publishers, critics, and public alike. He took this all very personally (as those strong in Cancer tend to do). Some commentators have suggested that his cultivation of a very visible, manly image is a result of over-reaction to this lack of acceptance and recognition.

As is often the case with Cancerian men, his mother was a powerful influence. Long into adulthood he remained a devoted and dutiful son. Similarly, he is a very patriarchal figure himself. He is father of eight children and has been husband to six wives.

... his understanding of new sociological forces at work in American society.

... by audaciously seeking out the most revolutionary antidotes to establishment strictures ... (he) helped shape the rebellious ideology of a new postwar radicalism.

Mailer's entire career has been like an elusive comet, shaking literary traditions and conventional mores in a blast of brilliance.

A connoisseur of experience (and) deeply suspicious of anything that takes place beyond the boundaries of his own first hand observation.

He's very loyal to his friends and courtiers and has a kind of paternal relation to them. He takes care of them and looks after them.

The story of Norman Mailer is one of an ego of large, sometimes outrageous proportions. Mailer has exercised that ego in his conflicts with the political and literary establishments, in his work, and in his relations with women. The symbols of masculinity — drinking, womanizing, and the combative sports — were especially appealing to him.

Source/reference:
Hilary Mills, *Mailer A Biography*, New English Library.

Mary I.

(Mary Tudor) Queen of England 1553-58. Earned the epithet 'Bloody Mary' for her cruel persecution of heretics.
Born: 28 February 1516 (ns), 04.00 LT, Greenwich 51N29 0W0.
Source: Official record; copy published in *Letters and papers of Henry VIII*, vol 3, no 1573 (I'm indebted to Jasper Ridley for this information).

Mary Tudor was a religious fanatic. She authorised the execution of hundreds of people whose beliefs differed from hers. She did so convinced that this was God's will and her duty. There seems little to be said in mitigation of someone who orders to be burned alive some 238 people, save perhaps that this figure palls when compared to the numbers zealously tortured and killed by her Spanish and French counterparts. The Counter-Reformation was one of the blacker spots of European history.

Queens are often looked upon as mothers of the nation. This was so with Mary's sister Elizabeth. As we have seen, what she incarnated for her people, appropriately for a Virgo Sun, was the image of the Virgin Mary. But Mary Tudor was a dark, devouring mother, and if she incarnated any archetype it was that of Kali. In this regard it seems fitting to find Pluto exactly conjunct the ascendant of the chart.

Fanaticism of one sort or another is generally associated with Jupiter and its signs and we have here a strong 'Jupiter chart'. Sun and Venus are in Pisces; Jupiter is conjunct the descendant and closely aspecting the Sun and Moon; the ruling planet Saturn is in Sagittarius, and the Moon is in the 9th house (by equal division). This all reminds us that Jupiter has a dark as well as a bright face. A strong Jupiter and a Capricorn ascendant suggest a rather impersonal nature, so that the suffering of individuals counted little against the greater cause. Had she been anything other than a monarch, Mary would likely have lived a quiet, uneventful life. As it was, she inherited power and became an instrument of Destiny. Like many of the Tudors and Stuarts she ruled in a broad period of transition when one world was dying and another struggled to be born. In a perverse way she hastened the transformation. Her terror turned people against the old faith. In future years the memory of Bloody Mary was often invoked in anti-papist hysteria.

It was only with regard to religion that Mary was ruthless and uncompromising. In secular matters she was, for her time, merciful, exhibiting the common Piscean tendency to forgiveness. Also, she was

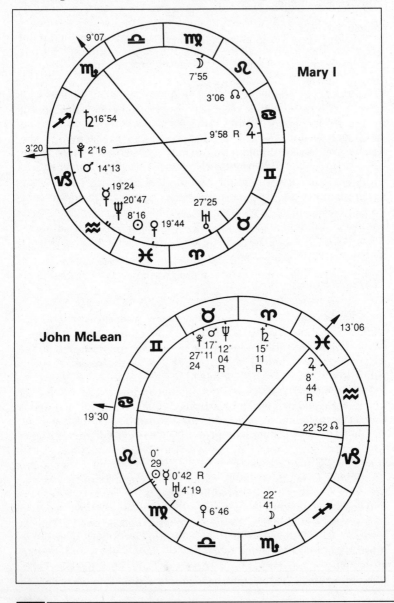

kind and considerate in small ways (reflecting, perhaps, the Virgo Moon). She visited the poor in their dwellings, listening to their troubles and distributing food and alms. However, she did nothing to instigate broad social reform. It seemed her Jupiterian side was wholly commandeered by the Roman Church.

In her daily life she was very pious, but here too she could be extreme. There were formal occasions when the sick were brought before the monarch for a ritual blessing. The Court was horrified at the fervid way Mary went about the ritual duty, embracing the supplicants and kissing their scrofulous sores. Such self-abasement is a singularly Piscean trait.

Mary was an intelligent and well-educated woman. She was an accomplished linguist and skilled in the many graces deemed essential to the Tudor gentlewoman. She had the anxious disposition sometimes found where Virgo is strong. She exhibited also the hard-working and abstemious qualities associated with this sign, along with the shrewdness and caution associated with Capricorn. She had a strong distaste for sex. She married the King of Spain, but it was a barren union and he later deserted her. Her childhood was notably insecure. She drifted in and out of favour with her father, and there was an ever-present possibility of imprisonment, even death. In short, she had a lonely, unhappy life and died perhaps the most unpopular monarch in English history.

Sources/references:
1. Jasper Ridley, *The Life and Times of Mary Tudor*, Weidenfeld & Nicolson.
2. Beatrice White, *Mary Tudor*, Macmillan.

John McLean.

Revolutionary. Educator.
Born: 24 August 1879, 00.50 LT, Glasgow 55N55 4W16.
Source: Birth certificate. Note: the records spell his name *Mc* and not *Mac-*, although the latter spelling occurs commonly in biography.

McLean is widely held to be one of the more important Left-wing revolutionary figures to emerge from Great Britain. Lenin was one who subscribed to this view, making McLean an honorary president to the first Congress of Soviets, and appointing him Bolshevik Consul to Scotland (an appointment not recognised by the British government of the time). McLean was a fighter for a cause, and political propagandist, organiser and agitator. But most significantly, in his own eyes, he was an educator. He believed that true revolution would not come about until the working-class masses had become thoroughly grounded in

Marxist principles, and to this end he devoted a good deal of his time and energy.

Perhaps the main indication of McLean's revolutionary zeal is the close Sun/Mercury/Uranus conjunction opposed to Jupiter on the MC. Uranus has come to be regarded as the revolutionary planet, but in an individual's chart it is not always a reliable indicator of political activism. There are plenty of radicals who do not have the planet or its sign accented, and in my experience, plenty of reactionary Conservatives who do. However, McLean was a man who pitted himself against the establishment, was considered an enemy of the State, and was persecuted accordingly. More specifically, Uranus relates to the urge to raise the awareness and consciousness of the 'unenlightened', and this is clearly enough reflected in McLean's educational ideals.

With Jupiter strong, he was a man of faith, not in religion (he was an avowed atheist), but in Marxism. We note also a Scorpio Moon (opposed by Pluto and Mars) which symbolised a vigorous fighting spirit, and single-minded determination. He was a man who made sacrifices and who suffered for his beliefs, again suggested by the strong Pisces Jupiter, and by Mars conjunct Neptune. He sacrificed the possibility of a comfortable, conventional existence, for he had a university education, and a teaching post. The strong Uranus-Sun conjunction is another symbol of his willingness, perhaps need, to abandon a conventional lifestyle. In the end, however, he sacrificed his physical and mental wellbeing. He was a victim of the ugly nationalism that infested Britain during the Great War years. McLean, like many of his socialist contemporaries, was opposed to what he saw as a ruling-class war. He spoke vigorously against it, and was imprisoned on a number of occasions because of this. He suffered a great deal from what was at the time a primitive and brutal penal system. His six terms of imprisonment undoubtedly contributed to an early death in 1923, but made of him a martyr and a working-class hero.

From biography we learn that McLean was a great idealist, and a charismatic public speaker. He was serious, earnest, studious, short on sense of humour, and abstemious, neither smoking nor drinking. His political ardour was beginning to mount around the end of 1900. By September of that year he was a convinced Marxist', and by 1903 he was 'devoting the larger part of his energy to the socialist cause'. Perhaps his awakening to his life's purpose was a reflection of the progressed new Moon, which was exact at the end of 1902, at about 23 degrees Virgo.

> (He) was very dogmatic and unyielding in his opinions ... almost completely devoid of sentiment.[1]

A man who found it difficult to relate to people, even those close to him, on an emotional level. But his puritanism has to be set alongside his unfailing generosity and humanitarianism, which impressed all who came in contact with him.[1]

One of MacLean's leading characteristics was his superb self-confidence.[2]

He was like a charged body ... a young, vigorous man, who had undergone an almost religious conversion to a noble doctrine, and the whole remainder of his life was the incessant pouring out of this charged energy in a sustained series of street corner meetings.[3]

One of MacLean's outstanding qualities was his complete moral integrity.[4]

... very much of his time and place, in spite of his advanced ideas.[3]

Whether his own conscious efforts had anything to do with it or not, there is no doubt that he was outstandingly successful in maintaining good health. In later years his extraordinary energy and strength were to astonish all who knew him.[3]

Sources/references:
1. *Scottish Labour Leaders 1918-32*, Mainstream Publishing.
2. Hugh MacDiarmid, *The Company I've Kept*, Hutchinson.
3. Nan Milton, *John MacLean*, Pluto Press.
4. John Broom, *John MacLean*, Macdonald.

Maria Montessori.
Founder and propagator of a method of education.
Born: 31 August 1870, 03.30 LT, Chiaravelle 43N36 13E19.
Source: Birth records (Gauquelin collection).

Maria Montessori was the first woman in Italy to receive a medical degree, graduating in July 1896, when transiting Jupiter was conjunct her ascendant. It was an extraordinary achievement, for in 19th century Italy it ran against the grain just for a woman to be anything other than mother and wife, let alone to succeed in a male-dominated profession like medicine. There was a good deal of hostility to be faced, but no doubt her Scorpio Moon welcomed the challenge, and furnished the courage and resolution to overcome it.

Her reputation, however, was made in education and not in medicine. In 1901, she gave up medical practice, first to re-educate herself, and then to devote her energies to the problems of teaching young children. From her own work and observations she developed a method, which grew into a movement, attracting large numbers of disciples and spreading to many parts of the world. Her method as such is not as popular today as it was during her own lifetime, but some of her ideas have infused into the general thinking regarding the educating of infants.

One reason why the method didn't survive is because it was very much the child of its founder, and she proved a very possessive mother. She jealously guarded the purity of her method. It was not common intellectual property, and there was no scope for cross-fertilisation. She was insistent that it couldn't be changed or modified in the light of others' experience, nor adapted to the demands of different circumstances. These strictures hindered its assimilation into State systems at large, and precluded its acceptance by the academic world. This rigidity is suggested by the strong Fixity of the chart, and perhaps also by an unaspected Mercury (a planet which symbolises the general principle of interchange and exchange). Saturn in Sagittarius closely opposed by Jupiter speaks the same theme, and suggests in fact that her method became something of a faith and a dogma.

She first described her ideas in *The Montessori Method*, written in the summer of 1909 (when transiting Jupiter was conjunct her Sun). On examining her ideas we find them very Virgoan. Like most creative thinkers, what she hit on was a little rather than a great truth, and these personal truths reflect the astrological Sun, which itself represents the individual analogue of a greater spiritual whole. The Montessori Method is a very sensual and pragmatic method of education. Learning, she states, starts from observation of the material world, and self-confidence in a child comes from the mastering of its environment. She devised teaching apparatus that allow abstract skills, like reading and writing, to be approached through concrete forms. Great stress is laid on sense training in general. 'The education of the senses', she notes, 'has as its aim the refinement of the differential perception of stimuli by means of repeated exercises.' The child was taught to distinguish ever subtler gradations of colour, sound, weight, shape and texture, and then to fix the distinctions in words.

Importance is attached to work, to performing common, simple tasks well (and she herself never lost her taste for chores). There is an emphasis on self-education, and improvement through self-correction. She recognised that understanding, at the end of the day, is not something that can be administered like a pill, but is a 'magical' process that takes place within an individual. One can only repeat an action — like the forming of letters — conscientiously and in the faith that sooner or later a transformation will occur and all the practice cohere into perfection. In effect, we have a quantum jump from one level of being to another, and anyone who has ever mastered a skill has crossed this boundary. This all touches on the meaning of Mercury and Virgo at a deep level.

Whatever generality the Montessori Method may have, we can opine that the Mercurial, or Earthy child is going to be more responsive to it than say the Jupiterian or Watery child. Indeed, there

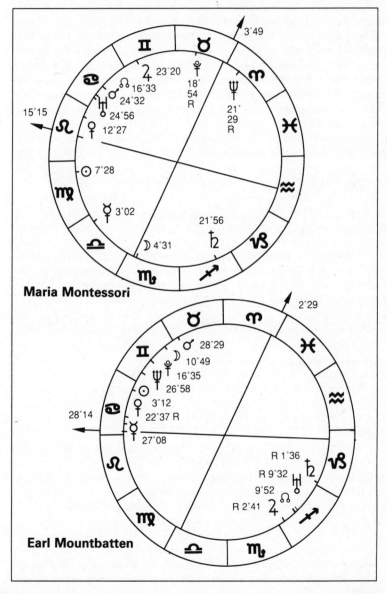

Maria Montessori

Earl Mountbatten

is no real scope for the imagination in this pragmatic Virgoan system (and this is a criticism often levelled at it). Plainly we should be looking to establish a plurality of educational methods rather than a single system, and astrology represents a valuable tool for matching child and method.

On the personal level, Montessori was a compelling and dominating personality. Leo more than any other sign seems to inspire the sort of affection, respect and admiration that she did. She was a social lion, and wherever her extensive travels took her she was honoured and rapturously received. People spoke of the majesty of her presence , and also of elegance, charm, and a strong femininity (Venus on the ascendant). She remained single, but like many Virgoans, was married to her work.

> Self-direction, stubbornness, and intuitions that proved valid as well as original were characteristics that appeared early in her life.[1]

> The eternally feminine was splendidly incarnated in this graceful Roman.[1]

> The core of her sense of self was her work; it had always mattered more to her than anything else in her life.[1]

> Even her most devoted and loyal followers recognized a certain imperiousness in Montessori ... She made royal entrances; she expected to be courted. She always expected to be the centre of attention.[1]

> ... a kind of loneliness that she seems occasionally to have acknowledged beneath her independence, her self-sufficiency.[1]

Sources/references:
1. Rita Kramer, *Maria Montessori*, Basil Blackwell.
2. William Boyd, *From Locke to Montessori,* Harrap & Co.

Earl Mountbatten.

Naval commander, statesman, supreme Allied commander SE Asia 1943-46, last viceroy of India.

Born: 25 June 1900, 06.00 GMT, Windsor 51N28 0W37.

Source: From his mother, as recorded in reference below.

Earl Mountbatten was a very ambitious man, always eager to advance his career, and taking a good deal of pride in his achievements. He was anxious also to achieve on his own merits rather than through advantage of position. He always maintained that his determination to succeed was rooted in the wrong done to his father, who, because of German ancestry was removed from his position as First Sea Lord at the outset of World War 1 (October 1914). The shock and humiliation of this deeply affected the young Mountbatten. The memory of it was only finally exorcised in 1954 when he himself became First Sea Lord. This is all accurately described in the chart by the close Sun-Saturn opposition, with Saturn strong in its own sign Capricorn. In October 1914, the date of the original incident, transiting Saturn (and Pluto) were conjunct natal Sun.

This is a chart strong in Cancer and biography makes plain that Mountbatten exhibited some of the qualities of this sign. There was kindness, sympathy, sentimentality and subjectivity. Also, under the self-confident playboy mask, it seems he was sensitive and vulnerable. But what is most apparent from biographical description is a Mercurial nature (Moon in Gemini and the planet conjunct the ascendant). He had a very active, inquisitive, enquiring mind, being very interested in things and people. He had a fascination for gadgets. There was a flair for — but also an obsession with — detail. He was very versatile, loquacious and eloquent, with a good deal of vital energy and boyish enthusiasm. He was somewhat dilettante in his approach to life. He was a great traveller, a reflection, perhaps, of the Mercury overtone and Jupiter in Sagittarius.

He was considered a vain man, with a tendency to claim too much of the credit for anything. He was fashion conscious and well-groomed. As a leader of men he was popular and inspiring, but there were too many errors of judgement for him to be accounted a good wartime commander. His greatest achievement was his work in India leading up to Independence. His was the Gemini ability to communicate with a wide variety of people. With Venus conjunct the ascendant he had diplomacy and negotiating skills, the ability to find the harmony and common ground amongst antagonistic factions.

For a good deal of his adult life Mountbatten's energies were focused on the public world. Part of the reason for this was his unsatisfactory marriage. Like many strong in Cancer he yearned for closeness and cosy domesticity. However, the woman he married was unwilling or unable to provide this. She, Edwina, was born 28.11.01, and her noon chart shows a Sagittarian Sun and a Cancer Moon. Her natal Moon was conjunct Mountbatten's Sun, traditionally regarded as a good cross-contact, but there was little connection at the feeling level. It seems she was emotionally very self-contained (as Cancer can often be). She couldn't look beyond her own needs, or let anyone close to her. She was unable to reveal the vulnerability that is always there when Cancer is strong. As one biographer put it: 'She was doomed to live alone in a fortress whose walls Mountbatten could never breach.' Edwina seemed to relate much more to her Sagittarian nature. Her Sun falls conjunct Mountbatten's Jupiter, and on this level they seemed to connect. For the most part the world knew them as a glamorous, dashing couple who travelled widely and were on easy terms with the famous and mighty. But at the core there was unhappiness and infidelity. He did, however, take great solace and comfort from his relationship with his daughters.

He first met his wife in October 1920, at which time progressed Sun had moved to conjunct natal Venus. They married 18 July 1922 — transiting Mars was stationary opposed to his natal Moon. He died violently, murdered by the IRA, 27 August 1979, with transiting Saturn square natal Pluto.

That his ambition was intense and naked could be attested by anyone who knew him.

His energy, his dedication, his flexibility of mind, his power of leadership, his charm, his phenomenal memory ...

Ranks, titles, honours held extravagant significance for him.

He was generous and loyal, putting himself to endless trouble for anyone who had any claim on him. He was warm-hearted, predisposed to like everyone he met, quick-tempered but never bearing grudges.

A powerful analytical mind of crystalline clarity, a superabundance of energy, great persuasive powers, endless resilience in the face of setback or disaster.

The least reflective of men ... Religious speculation was as alien to him as political philosophising.

Charm of manner ... one of his greatest assets.

Preserved the spirit of a boy, with all that this implied in the way of impetuosity, energy, enthusiasm, the urge to find out how things worked ... he remained startlingly naive, incapable of concealing his intentions.

He loved the company of women, sought their affection and had an almost irresistible urge to use them as confidantes.

Source/reference:
Philip Zeigler, *Mountbatten, The Official Biography*, Collins.

Muhammad Ali

(Cassius Clay). Boxer. Three times world heavyweight champion.
Born: 17 January 1942, 18.35 CST, Louisville 38N15 85W46.
Source: Birth records (*The Gauquelin Book of American Charts*).

Muhammad Ali boasted he was the greatest and then went on to prove it. From his first professional fight (29 October 1960), through winning the world title (14 February 1964), to when he was stripped of his crown for refusing to join the army (20 June 1967), he was unbeatable, and the ease with which he won his victories put him in a class above anyone else. Through the 1970s he went on to win and lose the title twice more.

Ali is accurately described by the main features of his chart. The Leo ascendant reflects the swaggering, self-publicising, self-confident side that the world came to know and (eventually) admire. With Leo rising, he was an outstanding personality as well as an outstanding sportsman. He also has a great way with children, a not uncommon trait when Leo is strong. The Capricorn Sun concurs with a 'devouring' ambition to be world champion, as well as the necessary self-discipline that achieved this. The elevated Saturn-Uranus conjunction is suggestive of his conflict with Authority over his refusal to enlist. Boxing is the most Martial of sports, and it is unusual for fighters at the highest level not to have Mars or its signs accented. In Muhammad Ali's case, Mars is conjunct the MC, and despite his casual, even lazy style of fighting, there was aggression and venom when required.

Mercury is strong in this chart, closely conjunct the Moon and conjunct the descendant, and this reflects his ability to talk intelligently, wittily, and seemingly endlessly. It is also possible to relate his unique skill to this Mercurial overtone. Mercury relates, among other things, to co-ordination, to the speed and clarity of interchange between mind and muscle. All boxers need well-honed reflexes, but Ali was exceptionally quick in both attack and defence. In his first period as world champion he often emerged virtually unmarked from a fight.

The writer Norman Mailer has a fascination with pugilism and has himself sparred with world champions. In his book *The Fight* he puts forward his own theory as to why boxers are knocked out, why Ali (in his prime) never was, and why, even when past his best, he could absorb a lot of punishment. He suggests that a knockout results, in effect, from failure of communication. The blow that floors a boxer is the one that isn't seen. Simple observation shows that there is substance in this view. If we watch fight footage we see the most common expression of a man dealt a knockout punch is surprise and perplexity, rather than pain. If a boxer sees a blow, information is communicated to the body, and power can be absorbed and dissipated. In Mailer's view, this is why it is often a swift combination of punches that effects a knockout. The victim's 'message centre' can not deal with all the information, and the result is overload, confusion, and coma. He goes on to suggest that Ali's success stemmed from his

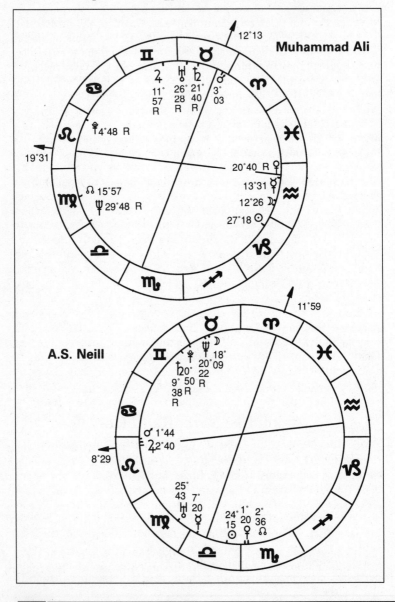

ability to 'assimilate punches faster than other fighters.' He could 'literally transmit the shock through more parts of his body, or direct it to the best path.' Basically, he could digest punches, could efficiently translate the blow from a mental to a physical experience, and this is all very suggestive of the Mercury function.

Ali's career was one of two halves, and if the younger was quicksilver Mercury, the older was more Saturnian lead. The man who returned to the ring after his enforced stoppage was a slower, less fluent fighter. It took a good deal of courage and dedication to come back as he did, but he was altogether a more ordinary boxer, one who was hit more and hurt more than previously. His career is not particularly well delineated by the common transits and progressions (plainly promoters are not in harmony with the cosmos). However, the two phases are separated by a Saturn return and by a progressed new Moon (which fell exact at the beginning of Pisces, shortly after he regained his world crown in October 1974).

A humorous young man with the overwhelming personality of a great extrovert.[1]

From the beginning, young Cassius loved the limelight. He was a show-off.[1]

The supreme exhibitionist, putting himself on parade at all times.[2]

Impulsive talking and the attention of an audience were his life blood.[2]

Sources/references:
1. Frank Butler, *Muhammad Ali*, Hamish Hamilton.
2. Gilbert Odd, *Ali The Fighting Prophet*, Pelham Books.
3. Norman Mailer, *The Fight*, Granada.

Alexander Sutherland Neill

'Neill of Summerhill'. Revolutionary educator. Author of *Summerhill, A Radical Approach to Child-Rearing*.
Born: 17 October 1883, 23.00 LT, Forfar, 56N39, 2W50.
Source: Birth certificate.

The teacher's job is to evoke love. This he can only do by loving.
(**A.S. Neill**)

If children anywhere are happier nowadays in school than their elders sometimes were, it is due in no small measure to this craggy, lovable Scot. (*Times* **Obituary**)

I know of no educator in the Western world who can compare to A.S. Neill. It seems to me that he stands alone. **(Henry Miller)**

Nineteenth century education, particularly in the English public schools, was largely about values. These schools were not out to foster any sort of academic excellence. Nor were they about the nurturing of individual potential. Rather, they set out to produce a certain 'type', an adult male imbued with a certain set of values that would enable him to function smoothly as a cog of Empire — as an administrator, diplomat, or policeman. Given this end the schools functioned perfectly well and the values they vaunted were apposite. The nature of these values is encapsulated in *Tom Brown's Schooldays,* significantly a book written by a Libran.

Generally speaking nineteenth century education ('to lead out') is more accurately termed inculcation ('to stamp in'). It was altogether more Spartan, Prussian, Martial, Saturnian. Nineteenth century attitudes spilled over into the twentieth, but that they no longer dominate is perhaps due, as his obituary suggested, to the work and example of A.S. Neill. He was the embodiment of a new ideal in education, and Summerhill was an embodiment of A.S. Neill.

The Summerhill philosophy was one of love, and of partnership and co-operation between equals — all very appropriate considering the strong Venusian nature of Neill's natal chart. Central to his school's routine was the meeting, when staff and pupils came together — as equals — to make decisions and to discuss problems and differences. As much as anything these meetings were exercises in sociability for within its structure children could come to understand the limits of their freedom. They learned that their own actions as individuals had wider ramifications and that they affected both the wellbeing of others and of the school. The individual child had to learn to sacrifice some of his or her will for the good of the community. And on a very basic level this is what Libra is all about. Not every child benefited from a Summerhill education, but many seemed to. The most notable successes were in the rehabilitation of so-called problem children, those that conventional schools were not able to deal with.

In Neill's life work and philosophy, then, we observe his strong Libran nature. Summerhill was a Venusian school. The emphasis was on co-operation rather than competition. To those critics who opined that Summerhill didn't prepare children for the real world Neill replied that it was Summerhill that was real. As well as being the embodiment of an ideal — something which Librans seem to do well — he was a revolutionary in the Nietzschean sense, a re-evaluator of values. Neill attacked and to an extent changed conventional attitudes and this is a very Libran role. For Libra is a sign that relates to moral codes, to those values adopted by a society because they are held at a basic level to be right and proper and conducive to the common good. Indeed, such codes, when they are believed, do stabilise a society. But all codes become outmoded, at first irrelevant and then positively destructive. Those values vaunted in *Tom Brown's Schooldays* seem risible and ludicrous to us now, and yet in their day were perfectly acceptable. Libra, on the whole, is a conservative sign, one that readily defers to the mores. It is when these dearly-held beliefs are perceived to be detrimental to the overall health of a society that the Libran rebel comes to the fore and seeks to change them.

At the fundamental level Libra is about a balance between individual desire and deference to an outer morality. Neill perceived how damaging, how fear and guilt-inducing, was the imposition on children of an often hidebound adult morality. He knew this more poignantly through his own childhood experiences. His father, the local school-teacher, bullied and ridiculed him. His mother was a cold person, more concerned with respectability and appearances. It was altogether a childhood clouded by the acerbic pall of Calvinism, one where joy and spontaneity were taboo.

Neill suffered the emotional immaturity not uncommon in strongly Venusian men. It seems there were problems with physical sex. Like J.M. Barrie, he had a hopelessly idealised view of women, and this seemed to hinder relating with real women. He avoided any sort of emotional confrontation or entanglement. As his biographer notes: '(he) never quite mastered the art of moving easily in the complex adult world. One view expressed ... was that Neill was only comfortable in carefully structured situations and relationships.' This again is very suggestive of Libra, a sign which symbolises a ritualistic, courtly sort of love, and the *I Ching* world and its time-honoured and formalised structure of relationships. But he did have an outstanding ability to relate to children, and particularly to disturbed and difficult children.

Certain of his characteristics relate to his Leo ascendant. He was a compelling speaker and enjoyed playing to an audience. He had an intuitive and lucky side. Leo is notably paternal and Neill was surrogate father to many children.

There was kindness, gentleness, and 'a warm, undemanding benevolence', which seems to reflect the Moon-Neptune conjunction in Taurus. Like other Librans he had difficulty in being firm and laying down the law. Yet, at the same time there was courage and determination to establish his school in the face of general disapproval and often local hostility (which suggests Leo fixity of purpose). People remarked on his great tolerance. There are two basic types of tolerance: the Piscean/Neptunian sort, which empathises with suffering and can forgive weakness; and a Libran sort where there is a more detached capacity to understand the reason for another person's behaviour. Both seemed to be at work in Neill. He liked to keep busy and discouraged idleness in others. He was an accomplished writer, producing a number of successful books.

Source/reference:
Jonathan Croall, *Neill of Summerhill: The Permanent Rebel*, Routledge & Kegan Paul.

Diana Ross

Singer, actress, entertainer.
Born: 26 March 1944, 23.46 EWT, Detroit 42N20 83W3.
Source: Birth certificate (*The Gauquelin Book of American Charts*)

Diana Ross first came to prominence with *The Supremes*, a group who enjoyed ten number one hits in the American charts between 1964 and 1967 (and a number in the British charts in the same period). Success continued as a solo performer and she has become a luminary in the glamour world of American show business. She has also developed a career as an actress, receiving considerable acclaim (and an Oscar nomination) for her portrayal of Billie Holiday in *Lady Sings the Blues*.

Her chart shows a strong 'Mars' overtone, with Scorpio rising, and Sun and Mercury in Aries. There is also a significant 'Venus' overtone, with the planet conjunct the IC and the Moon in Taurus. This mix of Mars and Venus is well summarised by the writer who described Diana Ross as 'part guts, part geisha.'[1] We see Venus in the image of rather cultivated femininity she projects (and in her early vocational interests of modelling and fashion design). But it is a ferocious Martial drive that has powered her rapid ascent from the Detroit slums to the peaks of super-stardom. The impatient ambition to escape her background was evident from an early age, as was the energy, determination and single-mindedness necessary to do it. Also in abundance is Martial magnetism — her undeniable stage presence. People have commented that she is a great example of positive thought in action. She has great belief in herself, in her ability to achieve whatever she sets out to. Her philosophy has been, if you *act* the part then you will become it. In other words, you create your own identity and your own reality. This is not a philosophy that is going to work for everyone, but it is sound enough for an Aries.

The ambitious, self-seeking side of Mars has its shadow, and there are those who have testified to her vanity and selfishness. A strong Mars chart like this speaks a very tough side, and an aggressive, even ruthless one when people oppose her will.

We can see her Aries side manifesting in a broader way. She very much functioned as a spearhead for the Motown music empire, the recording company that pioneered mass-market black music (we should remember that when *The Supremes* were first formed there was still apartheid in some States). The close sextile of Uranus to her Sun is perhaps relevant here — the breaking down of caste barriers — but more so is the opposition of Neptune. The phenomenal success of the group was due in no short measure to extensive marketing. If she and her music became more acceptable to white audiences it was because they were sanitised and glossily packaged for the easily fooled and satisfied middle-of-the-road palate. The music was scrubbed until tepid and inoffensive, and free of all but a trace of essential black qualities — the more pagan and emotional elements that are traditionally associated with negro music.

Living out the real meaning of a sign involves a process of polarisation and balance. Dane Rudhyar[3] has spoken of Aries in terms of adaptability, telling us, in effect, that force becomes power through the balance of individual and environment. This is how Diana Ross has succeeded: by coming into harmony with the status quo. She has adjusted to the entertainment world on its terms. She has taken standard forms, breathed new life into them, and made them her own. Aries does not create forms, but is, rather, a fount of life and energy. In her case the energy has been guided, channelled, and given definition by others. People have spoken of the chameleon-like way in which she has adapted herself, which is once more suggestive of Neptune opposed the Sun. This reflects particularly, I think, the ease with which she has become what a glamour-hungry public wanted her to become.

She signed up with Motown in 1961, but success did not come until June 1964, with the release of what became their first number one hit. At this time in her chart we note transiting Jupiter conjunct Moon, and Saturn stationary on her IC. The group received a huge amount of media attention throughout 1965, which corresponds to Neptune transiting her ascendant. April 1967 marked another milestone in her career when she was given lead billing in the group. It was a time of testing, when her popularity and talent were on the line, and this is adequately described by transiting Saturn conjunct natal Sun.

In October 1972 her first film was premiered. It was poorly received, but she was praised for her part in it. Her biographer notes of this time: 'The Holiday role was conceivably the most crucial turning point in Diana's professional life. Many critics have said that it was a springboard for a fruitful and long career.'[2] In short, critics agree, taking on the challenge of a demanding role in the face of considerable hostility was something that matured her. It is apt, then, that this time coincided with the return of Saturn to its own place in her chart.

There was no task too difficult for Diana Ross when it came to expanding her artistry. She would take on any musical challenge if it meant the opening of a door to something new and exciting.

In everything she ever did and in any way she did it, Diana was determined to make it work.

A complex, voracious personality that could find happiness in no

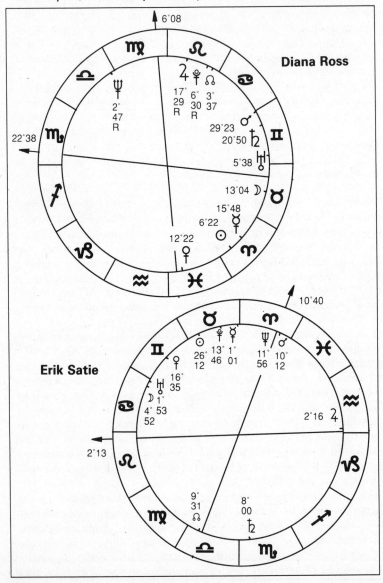

other way than to be loved by millions.

Her natural need for attention and innate ability to achieve at an accelerated pace.

Very much a perfectionist and always anxious to be the best at her craft.

Source/references:
1. Rona Jaffe, cited below (page 67).
2. J. Randy Taraborelli, *Diana: The Life and Career of Diana Ross*, W.H. Allen.
3. Dane Rudhyar, *An Astrological Triptych*, p.7, ASI.

Erik Satie.

Composer, musician, eccentric.

Born: 17 May 1866, 09.00 LT, Honfleur 49N25 0W13.
Source: Birth records (Gauquelin Collection).

Biographical description of Satie relates most obviously to his natal Moon-Uranus conjunction in Cancer. But there is also the distinct colouring of Neptune (or, more broadly, a 'Piscean' overtone with Neptune on the MC, Jupiter conjunct the descendant, and Moon in the 12th house). He was a very singular man, noted for his eccentricity, unconventionality and independence. He had a marked disregard for the bourgeois mentality, and was no friend of the music establishment. He seemed most at home scoring zany Dadaist films, or otherwise embracing the avant-garde currents of his day.

Satie was noted for his sense of humour, which was by turns droll, whimsical, cutting and wounding. The strong Mars (conjunct the MC) no doubt contributed to the latter, as it also did to the violence of his temper. He was notably volatile, possessing the characteristic Cancerian touchiness with its strange blend of hypersensitivity and aggressiveness. He had a strong unworldly streak. He renounced money, possessions, respectability and companionship. Although there was in him a Leonine taste and flair for self-publicity, for the most part he was governed by humility and, it seems, a Neptunian need for self-abasement. The greater part of his life was spent in poverty and solitude.

He had a strong imagination, but of a cast better suited, perhaps, to film or writing than to music. It manifested itself in nonsensical rhymes, maps of fictitious countries, plans of imaginary houses, bizarre inventions and other baroque fancies. Thousands of these drawings were found after his death, bottled messages thrown from the window of a rich and intricate inner world. This sort of fanciful fertility seems most often to be a product of Lunar and Neptunian factors.

He did have an affable and charming Taurean side, but for the most part it remained hidden behind a prickly Cancerian carapace. This combination of influences also reflected in a childlike nature, evident in the freshness of his imaginative cast, but also in a difficulty in relating to others in a mature way. There was something of the spoiled child in the temper outbursts, and he was shy and fearful of women. On the other hand he related very well to children, and loved animals. We note also, perhaps reflecting the 'Piscean' overtone, a marked religious nature, and an over-fondness for alcohol. He died from liver failure after 40 years hard drinking.

> Childlike by nature himself, attached forever to the mood of those early years that had vanished so quickly but had conditioned his mind for the rest of his life, he could sympathise instantly with boys and girls.

> He concealed his shyness beneath a facade of elaborate mockery. In his life, as in his work, the deepest feelings were encased by a protective covering of humour and jest.

> Satie claimed that he never married for fear of being cuckolded. This is significant. He was afraid of committing himself, afraid of being duped, afraid of attracting derision. He would not dare to take a first step that might reveal him without defences. So he lived alone, choosing to meet friends under circumstances of his own choosing and at times when he knew his mask was well adjusted. A terrible insecurity haunted him. It drove him to furious rage over trifles. He was ultrasensitive to imagined slights. He detected insult in the lightest remark and denigration in a passing phrase.

Source/reference:
James Harding, *Erik Satie*, Secker & Warburg.

Mary Shelley.

Writer. Creator of Frankenstein.

Born: 30 August 1797, 23.20 LT, London 51N32 0W0.
Source: Recorded by her father, present at birth.

This is the sort of birth-pattern that makes many astrologers involuntarily wince, with Saturn on the ascendant and a strongly aspected Pluto conjunct the MC. And it is true enough that, taken as a whole, her life can be seen as a sea of tragedy, loneliness and unhappiness with only here and there small islands of joy or serenity.

Her mother died in childbirth and so from the start there was a hole in her life. She idealized her father — a celebrated figure of his day — and while he did much to develop Mary's strong intellect, he was rather dry and distant and could offer no emotional sustenance. This early home atmosphere left its mark (as is often the case when Cancer/4th house are strong) and for a good deal of her mature life she carried a strong yearning for the warmth and intimacy of a stable domestic environment. Being starved of human warmth for a good deal of her childhood seemed to limit her capacity to express her strong emotions, and to many people who came in contact with her she appeared cool, aloof and self-sufficient. As is often the case when Cancer is strong, a warm, caring but vulnerable and sensitive nature is trapped beneath a self-protective carapace.

In July 1814 (transiting Jupiter conjunct natal Sun) she was catapulted from her rather dull, humdrum existence when she eloped with the poet Percy Bysshe Shelley and for eight years pursued with him a wandering, bohemian lifestyle. It was certainly an unorthodox departure, and one which was to set her apart from her peers for the rest of her life. It is suggestive of her Sun conjunct Uranus. Both she and her husband (who also had Sun conjunct Uranus) exhibited an Aquarian/Uranian idealism, flowing with the libertarian currents of the time, fired by schemes for the betterment of society, and by hopes for the future. It was a period when it must have seemed as if she dwelt with gods and heroes at a level far above that of the common herd. It was a period, at its best at least, marked by the intoxication of freedom, by Sagittarian enthusiasms, by euphoric creativity, impassioned learning, spectacular sights, romantic adventure, and the stimulating company of men like Byron and Shelley. But it was also a period of dramatic extremes, of physical hardship, persecution, and the grief of losing three children, a husband, and a sister. This focus on death is perhaps a straightforward reflection of the strong Pluto-Mars opposition (which also aspects Sun and Moon). We note at the time of her husband's death by drowning (8 July 1822) transiting Neptune conjunct her descendant, transiting Pluto quincunx Mars, and progressed Moon square Pluto.

Following her husband's death, and the drama and intensity of the life they led together for eight years, everything else was an anticlimax. It was back to the shadows. Writing became simply a living and not a creative pleasure, and there was little that could inflame her enthusiasm. All she really yearned for was a cosy, quiet life, with a family and a few intimate friends. But, as Jung reminds us, having once woken to a greater awareness it is not possible to abandon it and resume the sleep and security of instinct. Hers was essentially a long, lonely widowhood, struggling to support herself and her one surviving child, and prone to bouts of melancholy brooding and deep depression (Saturn conjunct Cancer ascendant, and a 'Scorpionic' overtone). However, she continued to get pleasure from foreign travel (Sagittarian Moon).

She is best remembered for her novel *Frankenstein*, written when she was only 19. It was published in March 1818, when transiting Jupiter trined Sun, Saturn opposed Uranus and a progressed new Moon fell conjunct Mercury. In *Frankenstein* she succeeded in creating a very potent symbol, one that has lodged in the collective consciousness (and this is the mark of Uranus). It is the tale of a Faustian figure who through knowledge seeks power over nature. And a tale of hubris, of the consequences of man seeking to be greater than his nature will allow. This reflects the essence of Virgo, and also the 'Promethean' nature of Uranus. There is also a Cancerian overtone to the story. It is a tale of loneliness, of a being who wants to be loved and accepted, but who is doomed to wander the earth in lonely isolation. Like many first novels, it is essentially transfigured autobiography, and a paradigm of the author's own life (like Mary, the monster lacked a mother).

The strongest impressions to emerge from biography are the strength and originality of her mind (reflecting more the Sun/Uranus in Virgo, and a Sagittarian Moon), and the complex emotional nature of a strong Lunar side.

> A literate, cultured person ... the range and variety of her intellectual interests and tastes.[1]

> Indeed the placid front which she displayed to the world and even to her friends seems to have been from the very first a protective covering for those moods of depression to which she was always prone.[1]

> She was always, even from her girlhood, a lonely person. After Shelley's death her loneliness engulfed her.[1]

> Her memory and acute perception never let her down. Even in middle age she could recall events and impressions with such clarity that frequently she was overwhelmed with a sense of living it all again.[2]

> A shy, private person.[2]

> The essential elusive Mary, passionate and controlled, reserved and melancholy, yet ready to give everything for those she loved; the studious intellectual and loving mother, the working writer, the reluctant solitary.[2]

Sources/references:

1. Elizabeth Nitchie, *Mary Shelley*, Rutgers Univ. Press.
2. Jane Dunn, *Moon in Eclipse: A life of Mary Shelley*, Weidenfeld & Nicolson.

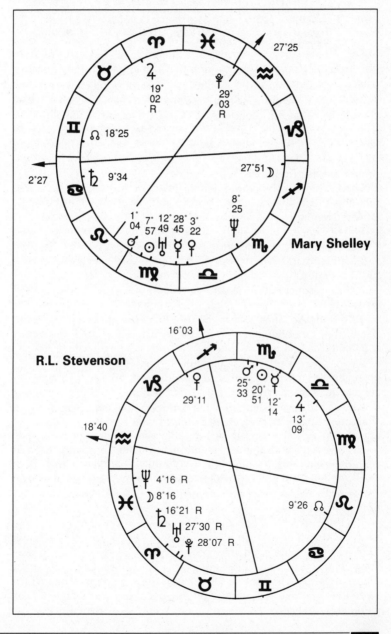

Mary Shelley

R.L. Stevenson

Robert Louis Stevenson.

Writer, famous for works like *Dr Jekyll and Mr Hyde*, *Treasure Island*, and *The Master of Ballantrae*.

Born: 13 November 1850, 13.30 LT, Edinburgh 55N57 3W11.
Source: Originated from his parents (see Alan Leo, *The Art of Synthesis*, p.112, 1912 edition).

Aquarius and Uranus relate to universalism. Writers with the sign and planet accented are more capable than most of producing stories or characters that are universally appreciated, that seem to reach that part of a person that transcends class, age, culture, or nationality. We noted it earlier in the case of Conan Doyle, and Stevenson, with Aquarius rising, is another case in point. His characters are among the best known in English literature; the books in which they figure are among the most popular.

Often evident with Scorpio writers are themes relating to the deep, subtle, sometimes dark side of human life. The nature of evil is often explored, and the crisis of subscendence whereby characters come to experience life at a more vital or compassionate level. Stevenson's Sun is in Scorpio, and we note these same themes in his writing. *Dr Jekyll and Mr Hyde* and *The Master of Ballantrae*, for example, are both about the intermingled light and dark in the human psyche. *Catriona* is about redressing injustice — another common Scorpio theme, both in art and life.

We see the Aquarian side to the fore in Stevenson as a young man. He cultivated a bohemian lifestyle, and rejected the values of his class and family. For many years there was a fundamental rift with his father, who expected his son to take up engineering, as previous generations of Stevensons had done. But Stevenson himself, from an early age, was certain he wanted to write. He at first acquiesced, but soon grew restless and depressed in his studies. We seem to have a straightforward description of this in the close Saturn-Jupiter opposition. He experienced the Jupiterian sense of despair that comes from confinement of the future, and the limiting of possibilities. To Stevenson a career in engineering loomed ahead like a long, dark corridor. It was Saturn, through his father, and beyond that, the conventions of class, that were doing the restricting. In early April 1871 he confronted his father and told him he was giving up his engineering. This marked a quite conscious break with his past, and a decision to be his own man and follow his own path. This new start was marked by a progressed new Moon. Also underlying the rift was Stevenson's rejection of his father's religious values. One suggestion of this in the chart is again the close Saturn-Jupiter opposition. But on a more essential level it is another playing out of the Scorpio theme. For father and son liked each other; on the feeling level there was a strong bond. What divided them was principle. Part of the lesson Scorpio must learn is that human feelings and welfare are more important than abstract principles (be these religious, political, or moral). The two were eventually reconciled.

This same idea underlies Stevenson's attraction to the low life of Edinburgh. His own bourgeois culture he found sterile and hypocritical. It was just those facets of life they excluded from their world, the pains and joys, the fullness and mystery of life, that he found so fascinating. A more authentic life, he believed, was the coarse-textured, passionate existence of the Old Town whores and reprobates. It was this same authenticity that he pursued throughout his life, and which took him to the primitive world of the South Sea Islands. What Stevenson experienced here was what has been called participation mystique, the sense of being rooted in life, and of belonging to the mysterious whole to which the natural world also belongs — a sense which comes more to Scorpio than any other sign.

Stevenson was a sickly child and throughout his life he was never really free of illness (it was his lungs that troubled him). It is not fanciful to say that, so precarious was his health, that death was a companion for long spells. One outcome of this was that he appreciated life more. It concentrated his mind, and generated the intensity of perception that is common among Martial types, particularly Martial artists. His first real touch with death came when he was travelling in America, at the end of 1879. It was the time of a Saturn return, transiting Pluto opposed his natal Mars, and Uranus his Moon. He was never really healthy after this time, and the awareness of his own frailty focused his energies, and overall deepened his view of life. In short, the experience has about it the quality of a Scorpionic 'fall'. A second major spell of invalidism spanned 1882-7. Transiting Neptune was active at this time, moving back and forth opposite his Sun/Mars conjunction. It was exactly opposed the Sun in May 1884 when he suffered his most severe lung haemorrhage (and we also note progressed Moon opposite natal Mars).

Accounts of Stevenson's character are many. There is general agreement that he had both the magnetism and the strong-willed egotism associated with Scorpio. With Mars also in Scorpio, and conjunct his Sun, we have a sort of double Scorpio effect, and it is not surprising to find this sign so evident in his life and character. Much of the immediate character seems to return to the Moon conjunct Neptune in Pisces in the 1st house. He was volatile and moody, easily swaying from joy to despair (indicative of the Pisces Moon). He had a rich, active, inner world which he had difficulty containing. It would bubble forth in effusive, fanciful conversation. As a child it would plague his sleep, producing troubling dreams and subsequent insomnia. As a young man he was enthusiastic and exuberant, somewhat dissolute and irresponsible — again we look to Jupiter ruled Pisces. He was very restless, and something of a rootless wanderer. It seems as a boy he was fed religious instruction of the more dogmatically moral sort, so that as a young man there was an obsession with virtue, a concern that he was being 'good'.

He had the sociable nature that often goes with Aquarius, but at the same time Scorpionic reticence. He avoided talking about his feelings, as the following extracts from his letters suggest: 'I have yet to learn in ordinary conversation that reserve and silence that I must try to unlearn in the matter of the feelings.' And in another he admits: 'I hate to speak of what I really feel, to the extent that when I find myself cornered, I have a tendency to say the reverse.' His marriage was happy and fruitful. He first met his wife in September 1876 and they married 19 May 1880. He died, suddenly, of a brain haemorrhage 3 December 1894 (progressed Moon opposite natal Uranus and Pluto).

Sources/references:
1. Janet Adam Smith, *Stevenson*, Duckworth.
2. Paul Binding, *Robert Louis Stevenson*, Oxford Univ Press.
3. J. Hammerton (ed), *Stevensoniana, an anecdotal life of Robert Louis Stevenson,* John Grant.

Marie Stopes.
Pioneer of birth control. Author of books on sex education.
Born: 15 October 1880, 04.10 LT, Edinburgh 55N57 3W11.
Source: Birth certificate.

Marie Stopes is another example of a Libran Sun whose life purpose was connected with the re-evaluation of values. She worked to alter society's attitudes towards sex, marriage and women, and through this quite possibly hastened the transition from the prissy and hypocritical values that characterised the Victorian era. In 1920 she opened the first birth control clinic in Britain. From about 1918 onward she produced a quantity of books on the broad subject of sex that, although often hopelessly idealistic and woolly did bring the subject into the open and did afford some comfort for a generation steeped in sexual guilt and repression. These books also made of Marie Stopes a public and highly controversial figure.

As a child and young woman, however, she seemed to reflect the more introverted side of Pisces and Virgo (her Moon sign and ascendant), being passive, rather colourless and diffident, and suffering the Libran guilt at putting self before others. It seems she suffered a difficult relationship with her mother, who refused or was unable to offer any encouragement or affection. So it is not surprising that Marie Stopes developed an inferiority complex, which turned in maturity to a pugnacious over-compensation. With achievement and fame came arrogance, conceit and self-praise. With old age and a consciousness of the waning of her power came messianic megalomania.

Her maturity speaks more the dynamic side of the chart — the Moon opposed to Uranus, and the Sun closely conjunct Mars. These reflect the determination to prove herself in difficult circumstances and the willingness with which she cut across the grain of convention. She was very ambitious (and we note Saturn opposed to Sun/Mars), very energetic and aggressive, particularly towards those who opposed her will. But there was forcefulness, vigour and courage. She cut through taboos, didn't baulk at taking on the combined forces of the (male) medical profession and Church, nor flinch at the barrage of vilification and hostility her views produced. In much of this there is Mars, an archetype she strongly embodied for better and worse, as the following suggests:

> What appeared to many as her vanity, lack of humour, paranoia and aggressiveness were perhaps an inevitable counterpoint to the obstinacy, courage and pertinacity that gave her the strength to go on fighting for what she believed in.

Despite a Libran Sun, the Mars conjuncting it precluded any sort of co-operation with others, even to further ends that were dear to her heart. She yearned for a perfect partnership — 'the fusion of two equal individuals into a higher exclusive unity' — and for a mystical sexual perfection. Needless to say both of these remained elusive. Her first marriage remained unconsummated through her husband's impotence. Her second, proved equally unsuccessful. No doubt she suffered great disappointment, the natural concomitant of a romantic and idealistic nature (a side suggested by the Pisces Moon, the Libran Sun, and by Venus opposed to Neptune).

Although in some ways an iconoclast she was in others quite conservative and illiberal. Sex was for marriage as far as she was concerned, and things like homosexuality she regarded as an aberration. Her passion for birth control was less rooted in compassion than in elitism. She wanted to control the breeding of the working classes. The quotes below for the most part emphasise how dominating an influence is Mars.

> Her unusual capacity to react with positive aggression to any challenge and adversity.

(A) ferocious ambition that was later to unleash such energy in pursuit of her ends.

A temperament that saw people not as they were, but only in relation to her own demands.

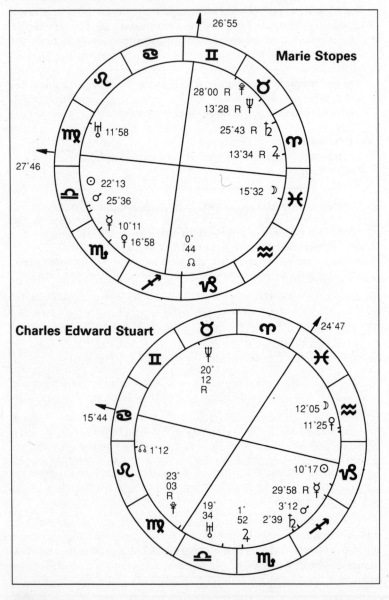

Marie Stopes

Charles Edward Stuart

Whatever else may be said of Marie Stopes, at least she had the courage to cut through the fears and prejudices that beset everyone else in England at the time, and to do what needed to be done.

Birth control, with which her fame became largely associated, was only one aspect of the wider reform she initially envisaged. This was nothing less than the total transformation of the apparently immutable nature of the sexual relationship between men and women.

Energy, intelligence, and enormous powers of concentration.

Her will to succeed was immediately evident.

Source/reference:
Ruth Hall, *Marie Stopes, a Biography*, Andre Deutsch.

Charles Edward Stuart.

Bonnie Prince Charlie. Claimant to the British Throne.
Born: 31 December 1720 (ns), 17.00 LT, Rome 41N54 12E30.
Source: Contemporary accounts. His birth took place amid much public interest and was witnessed by numbers of eminent dignitaries.

Charles' life was dominated by circumstances beyond his control, set in motion long before he was born (see Part 3 of this book). As the eldest son of James the Old Pretender, exiled heir to the British Crown, it fell to him to carry on the Jacobite cause, to undo, as it were, an ancient wrong. It was a duty he accepted without reservation, reflecting here the Capricorn Sun, a sign noted for its willingness to shoulder burdensome responsibility.

His life was of two halves, defeat and failure at Culloden marking the great divide. A progressed New Moon fell exact in February 1748 and this marks well enough the watershed. After this date his cause was a lost one and his character deteriorated rapidly. He lost many of the princely attributes that had won him support. Underneath the princely persona that he had carried so well was revealed a weak and unattractive human being, bad-tempered, selfish, depressive and suspicious.

He had a pampered upbringing. From an early age he was made to believe he was something special, and this was to become a conviction that never left him. This sense of specialness is suggested by the Solar nature of the chart, with the Sun conjunct the descendant. This Solar influence no doubt contributed to a striking regal nature and to his charismatic qualities of leadership. He was greatly admired and loved by his followers and by the Scottish people. After Culloden a price of £30,000 was put on his head, a phenomenal sum for the times. But there were no takers. As a youth and young man he was noted for his charm, but also for his vitality, and enthusiasm and aptitude for manly pursuits. There was courage and toughness, which enabled him to survive when he was being hunted like an animal after Culloden.

Charles' chart demonstrates the importance of close conjunctions in the horoscope. Moon and Venus are within a degree of each other in Aquarius, and likewise Mars and Saturn in Sagittarius. The first of these suggests the charm that was such a noted part of his character. There was a kind of chivalrous gentility about him that appealed to a broad spectrum of people (and made him very attractive to women). At the same time, there was the characteristic Aquarian coolness. He kept a distance and had few, if any close friends. And, despite his appeal to women he felt uncomfortable in their company, and was unable to relate to them in anything other than a mannered and formalised way. With his strong Solar side he was better at receiving affection and favour than giving it. People sacrificed greatly for him and his cause, but he considered it his due.

A Moon-Venus conjunction is a double-edged influence for a leader of men. It is a charismatic aspect but one which seems to preclude the incisiveness and ruthlessness necessary for the leader of a wild Highland army. Charles was often too chivalrous and considerate of the enemy. He lacked any of the practical qualities necessary for a field or campaign commander, though what proved critical in the end was a lack of real self-confidence. He was indecisive and easily swayed by the majority. In short, Venus overpowered Mars in his chart. His general inability to express Mars is perhaps a reflection of the conjunction with Saturn. In his own day an astrologer would have seen this combination as decidedly malefic, and seeing it in Sagittarius he might have predicted tragedy and misfortune in foreign matters (and wouldn't have been wrong). A modern, psychological interpretation, such as that offered by Liz Greene[1], is more illuminating. She suggests that this is a combination that affects a man's 'confidence in himself as lover, aggressor, conqueror, and leader; it is in these areas that the frustration is felt.' The Prince's sense of manhood (Mars) was coupled with the need to discharge his karmic duty. He was presented with the opportunity but failed to take it. Consequently 'the intense inner frustration and ... feeling of weakness and powerlessness'[1] associated with this aspect mounted in the years after his defeat. A good deal of it seemed to find vent in cruel and violent treatment towards his wife.

We do note a number of major cross-contacts between Charles' natal chart, and the 1707 British chart and the founding chart of the Stuart Dynasty (see page 199) reflecting his role in the destinies of

England and Scotland. The most immediate outcome of his abortive expedition was the unleashing of brutal retributive forces on the Highlands, and the death of a culture and way of life. There is truth in the view that, like Mary Queen of Scots, he gave nothing to Scotland but his story.

Those amiable traits of disposition which had always distinguished him; and as he increased in years and stature his fascination of manner became even more marked, so much so, indeed, that few who came under his influence could withstand its powerful attraction.[2]

Charles exuded energy. His very presence revitalised those who came into contact with it.[3]

A young man of considerable grace, to whom manners and social accomplishments came easily.[3]

His strength lay in his tenacity, his weakness in his pride.[3]

Charles had always enjoyed meeting new people and prided himself on the ease and speed with which he made friends.[3]

His rashness and ambition.[5]

His royal air, flashing smile, indescribable dignity, vitality and glowing health probably were summed up in the loving epithet 'bonnie' which clings always to his memory.[5]

Sources/references:
1. Liz Greene, *Saturn*, Samuel Weiser.
2. W.D. Norie, *The Life and Adventures of Prince Charles Edward Stuart vol 1,* Caxton Publishing.
3. Margaret Forster, *The Rash Adventurer*, Secker & Warburg.
4. Hugh Douglas, *Charles Edward Stuart, The Man, the King, the Legend,* Robert Hale.
5. Winifred Duke, *Prince Charles Edward and the Forty Five*, Robert Hale.

Margaret Thatcher.

Politician. Prime Minister of Great Britain 1979-

Born: 13 October 1925, 09.00 GMT, Grantham 52N56 0W38.
Source: Private secretary (through AA Data Section).

This is a strong 'Mars' chart, with Scorpio rising and the ruling planet Mars conjunct the Sun. So it is that Margaret Thatcher, for better and worse, is a powerful living embodiment of the Mars principle. It permeates her policies and character; it is her strength and her weakness. As with any individual, there are a number of strands to the character, and these reflect in other facets of the chart. But Mars/Scorpio is the dominant overtone of a character that is more focused and rather less complex than most. Mars reflects in obvious character traits like vigour, incisiveness, energy, domineering aggressiveness, single-mindedness, arrogance, and her incapacity for compromise. More broadly, Mars is the champion of self-sufficiency and rugged individualism. It is the enemy of abstraction, excess and waste. It is a planet of direct action. Its major weaknesses are lack of subtlety, with subsequent difficulty in comprehending complex situations, and a tendency for unchecked strength to degenerate to harshness or ruthlessness.

Mars, along with Pluto and Scorpio, also relates to power and this forms an important theme in Margaret Thatcher's life. She has a thirst for power, an instinctive understanding of it, and has demonstrated an ability to grasp and keep it. If we look back over the last ten years it becomes plain that the way power is wielded in Britain has changed. It is much less dependent upon the consensus of Cabinet, Parliament, or Civil Service. The Government of the country is the product of a single will to a greater degree than at any time in modern history. If we chart her rise to power in terms of transits and progressions we find a marked emphasis on Mars and Pluto:

Feb 2 1960: Elected to Parliament — Pluto conjunct MC; transiting Saturn opposite natal Pluto.

Oct 1967: Seat in Shadow Cabinet — transiting Saturn opposite natal Mars; transiting Jupiter conjunct Moon.

June 1970: Full Cabinet member — transiting Pluto conjunct Part of Fortune; transiting Saturn conjunct descendant.

Feb 1975: Elected Party leader — transiting Pluto conjunct natal Mars; transiting Saturn conjunct natal Pluto.

May 1979: Prime Minister — progressed Mars conjunct ascendant; Saturn conjunct MC; Pluto conjunct natal Sun.

We note that Saturn also features strongly at critical times. As well as the above examples, we note the planet conjunct her natal Sun at the time of the Falklands War, and conjunct its own place and the ascendant on the occasion of the IRA attempt on her life in October 1984 (when transiting Pluto was closely conjunct the Sun/Saturn midpoint).

To date Margaret Thatcher has proved more 'reliable' than most when it comes to transits and progressions. When something is happening in the chart (especially involving Saturn, Pluto or Mars) there is invariably significant development in her life. We look with interest then, to the end of 1988 and early 1989, when Pluto will transit over ascendant and Saturn. This period is also marked by a progressed new Moon (exact in February 1989). Progressed new Moons occur every thirty years in an individual's chart and are one of the more reliable indicators of the onset of a significant new life phase. In Mrs Thatcher's case the last one fell in September 1959, broadly coinciding with the start of her Parliamentary career. This suggests, then, that she is fast approaching another critical point in her career. It is difficult to say precisely what this will be, although with Pluto involved it will likely concern power. It may be a phase where she seeks to concentrate more power in her own hands, or one where there are attempts, from within or without her Party, to wrest power from her. It should be said that to date challenging transits have worked well for her, advancing her in her life's purpose and consolidating her political ambitions.

What of the rest of the chart? There is a strong 11th house (Sun, Mars and Mercury here, by quadrant systems) and she has a very fixed and definite vision of what a society should be, and has set about imposing that vision on the country. Despite having three planets in Air signs, the Water of Scorpio, and the Fire of Leo predominate. She is a politician of the heart, not of the head. She has learned to trust her instinct and intuition. She is vague and evasive when it suits her, reflecting the accented Neptune of the chart (conjunct the Moon and the MC). This also reflects a propagandist nature, an ability to use the media and to project a glossy, populist image.

The Leo Moon amplifies some of the Scorpio traits, such as arrogance, autocracy, and single-mindedness. It suggests the showy side, her liking for the limelight. The Leo Moon also contributes to force of personality. She has imposed her will, first on the Conservative Party, and then on the country. It has become *her* party and Thatcher's Britain. In short, she has stamped her personality on the times.

Libra is apparently evident in her more private face, in a sort of brisk courtesy, and a mannered solicitude towards friends and staff. But the Libran Sun is also operative at a much more significant level. It reflects the concern with values and morality that form the substance of her mission. As we have seen in these profiles, Librans are often concerned with the mores, with the changing of values and attitudes. But Mrs Thatcher is unusual in being retrogressive. She would like to institute the essentially Victorian attitudes that prevailed in her own childhood home, and this more than anything is evidence of the simplistic narrowness of her mind. It demonstrates an essential lack of understanding of social dynamics. Suffice to say at this point that

Victorian values were apt for the Victorians, but they have lost their potency to instil order and harmony in the modern world, this much should be plain. A new age needs new values. The last twenty years or so has seen the evolution of new values, but these have not yet penetrated the centres of power.

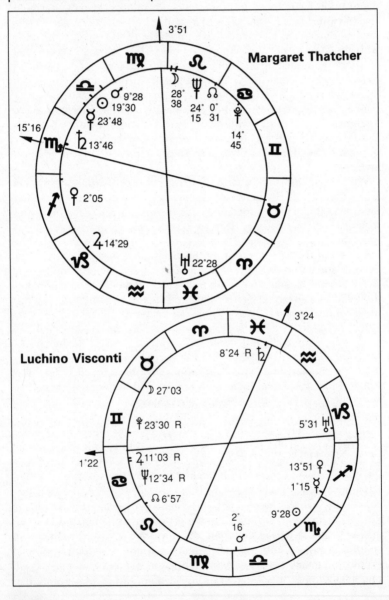

Thatcher has taken her early life and used it as a touchstone to identify the old fashioned values that she holds, admires and would like to restore to Britain.[1]

(When young she) ... never rebelled in any way against the strict mores of her father ... she had an intense, some have said, arrogant certainty that she was right; and she was never shy about declaring herself. She never shared the frivolity of her contemporaries, nor the gossip, but was always very serious and worthy, and as often as not gave the impression that she disapproved of their way of life.[2]

The codes of right and wrong lie at the bottom of every decision she takes. They account for the inflexibility, the black and white approach to life, and for the lack of imagination or real interest in debate.[2]

... zeal, industry, ambition, endurance, firmness of purpose.[3]

She is a political leader who hates admitting wrong or accepting reversals in fortune.[4]

The best part of her, not to be under-rated in the career towards which she was working, was her dogged determination to succeed in the face of difficulty and setbacks.[4]

Sources/references:
1. Nicholas Wapshott and George Brock, *Thatcher*, Futura.
2. Penny Junor, *Margaret Thatcher*, Sidgwick & Jackson.
3. Hugo Young and Anne Sloman, *The Thatcher Phenomenon*, BBC Publications.
4. Bruce Arnold, *Margaret Thatcher A Study in Power*, Hamish Hamilton.

Luchino Visconti

Acclaimed Italian film-maker and director whose work includes *Death in Venice*, and *The Damned*.

Born: 2 November 1906, 20.00 MET, Milan 45N29 9E11.
Source: Subject, cited in reference below.

Both Visconti's parents were involved with the theatre and very early on he also developed a taste for its glamour and excitement. Once more we note the importance of the early home life when Cancer is strong in the chart (as it is here, being the rising sign). His love of theatre and opera, and his ultimate work in film is suggested by the close conjunction of Jupiter and Neptune in the first house. It is also common to find Cancer and Taurus emphasised in some way in the charts of those skilled in the use of image, and as well as a Cancer ascendant we note the Moon well placed in Taurus.

Biographical description makes evident the strong Water of the chart. He possessed the complex emotional nature associated with this element. He was very volatile, with a fearsome temper, although at heart was a shy, reserved, private person, and a listener rather than a talker. He was sentimental and had the Cancerian home-loving side. He was paternalistic and liked to build a clique about himself, excluding those who refused to be dominated by him. He possessed the Scorpio will, vigour and energy. There was a strong personal magnetism that could captivate both men and women. He could be possessive, jealous, bullying, dictatorial, even cruel. He was courageous and self-disciplined.

In his personal relationships he exhibited an unusual combination of masochism and domination (a polarisation perhaps mirrored by Uranus conjunct the seventh house cusp). If a partner would not dominate and debase him, then he would dominate the partner. There could be no half-measures it seems. The Piscean elements of the chart — the first house Jupiter/Neptune, in a grand trine with Sun and Saturn in Pisces — suggest a passive side, while Scorpio, ruled by Mars, is associated with the urge to dominate. He was basically a guilt-ridden person and much of this focused on his feelings for his mother who he idealised beyond words. It seems likely this mother-worship formed the root of his homosexuality. 'He could not', notes his biographer, 'love women after having loved his mother passionately. His mother had been for him a continuous standard of comparison' (compare J.M. Barrie, whose chart also has Cancer and Taurus accented).

On 30 September 1929 his chauffeur was killed in a motor accident for which Visconti was partly to blame. He was riven with remorse and guilt. He wouldn't drive a car himself for the next twenty years. But more immediately he spent two months of solitude, a period of intense introversion and transformation, in the Sahara desert attempting to assuage his guilt. His chart was active by progression and transit at the time, with progressed Sun sextile Mars, progressed Moon opposite Mars and square Uranus, transiting Uranus quincunx Sun, transiting Saturn opposite Pluto, and transiting Neptune on the IC.

An important year in his life was 1935. It was the year he accepted his homosexuality. Early in the year he had his first serious love-affair with a man and some months later he broke off his engagement, thus abandoning all pretence of respectability. The Saturnian aspects prevalent at the time seem apt here. Saturn was conjunct its own place and the progressed Sun squared Saturn. Progressed Moon was opposite Venus suggesting it was a time of reassessing his relationships and his attitude to women in general. This year also marked the start of his film career.

The overbearing insecurity of his character.

He was a great conqueror and he wanted people to love him ... extremely jealous.

Worked with vigour, never troubled by doubt ... what he did he did with virile firmness.

The energy that Visconti consumed by being in love was frankly amazing. If the object of his passion did not humiliate him, Visconti would humiliate his partner; there were some terrifying scenes in which Visconti would reduce the momentary object of his love to tears ... it was Visconti's vengeance on the boy for not having been debased by him. His was a violent passionate nature and, in his constant need to be loved and humiliated, it was also a very insecure nature. He was the product of a disorderly family, of lack of real affection in his childhood and, however often he exalted his family in interviews and recollections, he felt towards it the masochistic attraction of the rejected, the only relationship which ultimately satisfied him.

Source/reference:
1. Gaia Servadio, *Luchino Visconti A Biography,* Weidenfeld & Nicolson.

Part 3

Astrology in action at the collective level

The outer planets

In astrology it is quite common to arrange the planets in the following way:

Personal: Sun, Moon, Mercury, Venus, Mars.
Social: Jupiter, Saturn.
Collective: Uranus, Neptune, Pluto.

We have an increase in scale of expression. The social planets are more concerned with the individual *vis à vis* society, while the collective planets operate at a transpersonal level, equating to strata of experience belonging to humanity rather than individuals. However, individuals with these planets strongly placed in the natal chart might act as a focus for the energies they symbolise. So runs the conventional wisdom.

While there is substance and value in such a scheme, it is in my view oversimplified and in some ways misleading. Symbols have their own inner logic and can never be wholly contained by the approximate systems we devise to facilitate understanding. As Dennis Elwell points out in the excellent *Cosmic Loom*, the categories we invent are not necessarily recognised by the universe at all. It seems to know nothing of malefic or benign; or of trivial and profound. It all comes back to what was said in the introduction about astrological symbols being three rather than two dimensional. Each of the planets has a personal *and* a greater-than-personal dimension. As we have seen already with the profiles, the collective planets do equate with what we call personality traits. There is, for example, a certain type of behaviour specific to Neptune. Its principle can be acted out on an individual level, in an essentially small and trivial way. This is not to deny that it can manifest also in an overwhelming and epic way in an individual, or that it does have a transpersonal nature, equating with a broader and deeper pattern of history.

So it is with Mercury, Venus and Mars, who are anything but the lightweights they are often assumed to be. Each has a greater-than-personal dimension. These planetary principles can be quite clearly detected in collective life. Their meaning accords with the tone of certain social phases, and indeed of whole civilisations. It is difficult to read accounts of the ancient Spartans or Assyrians without thinking of Mars; or of the Byzantines without thinking of Mercury. In *The Literary Zodiac* I spoke of a pattern of alternating social phases that clearly accord with the nature of Jupiter and Mars. The Western world-view, that abstract idea that underpins our whole collective being, is essentially the Mercury principle. As a collective we are, in a broad way, living out this theme, in the same way that the Elizabethans seemed to live out a distinctly Venusian theme. Venus has a very definite social side, particularly through its Libra face, and we spoke of this in an earlier section. But I have to say, I have not to my satisfaction discerned the Solar and Lunar principles operative on the collective level. It is possible that these must operate on a wholly individual level. With the other planets, however, there seems no clear-cut distinction, although there seems to be truth in the generalisation that the outer planets are somehow more suited, can better express themselves, on a transpersonal rather than individual level.

This section of the book, then, deals with astrological principles as they manifest more broadly in a collective sphere of existence, with the focus on Uranus, Neptune and Pluto. The chapters on Uranus and Neptune are based on articles that first appeared in *The Astrological Journal* (Autumn 1983 and Summer 1984), although these are here significantly enlarged and revised.

Modern Planets.

Uranus, Neptune and Pluto have been discovered in modern times, and as such there is no meaning inherited from ancient times. Their meaning is a product of recent thought. Indeed it would be interesting and informative (and quite possible) to establish the genesis of the symbolism; to see just how a body of astrological knowledge comes to be established. However, this is a project I leave to someone else.

But modern or not, it is the case that ancient mythology has been used to render meaning to these planets. This seems to be justified, though certainly raises questions among more hard-headed astrologers. They point out that the names were chosen by scientists, that they might have been called anything — as indeed Uranus was otherwise called for a number of years. To them it seems most unreasonable to use arbitrary nomenclature as a basis for deriving planetary meaning. More intuitive astrologers console themselves with the fact that the universe is not 'reasonable' in the commonly accepted sense of the word, and that in some mysterious way the names were not arbitrary. Yet there is no real cause for dilemma, for it is possible to come to an understanding of the energies represented by these bodies without recourse to mythology.

Another question commonly raised regarding the outer planets is whether or not the principles they symbolise have always existed, or came into being only at the time of physical discovery. It seems to me a case, as so often it is, of both/and rather than either/or. Yes, as we will see shortly, Pluto does seem to be active in the charts of those born pre-twentieth century. Yes, at least some of the social phenomena symbolised by Neptune seemed to be present in the Ancient and Medieval worlds. Likewise there was a good deal of evolution, revolution and technology before Uranus was discovered in 1781. At the same time, when each of these planets was discovered there was a sort of quickening. The energies they represent became more real, and more of a focus of human affairs.

The coincidence of planetary discovery and world developments is an example of synchronicity, a concept formulated by Jung in which events can be understood as being linked acausally, that is by inner meaning rather than through cause and effect. The concept is not given much credence by the doggedly scientific mind, but we have only to think of Rostand's foolish cockerel, who believed his crowing actually *made* the sun rise, to keep a perspective on the matter. Much can be learned by examining the inner nature of the phenomena that coincided with the discovery of these planets. This has been remarked on by other astrological workers. But what has not been noted is the continuing correspondence throughout the planetary cycle; a recurrent flowering of the planetary principle at well-defined intervals.

Planetary cycles.

The application of cycles to astrology is nothing new. The ancients referred to them, and in contemporary times Dane Rudhyar is just one writer who has stressed their importance. In recent years many astrologers have incorporated cycles into their methodology, and the use of the progressed Sun/Moon cycle, and planetary returns has become increasingly common. Some cycles involve two planets, and the recurring conjunction of the two marks a starting point. But a return involves just one planet, and the start of its cycle is the zodiacal degree at birth. Thus, those periods when a planet returns to its natal degree are very often marked by a sort of recharging, so that its principle expresses in and through the individual in a marked way. That this is so is borne out by the experience of many astrologers.

In collective life we generally deal with two-planet cycles. However, in the case of Neptune, Uranus and Pluto we are afforded the opportunity of an extra cycle. Because, in fact, they have a 'birth point', the zodiacal degree at which they were discovered — approximately 24 Gemini for Uranus, 25 Aquarius for Neptune, 20 Cancer for Pluto. From these reference points it is possible to construct well-defined cycles, with four critical points. As with any cycle, we have an opposition 180 degrees from the natal point, and the first and last quarters, respectively 90 and 270 degrees from the natal point (figures 1 and 3 in the relevant chapters will make this clearer). So it is not only the discovery of an outer planet that corresponds to a marked manifestation of its principle in the world of affairs; but also the transit of the planet to its opposition, and first and last quarter degrees, and the return to the discovery degree.

The next two chapters, then, examine the Uranus and Neptune cycles in some detail. They represent, I believe, a very convincing demonstration of astrology in action. Pluto can not be effectively examined in this way, however, having not progressed far enough in this its first cycle. The final chapter in this section looks at Pluto in a different way.

Uranus
in action

Before considering the Uranus cycle we might first consider the astrological meaning of the planet in a little more detail.

The Uranian principle can be summed up quite simply: it always works to overcome the laws and limitations of space, time and matter. Symbolically speaking, Uranus pits itself against Saturn. From this one principle stem a number of related phenomena and concepts such as evolution, social amelioration, technology, democracy, internationalism, common language, universalism, speed, accidents, and rebellion. Contemporary opinion tends to overstate this last category. We do find Uranians (and Aquarians, through which sign this principle also manifests) who are provocative and challenging in their ways, and who hope thereby to awaken their peers to higher potential. We do find Uranians who pit themselves against some sort of establishment structure. But equally there are many who do not fit the colourful or radical mould, and who express the principle, if at all, through other of the listed avenues. This must be evident from the individual profiles in the previous section.

Uranus breaks down divisive barriers, thus creating the conditions where what is separate can come together and move towards one end. It breaks down class and caste systems to bring about democracy, and national barriers to create a unified body of humanity — thus the association with internationalism and common language. It is Aquarius' polar sign, Leo, we note, that relates more than any other to nationalism. Ideas of race and racial superiority relate to Leo and the Sun. Uranus's race is the human race; it doesn't discriminate within this. It doesn't register terms like 'American,' 'British', etc. because these are simply transient political and administrative categories. It does not recognise terms like 'Celt', 'Anglo-Saxon', 'Negro', because these are racial categories rooted in the Earth, and Uranus is a sky-god. One thing that has helped create an international world is speed. Trains, automobiles, aircraft all overcome man's inherent immobility, and have catalysed the intermixing of the separate races of the world. It is the speed of a rocket that allows it to escape from the Earth's (Saturnian) gravity.

The Uranian/Aquarian capacity to transcend barriers of time and space can manifest in the creative or performing arts in a characteristic way. Writers with these influences strong are often able to achieve both critical and popular acclaim — and a popularity that goes beyond lowest-common-denominator, tabloid appeal (which relates more to Neptune and Pisces). What the work essentially does is transcend generation, class, or nationality. The writing is not restricted to time and place. It strikes to some fundamental and common level in human beings everywhere and at all times. Those British writers most popular internationally often have the sign or planet accented. Carroll, Dickens, Maugham, Byron and Burns were all Aquarian Suns; Wells and Stevenson have Aquarius rising; Rider Haggard and J.B. Priestley have the Moon in the sign; Kipling, Conan Doyle, John Buchan, and Mary Shelley have Uranus strong. Humour is one of the more difficult commodities to export. The British comedian who has succeeded more than any other, at least in America, is Aquarian Benny Hill.

Uranus has come to be related to accidents, and indeed, there is that about accidents that is a faithful reflection of the Uranian principle. Once again, it is a case of the ancient conflict between Uranus and Saturn. The Saturnian laws of matter are well-defined. In the world of time and space only one object can occupy a particular place at a particular time. Indeed, it would be confusing if this were not so. But accidents are very often the consequence of two objects, one of them usually a person, attempting to do just that.

However, the most important aspect of Uranus, particularly with regard to our current epoch, is a connection with social amelioration, technology and evolution. At a basic level Uranus and Aquarius are about the improvement of life, about the creating and sustaining of those conditions in which human potentiality can flower. Evolution represents an ongoing leavening process. It is in effect a sort of alchemic conversion of matter into energy, or 'Earth' to 'Sky'. In progressing from one to the other the burden of survival is lessened, and an essentially more human, refined, spiritual level of existence attained. More specifically, Uranus relates to the evolution of the mass. Again, it is the polar influences, Sun and Leo, that equate to the raising of individual consciousness. With Aquarius and Uranus the concern is with moving the whole of humanity to some higher vibrational level as part of some larger cosmic purpose we can only speculate upon.

What, then, is the connection of technology with this process? In short, it is a means to an end; an essential *first step* towards a more spiritualised humanity. The opportunity for inner development is very limited if we are chained to the Earth, if the greater part of waking existence needs to be devoted to meeting the basic human demands of sustenance and shelter. At one time each individual had to do his or her own surviving (or at least be very directly involved as part of some group effort). This is the way of primitive cultures. That you or I do not have to do so is because ways have been devised whereby one person, in effect, can do the work of a hundred or even a thousand. The processes of labour have become hypereffecient, and, in the West, technology liberates us to a good degree from toil. It has created time and energy for the individual, thus providing the opportunity for getting on with the real business of living, that is, of developing our conscious potential as individual human beings. That most people do not capitalise on the opportunity is, of course, another matter. Perhaps one outcome of the Aquarian Age will be that increasingly large numbers of people will remember the end to which technology has been a means. It seems to have started already.

Uranus and revolution.

The discovery of Uranus in 1781 coincided, as other writers have pointed out, with the French and American Revolutions. In fact, these last decades of the eighteenth century saw a number of insurrections throughout Europe, but the two mentioned proved the most consequential. These two major revolutions were not isolated events, but, rather, critical and highly significant points on the curve of a vaster cycle. In simple terms, this period represents a crisis point in the change from the Medieval to the Modern world; from absolutism to democracy; from an ideational to a sensate world. Or, in astrological terms, from a Jupiter to a Mercury world (and here I believe the Gemini placement of Uranus at the time of its discovery is meaningful). The forces of modernity had been waxing at the expense of medievalism for centuries. The era of revolutions marked a sort of equinoctial point where, for the first time, the strength of the new (the power of democracy) surpassed the strength of the old (the absolutist power of Church, kings and aristocracy).

Revolutions were nothing new in the eighteenth century. However, there were many novel features regarding the revolutions that did occur at this time. Moreover, that which is unique about them relates to Uranus. In the first place, they transcended local or prosaic issues. The same refrains — the rights of man, the happiness and welfare of all — were on people's lips the world over. It was the revolutionary figure Thomas Paine (an Aquarian Sun, we note) who said that the cause of the American colonists was the cause of the human race. It was one of his contemporaries who added that America's oppression was the oppression of the world. What we had for the first time with the discovery of Uranus was the appearance of political and social awareness on a collective level.

When we read accounts of the mood of revolutionary France we can't help but see the Aquarian quality of it. There was an awareness of common ends among disparate groups. There was an awareness among individuals that a whole lot of people were thinking along the same lines. There was a prevailing belief that the time was 'right'. That the opportunity for change had come, and must not be missed. In hindsight it does indeed seem as if the end of the eighteenth century was one of those rare moments in history when the underlying architecture unfreezes and becomes fluid for a short time before resetting in a fundamentally new configuration. Such moments might be likened to earthquakes, but instead of the massive sliding of continental plates, we have sudden, sharp shifts on the conceptual level, the 'sky-world' of Uranus, where lie the great 'ideas' or principles that pattern collective life. History is an ongoing process, a continuum, but it seems as if we also need sudden shocks to help the evolution along, in the same way a Zen disciple needs the blow of the master's stick to help elevate personal consciousness.

The return of Uranus to its own place in 1863, and the subsequent unfolding first quarter, marked another milestone in the ongoing conceptual shift of European history. The alacrity with which the West latched on to Darwin's theories (despite their flaws) indicates that these were ideas whose time had come. Darwin (an Aquarian Sun) brought into focus the polarity of the old and new ways of thinking: the medieval/Jupiterian view of Creation as a one-off event by a single God, and the modern/Mercurial view of life as a process changing through its own momentum and not dependent on supernatural agencies. Darwin's theories did not bring about this conceptual change. What he did, was to function as a sort of seed crystal to what was in the 'Air' at the time. At some level he was alive to these conceptual currents, and they translated into a life purpose.

Uranus and Technology.

The discovery of Uranus in 1781 coincided with another revolution equally if not more important than either the French or the American. This was the Industrial Revolution. Uranus did not herald the birth of technology by any means. Technology, the application of mind to overcoming the challenges of living in the physical world, began with the earliest human beings. There were many important inventions and discoveries before this date, the wheel, fire, the plough, tools, printing, paper, rope, gears, pulleys, pumps, pottery, plumbing, to name but a few. What happened at the end of the eighteenth century was a great acceleration in the process, as figure 2 suggests. Uranus is not bound to Saturnian time. It makes more happen in a given time, which is what we call speed. There has been as much technological advance in the past 200 years as in the previous 10,000; as much in the past 50 as in the previous 150. The main reason for the acceleration is that technology at the time of the Industrial Revolution moved to the 'sky' world. The model of the material world that we call science had advanced to a point where it was possible to express diverse physical processes and problems in terms of common principles and concepts on the mental level. Technology acquired a common language, so that advances in understanding could be applied across the spectrum of separate industries.

We can turn now to the pattern of technology since 1781. What we find is that the critical points in the Uranus cycle (see figure 1) correspond very well to important technological developments. At the time of the discovery, and at the return of Uranus to the degree of

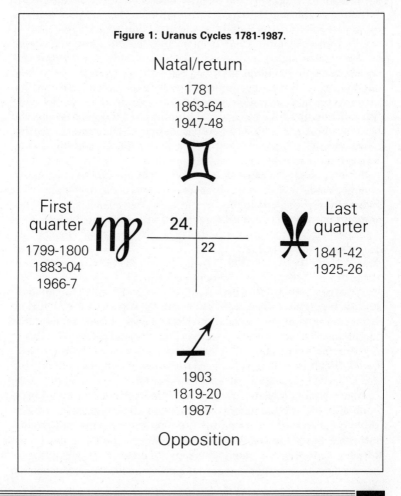

Figure 1: Uranus Cycles 1781-1987.

Natal/return

1781
1863-64
1947-48

First quarter

1799-1800
1883-04
1966-7

24.

22

Last quarter

1841-42
1925-26

1903
1819-20
1987

Opposition

discovery every 84 years, we get a new 'seeding' of Uranian energy, which then develops over the period of the cycle, with the quarterly points the most critical. It is over the first quarter period that we get the most visible development.

The first cycle, 1781-1863/4.

Popular myth has James Watt sitting by the fire in a rocking chair observing jets of steam from the kettle and being assailed with the idea of the steam-engine. In fact, there were working steam-engines long before this period (such as that of Savery and Newcomen in the 1690s). Watt's role was to radically improve what was essentially a primitive device to produce an engine capable of continuous, efficient performance. Watt's steam-engine basically *made possible* the Industrial Revolution, and most historians regard it as the foundation stone of the modern technological era. Watt himself, we note, had his Sun in Aquarius. He took out his first patent in 1769, though it wasn't until 1776 that the first commercial engine was sold. Over the next few decades, the unfolding first quarter of the Uranus cycle, the steam-engine became the primary power source of Industry, being used to drive mills, to power looms, to pump water, and to work metal. Essentially it made the processes of labour more efficient. The amount of work a person can do is limited by energy and muscle-power. The steam-engine transcends that physical limitation, and thus is a manifestation of the Uranian principle.

This first cycle also saw the start of modern transportation, though specifically that based on the steam-engine. It saw the development of locomotives, or steam-engines on wheels. Two names stand out as pioneers in this field: Richard Trevithick and George Stephenson. The latter, we note, was born 9 June 1781, the same year Uranus was discovered, and with his Sun conjunct the planet. Stephenson was building his first railway 1819-22, which coincides with the opposition phase of the cycle (1820). Commentators agree that it was Trevithick's application of a high-pressure engine to the problems of locomotion that *made possible* the commercial steam railway. He was engaged in this at the turn of the century (the first quarter phase), taking out a patent which covered the workings of his locomotive in 1802. Other developments include the first iron steam-ship, built 1819-21 (opposition); and the onset of the boom period of railways in Britain, so-called 'Railway Mania', in 1840 (last quarter).

Uranus has been related by many astrologers to the phenomenon of electricity, although as a bipolar phenomenon it has a connection with Mercury and Gemini. However, we do find a very convincing correspondence between the Uranus cycle and the development of the science (rather than the technology) of electricity.

We might take as a starting point Galvani's famous experiment in

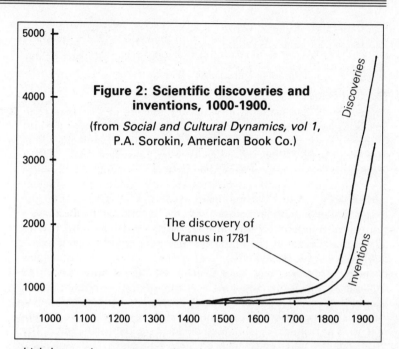

Figure 2: Scientific discoveries and inventions, 1000-1900.

(from *Social and Cultural Dynamics, vol 1*, P.A. Sorokin, American Book Co.)

The discovery of Uranus in 1781

which he used a current produced from unlike metals in contact to induce muscular spasms in frogs. He first performed this in 1780 (discovery phase), although he did not set forth his observations until 1791. This whole first quarter was, as the following comment suggests, one of great fertility in the science of electricity:

> In 1790 began one of the most brilliant periods in the entire history of science, culminating with Volta's discoveries of the battery and current electricity, of the relationship between electricity and magnetism, between electricity and matter, and with the birth of the modern electrical industry ... this extraordinary revolution.[1]

'The momentous discovery of Alessandro Volta'[2] (yet another Aquarian Sun) came in 1800 (first quarter). It was in March of this year that he described his voltaic cell to the President of the Royal Society. His discovery generated much activity in the scientific fraternity (often the sign of a true discovery). This phase of the cycle, from the first quarter to the opposition saw the development of his discovery, culminating in 1819 with The Royal Society's Great Battery, which utilised 4000 copper and zinc discs, and constituted a formidable source of electrical power.

The opposition phase marked another milestone in the development of the science of electricity. In 1819 Oersted showed that electricity and magnetism were connected (his findings were reported the following year). His results precipitated a frenzy of experimental activity so that by the end of 1820 many of the quantitative laws relating the two had been discovered. We also note the invention of the electromagnet by Arago in 1820. In 1821 Faraday showed that a magnetic pole can be made to rotate indefinitely around a current-carrying wire, thus demonstrating, in effect, the principle of the electric motor. The period from the opposition to the last quarter was one of continued discovery, most notably by Faraday, some of which, it has to be said, does not tie in with the critical quarterly points.

The second cycle, 1863/4-1947.

Electricity as a technology came with the second cycle. The dynamo was born in a practical form in the mid-1860s, but beyond this it is difficult to find correspondences. However, in other areas we do continue to find them.

In 1862 a patent was filed which covered the workings of the four-stroke internal-combustion cycle, the precursor of the universal petrol engine (although we note that such an engine was not built for some time). In 1885 (first quarter) Herr Benz, who has been called the father of the automobile, built his first vehicle. The opposition phase saw the formation of the Ford Motor Company, and the start of automobile mass production. It can not be denied that motorised transport has had a singular impact on modern life and indeed many governments today foolishly gauge the health of the nation on the number of cars it produces. Transportation has basically helped unfreeze the world. One is struck by the static nature of the old world and certainly part of the reason for this was the difficulty and expense of travel itself. Transport has overcome the barrier of physical distance, and consequently the world has become less of a fragmented, heterogeneous place. Mobility has helped erode national barriers. It has not brought about, though has made possible, a world united by common humanity and not divided by nationalistic difference and self-interest.

This second cycle of Uranus also witnessed the start of powered flight, again in machines based on the internal combustion engine. On December 17 1903 Uranus stood at 25.42 of Sagittarius, closely opposed to its natal position. This was the day of the Wright brothers' historic first flight. It was the most marginal of beginnings, but its importance is widely recognised. One commentator notes:

> This event is now accepted by responsible opinion throughout the world as the significant landmark identifying the beginning of the era of powered heavier than air flight,

which has become one of the most important technological developments of the 20th century.[3]

The last quarter phase corresponds to Lindbergh's historic flight, linking the New World and the Old, in May 1927, an event which captured the public imagination in an extraordinary way.

Lindbergh was an Aquarian Sun, and indeed a significant number of those individuals involved in releasing Uranian energy into the world in one form or another have the sign or the planet accented in some way. Similarly, important or highly symbolic events pertaining to flight and space travel often (but not always) have charts that highlight Aquarius, Uranus, or alternatively the discovery degree of Uranus. The charts accompanying show three examples:

(1) A chart drawn up for the first flight, shows Aquarius rising, and Sun conjunct Uranus on the discovery degree axis.

(2) At the time of the first liquid-fuel rocket launch by Robert Goddard, the Sun was exactly conjunct Uranus, and also involved in an exact aspect pattern with Saturn and Mars. This event also corresponds, we note, to the last quarter phase of this second cycle. Again, this event was the most marginal of beginnings. Goddard's rocket flew for only two and a half seconds. Yet it can be said that this was a first step which led to Neil Armstrong's big first step.

(3) The third chart is for Lindbergh's landing in Paris after conquering the Atlantic, and we note the ascendant axis falling across the discovery degree.

We note on the day of the Moon landing that Uranus was conjunct Jupiter on the MC of the USA national chart (the 12 Sagittarius rising version). The same two planets were conjunct on the IC of the chart on the day of Lindbergh's flight. The equivalence of these events, and the aptness of the planetary conjunction need not be commented upon.

Before leaving the history of flight, and passing onto the third cycle, we might note a final unlikely coincidence. The Montgolfier Brothers made the first free, controlled flight by man, in a hot-air balloon, in 1783, corresponding to the discovery of Uranus. Saturnian gravity has never been the same since.

The third cycle, 1947/8-2031.

Each new cycle of Uranus seems to mark a shift of geographical focus. In each cycle one nation more than others seems to be taken by the urge to industrialise. In the first cycle it was Britain, in the second America, where, by the second half of the nineteenth century both population and industry were burgeoning. Before the end of the century production was outstripping any European nation, so that in 1886 steel magnate Andrew Carnegie could write with truth: 'The old nations of the earth creep on at a snail's pace. The Republic thunders past with the rush of an express.' The third cycle saw Japan emerge as the nation to most vigorously embrace the technological spirit.

The return of Uranus to its discovery degree in 1947 heralded the onset of the computer age. It is true that the principles of computing were known to earlier generations of mathematicians, but it was not until the 1940s that the first real computers were being built. We note that it was in 1946 that the first all electronic computer was completed. The computer has continued to develop throughout this cycle, although the take off period, in so far as one can be recognised was during the mid-60s, the first quarter phase. It has been estimated that the number of computers in use increased by a factor of ten over this period.[4] What facilitated this growth was the invention, in 1965, of BASIC, a sort of universal computer language. In terms of their effect, computer and steam-engine can be connected through Uranus. For while one took over the laborious work of muscles, the computer has released millions from the drudge of trivial, repetitive mental activity. Both devices reflect the Uranian evolutionary principle of relief from survival-oriented labour. The computer also ensured technological advance at a time when it seemed it might stagnate through sheer complexity and volume of data.

The other highly significant development corresponding to this third cycle seeding was the onset of the semi-conductor age. In 1947 the transistor effect was first isolated in the Bell Telephone Laboratories. This is a discovery from which many things, positive and negative, have stemmed.

In conclusion.

Uranus will return once more to its own place in the year 2031. If past patterns are continued then the world at this time will experience a new influx of Uranian energy. But it does not follow that this period will herald a new technological dawn. Technology is not the Uranus principle, but simply one aspect of it. The Uranus principle relates to evolution in the sense of the ongoing elevation of the consciousness of humanity. For this to come about there has to be a loosening of the bonds of matter. This is what Uranus effects, and technology has been the means. Technology is not an end. It is amoral. There is not the purpose or meaning in it that writers like H.G. Wells seemed to assume. It is not a surrogate religion.

By the time of the last Uranus return in 1947 the bondage to matter had been loosened substantially, or so we can judge from the fact that part of the 'input' at that time has manifested in a non-material, essentially spiritual way. In the West there was an awakening, specifically in the mid-60s first quarter phase. We recognise that this was a unique period in modern times. I believe it is reflected astrologically in the coming together of two cycles, the unfolding first

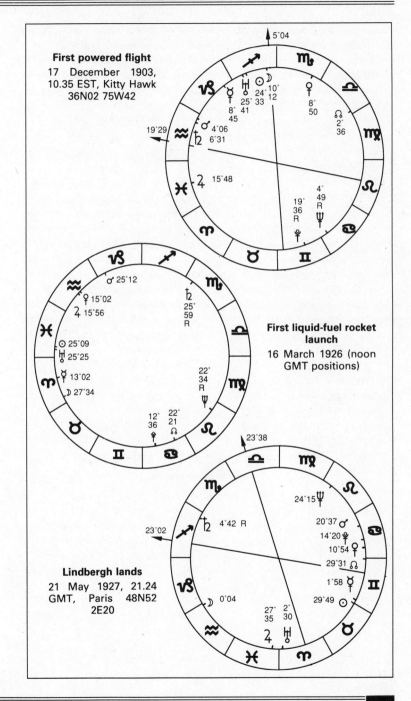

First powered flight
17 December 1903,
10.35 EST, Kitty Hawk
36N02 75W42

First liquid-fuel rocket launch
16 March 1926 (noon GMT positions)

Lindbergh lands
21 May 1927, 21.24 GMT, Paris 48N52 2E20

quarter of Uranus, and the last quarter of Neptune (and we talk about this in the next chapter). Some things at this time are best described by Neptune, others by Uranus. We can attribute to the latter the spread of the conviction that there is more to life than a work pattern determined by economic demands, and the realisation that technology blindly followed, without reference to a larger framework, can have evil consequences. The idea of alternative technology gained a good deal of acceptance at this time. This favoured working with, rather than against nature. It represents a wholesome philosophy, one which balances spirit and matter.

Whatever the nature of the spiritual wave of the 60s, it plainly failed to penetrate the centres of political power. In Europe there is one, highly marginal political party, the Greens, who seem able to see beyond work and industrial production as the sustaining drives of Western civilization, and who have a philosophy that sees in life a greater purpose than economic growth. They are thus the only party who can credibly claim to be the party of the future.

The late 60s was a time when many, mostly young, people came alive to a larger vision. It didn't take root in everyone, but substantial numbers changed their lives quite radically and today are working quietly towards their own, and the Planet's evolution. A few of these are astrologers.

References:

1. Rene Taton (ed), *Science in the Nineteenth Century*, Thames & Hudson.
2. *History of Technology* vol 5, p.177, Oxford Univ Press.
3. *Ibid*, p.391.
4. Gareth Ashurst, *Pioneers of Computing*, Frederick Muller Ltd.

Neptune
in action

Neptune has come to be associated with a variety of things, including religion, escapism, drugs, the creative imagination, the Theatre, and music. It is also said to have a relation to gases, oil, spiritualism, and anaesthetics, although it has to be said, valid correspondences as they may be, it is sometimes difficult to incorporate them in a meaningful way in a chart synthesis. There is substance in much of the astrological lore surrounding Neptune, but as with much contemporary astrology there is a need for clarification, and for a finer use of the discriminatory faculty. This chapter attempts to establish a clearer meaning of the Neptune principle, and furthermore demonstrates this principle in action.

The meaning of Neptune.

Neptune is said to rule Pisces, but this should not be taken to mean that the traditional ruler Jupiter has been usurped. There is that about Pisces that can not be explained without Jupiter. Nevertheless, as we saw in some of the profiles, where Neptune is accented in a chart there is very often a Piscean overtone evident in the individual's character. There can be an unfocused quality. There is often vagueness, evasiveness, secretiveness, sometimes mendacity and dishonesty. Neptune does seem to blur at the edges, make things less precise. Neptunian individuals can often have a diffuse and ambiguous cast. Sometimes there is the capacity to radiate a mysterious or glamorous aura. There can be an urge for self-surrender or self-denial. Neptunians can be victims but equally show great compassion for victims, or the underdog in general. There can be a refined quality to the Neptunian individual, with an urge to move beyond gross reality. Neptune relates to aestheticism, taste and connoisseurship; to the products of Art rather than the process of creation, which is a little too robust for Neptune.

Neptune and the Arts.

The connection of Neptune with the Arts has been overstated in my view. If we examine collections of artists' charts — painters, poets, musicians, writers and actors — we do not find a real emphasis on Neptune. This is not surprising if we think about it, for the nature of productive art is basically at odds with the nature of Neptune. Neptune is regarded as passive and yet creative art is a dynamic, assertive process. There are two distinct sides to creative art: the power to imagine, and the capacity to put images or ideas into compelling form. Indeed, we might add a third factor: the will and energy to create, without which the first two are of no value. This third factor is an essentially Masculine aspect of creating. In astrology it equates with Sun, Mars, and perhaps Uranus. I think Neptune does symbolise in part the imagination, but Moon and Venus are the more immediate symbols of this side of the creative process. The form-giving side is symbolised by Mercury and Venus, and in some senses Saturn. What we call creative art turns out on closer examination to be a multifaceted phenomenon, and this is just one reason why when we analyse a collection of artists' charts we get no clear cut results. Even when the result is statistically sound, in practical terms it is only marginal.

What of theatre, film and music, other spheres commonly related to Neptune? If we examine collections of musicians' charts we do not find a major emphasis on Neptune, or indeed on any single factor. Once again, this is at least partly because music is not one but a number of things, and not many of these things seem to me to be of the same essence as Neptune. It is true that music is the most subtle art form we have, and this is not at odds with the nature of Neptune. However, other facets are. It is dynamic, involving development through time. It is inherently ordered, almost by definition. If not ordered we simply have noise or sound. It is organised through time and rhythm (a function of Mercury), and more subtly through the Venus principle, which patterns sound in the way a magnet patterns iron filings. This is the inner order of music, which reflects some higher universal order, and which becomes crystallised and formalised in things like harmonic structure (and this Venusian ordering is specific to culture, so that Western music sounds 'right' or harmonious to the Western ear, but not so necessarily to the Oriental ear.)

If we examine the charts of actors and actresses we find factors other than Neptune emphasised, namely Jupiter, Mars and Mercury, which are not inappropriate if we think about it. We associate Mars with the capacity to translate into action, and what is called stage presence is also linked with this planet. Mercury like Neptune also has a slippery, chameleon quality, and traditionally is connected with an ability to impersonate and mimic. I have noticed in the charts of actresses that Mars/Scorpio factors are also very often accented[1], suggesting that what most of these women have is magnetism and old fashioned sex-appeal. Where we find strong Neptune is in those cases where individuals are able to fulfil collective fantasy and escapist needs. We saw this in the profiles in the case of Sean Connery. We can note it also with Clint Eastwood, Humphrey Bogart, and Marilyn Monroe, whose charts all show a strong Neptune. This planet, then, does not relate so much to the ability to act as to something which forms an integral part of the worlds of stage, screen, and television.

Neptune and illusion.

Neptune blurs the boundary between fact and fantasy, with positive and negative results. Like Jupiter it relates to some suprasensory reality that lies beyond appearances, and more specifically to the coupling of the two. This can relate to the refining and broadening of consciousness, to the incorporation of a mythic, spiritual, or 'artistic' dimension to life, and to the alleviating of the pain and ugliness of life. One possible manifestation of this is religion, but equally Neptune can relate to illusion, particularly to this on the collective level. It relates to legend rather than historical fact. Distorted and romantic tales seem to attach readily to the Neptunian or Piscean. Neptune relates to the fictionalisation of life such as is generated by television, film, public relations, propaganda, and the tabloid press. This is one of the more disturbing aspects of the Neptune principle, particularly as it increasingly infests public life so that secrecy, mendacity, and deception are now an integral part of politics.

Neptune is the symbol of that urge for a 'higher' dimension to life. It represents the need we feel to escape from the humdrum and oppressive, but more than that it's the need for mystery, inspiration, and wonder in life. Neptune is that part of us that is willing to suspend disbelief; that wants to believe the fantasy rather than the reality, simply because it makes us feel better to do so.

The following extract is taken from Thomas Mann's *Confessions of Felix Krull Confidence Man*[2]. It illustrates very well the things we have been saying about Neptune's relation to illusion and glamour. At one point in the novel, Felix, the central character, recalls the occasion of his first visit to the theatre, being enraptured by the magnificence of the auditorium, the music, the colour, the lights, and the power of the star singer's performance. The audience in its collective emotional response, Mann tells us, 'was like an enormous swarm of nocturnal insects, silently, blindly and blissfully rushing into a blazing fire.' Felix's father by chance is acquainted with the star, and he and Felix go back-stage to meet him. Rapid disillusionment follows. Instead of the splendour of the auditorium there is a small, cluttered, over-heated dressing room, smelling of sweat and grease. Instead of the glamorous Olympian who strutted the stage there is a rather coarse, vulgar man, looking slightly ridiculous with his make-up half off, and afflicted with all too human blemishes. What particularly offends Felix are the pustules visible in some number over the back and shoulders of the star: '... horrible pustules, red-rimmed, suppurating, some of them even bleeding; even today I cannot repress a shudder at the thought of them.'

Felix reflects at some length on his disillusionment, on the stark contrast between the magic of the theatrical performance and the man responsible for it:

> This grease-smeared and pimply individual is the charmer at whom the twilight crowd was just now gazing so soulfully! This repulsive worm is the reality of the glorious butterfly in whom those deluded spectators believed they were holding the realization of all their own secret dreams of beauty, grace and perfection ... But the grown up people in the audience, who on the whole must know about life, and who yet were so frightfully eager to be deceived, must they not have been aware of the deception? And that is quite possible. For when you come to think of it, which is the real shape of the glow worm — the insignificant little creature crawling about on the palm of your hand, or the poetic spark that swims through the summer night? Who would presume to say? Rather recall the picture you saw before: the giant swarm of poor moths and gnats, rushing silently and madly into the enticing flame! What unanimity in agreeing to let oneself be deceived! Here quite clearly there is in operation a general human need, implanted by God himself in human nature, which (the Star's) abilities are created to satisfy.

Thus the early impressions of a confidence man, whose trade is deceit, and who must master the art of appearing to be something he is not. This is a talent that finds outlet in public relations, politics, on the stage and in the criminal underworld. I have never seen a chart of a criminal confidence trickster, but I would be disappointed if Pisces or Mercury factors were not emphasised.

Another manifestation of the Neptune principle is advertising, because this is basically about the linking of the ordinary with the fantastic. We must distinguish here between wholly functional advertising (such as small-ad columns), and the sort that relies on benign deception, and seeks to command loyalty or sway opinion.

Neptune relates to the latter. Advertising seeks to infuse functional objects with an essentially false patina of glamour. Soap is basically fat and caustic soda, but in the hands of the ad-man this useful but mundane substance becomes interwoven with irrelevant abstract notions such as romance and maternalism. Coca Cola is basically carbon dioxide, sugar and water, but you wouldn't think so to see it ludicrously inflated and romanticised on the television screen. The following self-parodying doggerel appeared in an advertising journal in the 1930s.[3] It illustrates well this point about advertising being a blend of the prosaic and the romantic:

Glorifying pink chemises, eulogizing smelly cheeses,
Deifying rubber tires, sanctifying plumbers' pliers,
Accolading rubber panties, serenading flappers' scanties,
Rhapsodizing hotel fixtures, sermonizing on throat mixtures.
Some call us the new town criers,
Others call us cock-eyed liars!

For centuries people have bought, sold, and exchanged goods, without recourse to images and without pretending that goods were anything other than what they were. It used to be called commerce, and is symbolised in astrology by Mercury. Today we have commercial*ism*, which is symbolised by Neptune. Like any -ism it involves exercise of the irrational and romantic function. Advertising commandeers some of the more ennobling facets and products of human nature and couples these with mundane products. It asks us to believe that, by some alchemy or other, the one is infused with the inspiring qualities of the other and thus made more worthy. It also panders to populist fantasies of a baser kind, so that sexual attractiveness becomes a function, not of personality, but of some manufactured item. It may all be transparent, and a foolish deceit, and yet hard-headed businessmen spend billions every year perpetuating the hoax.

Advertising is not one thing, but a number. Another major aspect of it is association on the subconscious level. An advert will commonly juxtapose a product with scenes of security, contentment and happiness rather than with romantic elements. If the technique is refined enough, and if the scenes are appropriate to our own experience, then a positive feeling is invoked from our memory, and by extension this becomes associated with the product. This sort of unconscious association is symbolised in astrology by Taurus, Cancer and Moon.

Neptune and collectivism.

Neptune is a collectivising energy. It is one that erodes differences and draws individuals together into ever larger groups, often in the name of some cause, or in common surrender to some religious or pseudo-religious ideal. Neptune thus symbolises things like the anonymous mass, particularly that resulting from urbanisation and industrialisation. It stands for the general degeneration of life-quality — the poverty, suffering, and exploitation — that most usually results from these processes. But Neptune also symbolises the collective response to this erosion of individual wellbeing. It stands for strength through unity, and for the power of mass movements.

In some ways that energy which is Neptune behaves like a gas. If pressure is applied to gas in a confined space then it will yield. It will decrease in volume, and go on doing so in proportion to the pressure applied. But only up to a point, whereupon it will liquefy, and then no amount of pressure will decrease the volume further (a distinguishing characteristic of the liquid state is this incompressibility). In the same way, Neptune and Pisces will absorb a lot of pressure. They symbolise a large, though not limitless capacity for suffering. They will never yield finally, but will 'liquefy' into a unity of fellow-feeling, and in this there is the strength to move mountains. Then we have phenomena like unionism, socialism, and communism whereby the amorphous mass gains definition, and the power to resist oppressive forces.

Another thing can happen if we compress a gas. If the pressure is strong, and the walls of the container weak then an explosion results. The equivalent in collective life is mob insurrection and anarchy, particularly associated with the lower strata of an urbanised society. Such revolts are short-lived, a sort of reduction of pressure. We do not get a fundamental change in the underlying architecture as we do with Uranus. But they tend to serve as a warning to governments to hasten social improvement. They also bring about a levelling of society, at least some movement toward more equitable distribution of wealth and privilege.

The Neptune Cycle

We can look now to the critical quarterly phases (see figure 3) associated with the Neptune cycle. What we find is that Neptunian phenomena of the type described do indeed seem to manifest strongly in collective life at these times. The planet was discovered in 1846 when it was at about 25 degrees of Aquarius, so it has not yet completed the first cycle. It will not do so until the year 2009, around which time we can expect a significant influx of Neptunian energy, and phenomena and events that will mirror the essence of the planet as we have described it here.

The 'natal' phase, 1846.
The discovery of Neptune in 1846 coincided with industrial depression

and severe economic and agricultural crisis. It was crop failure that provoked the proletarian uprising in Paris in 1848. This alarmed many Western governments, and the long-term impact was a quickening of social reform and moves towards universal suffrage. Indeed, across the world at this time there were many acts of popular insurgency. Britain was spared violent revolt, but the period around the middle of the century was one of intense political agitation, focused through Chartism, a vast, popular movement aimed at electoral reform. An event of great consequence at this time was the publishing of the Communist Manifesto (1848), a document that ends with the suitably Neptunian directive: 'working men of all countries unite.'

The discovery of Neptune also coincided with the onset of what historians term modernism. The mid-nineteenth century is often taken as a dividing line between an old order, and the industrialised world

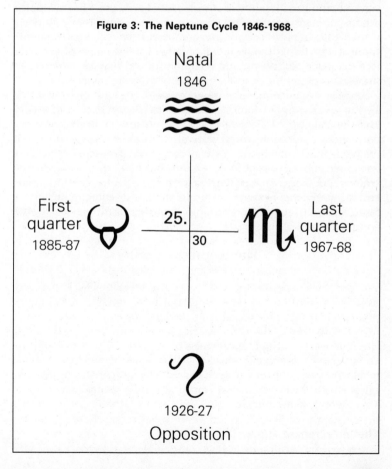

Figure 3: The Neptune Cycle 1846-1968.

we know today. One event which symbolised this divide was the radical modernisation of Paris by Baron Haussmann following the uprising of 1848. But more generally it was a period marked by more diffuse flux rather than specific events. It was more the spread of the conviction that the world was changing in a profound and irrevocable way. In one sense it was a very Piscean time, with one world dying and another being reborn. Pisces has twin fishes for its symbol, and at this time people looked forward, albeit uncertainly, to a rosier future, but also backwards, nostalgically, to a stable and valued past. The time-honoured rural world was being eroded by industrialisation; people were migrating in increasing number to the cities and industrial centres; mass production and commercialism were superseding traditional working methods. Indeed, the whole basis of the economy had changed, from land and agriculture to manufacture. Consequent to this shift in the wealth-base, was a shift in the power-base, from landed aristocracy to the middle classes growing rich on industrial production. It was these middle classes who were being enfranchised at this time. Once more we see Neptune as a leveller, and we see money instrumental in dissolving hierarchic structures.

Modernism introduced new sorts of fears into collective life. Neptune is a symbol for the sense of helplessness and confusion experienced by the individual in the face of the complexity of modern urban life. It represents the impotence of modern urban man, who is prey to forces over which there is no individual control — the tides of economic fortune that throw a person out of work, no matter how skilled and diligent. We detect something of a turnabout here. Primitive man was beset by fears of the hostility and contingency of Nature. These fears were alleviated, first by magic, then by science and technology. Life progressively became more certain and secure until the onset of modernism, at which point the progress seemed to turn back on itself. Neptune eroded the Mercurial order and once more the individual is beset by powerful, irrational forces. This sense of impotence has been countered largely by mass political movements so that something of an equilibrium has been attained.

The first quarter: 1885-87.
At this time, in Europe and America, there was significant activity in Left wing politics and unionism. In Britain, for example, there was the formation of groups such as The Fabian Society, and The Scottish Labour Party, that were the precursors of the modern Labour Party. The 1880s saw the mushrooming of Friendly Societies, once more a manifestation of the urge in the working classes to relieve oppression through common action.

The first trades unions were appearing in the early decades of the

19th century, although these did not embody the Neptunian principle, being largely based on the ancient guilds system, exclusive and composed of skilled craftsmen. In the 1880s, however, there occurred a new wave of unionism. It was one which absorbed the mass of working men, and one which was markedly different in tone from the first wave. As one commentator has noted: 'compared with the earlier unions the movement was militant and political in its objectives and more closely linked with political creeds.'[4] Working men and women were also organising in America at this time, and in 1886 The Federation of Labor was formed. We note an earlier development, in 1850 (natal phase), when the so-called Junta was formed in an attempt to effect co-operative action among fragmented, localised unions.

This first quarter phase marked significant developments in cinema, television, and advertising. In 1884 the patent was taken out for the first complete television system, the so-called Nipkow System (after its German inventor). In 1888 John Logie Baird was born who was later to play a significant part in the development of television. In 1888 the first modern cine camera was built by Marey, an achievement singled out by one historian as providing 'the greatest single impetus'[5] for the establishment of cinematography. In 1886 Pears bought Millais's picture *Bubbles* for use in their soap advertisements. This, it seems, was the first occasion when a commercial product was coupled with a romantic image.

In 1886 a linotype typesetting machine was used for the first time (on *The New York Tribune*). We note in 1846 (the natal phase) the construction of the first successful rotary press. Both inventions represent major developments in the growth of mass-circulation newspapers.

The opposition phase: 1926-27.

A landmark in the history of British unionism (and politics) was the General Strike of 1926, which brought the country to a standstill for ten days. There were also major strikes and uprisings in other parts of the world at this time. The year 1928 marked the fruition of the political agitation of the mid-nineteenth century, with all adults, men and women, given the right to vote.

This opposition period was a very significant one in the history of Communism. In 1927, threatened by Chiang Kai-shek, the Chinese communists retreated to the rural interior. The period 1927-34 was one of gestation when Mao was gaining experience in the mobilisation of the peasantry. It ended with the legendary 'Long March', and the communists established in power. In 1924 Lenin died, and Stalin assumed control a year later. This opposition phase marked the start of the communist state as such. The first Five Year Plan, aimed at rapid industrialisation and collectivised agriculture ran from 1928.

Television as a practical technology came at the opposition phase, largely through the work of Zworykin in America and Baird in Britain. In 1926 Baird gave what is regarded as the first demonstration of true television by electrically transmitting moving pictures in half-tones. A significant development in Cinema history at this time was the introduction of panchromatic film (in 1925). Another, in 1927, was the introduction of sound; the movies became the talkies.

In the United States this opposition period was one of marked urbanisation and industrialisation. Factories were increasing in size, the large chain store was coming into being, and through the 1920s industrial production doubled.

This period also marked the birth of the advertising industry. Advertising expenditure doubled over the period 1919-29; magazine advertising increased 600% through the early 20s. The phrase 'Madison Avenue' came into being in the mid-20s as a generic term for the industry. In 1926 *The Saturday Evening Post* began to carry an index of advertisers. In 1927 the last 'non-believer' in advertising, Henry Ford, succumbed and embarked on a massive campaign for his Model A. The early 20s saw a rise in the status of advertising to the extent that in 1926 President Coolidge addressed the Convention of the American Association of Advertising. One thing he said in his address was: the advertising industry has taken on 'the high responsibility of inspiring and ennobling the commercial world.'[7] So saying, and almost certainly without knowing it, he highlighted the Neptunian dimension of advertising. It was a period overall when advertising took on its modern cast; became less foot-in-the-door, more subtle. It was the time when the industry came to presume 'that the public preferred an image of life as it might be, life in the millennium to an image of literal reality.'[6]

This same period also saw a marked growth in the tabloid press, and presumably in the tabloid mind that prefers pictures to words, sensationalism rather than truth. Cultural barbarism is one of the more negative outcrops of Neptune, and yet still a faithful reflection of its principle.

The last quarter: 1967-68.

In the world of communism this last quarter phase corresponded to Mao's 'great proletarian cultural revolution.' This was the time of the Young Red Guards, and marked hostility towards Western values. Mao intended a revitalisation of communist ideals. He believed the party was becoming too elitist; failing to serve the people. In Britain at this time the political pendulum was strongly socialist. The franchise was again extended, to take in the 18-21 age group.

This last quarter phase, the late 60s, corresponded to an unusual time the world over, with political and civil unrest in many countries.

In America there were civil rights protests, race riots and political assassinations. There was civil rights protest in Ireland, and vigorous student protest the world over, notably in Paris, where once more anarchy reigned. It was also the era of flower power, when a whole generation were eager to imbibe non-material dimensions of reality. There was more than Neptune to the spirit of the late 60s. We have noted already that this period also corresponds with the first quarter of the Uranus cycle (based on the 1947 return), and indeed some facets of this era are best symbolised by this planet.

This period marked the onset of the era of satellite transmission in television. The concept of the global village and one world was made more real when images from one part of the world could be instantly beamed to any other part. (We note a similar phenomenon in America in the 20s opposition phase when radio and cinema helped engender, for the first time, a sense of one nation and one people).

The first return: 2009.

Neptune, it is widely said, spiritualises and refines, but what generally has happened this first cycle is that, rather than spiritualising, it itself has been materialised, and hence some rather bizarre manifestations. We should ask ourselves: is the world today a more spiritual and refined place than it was in the middle of the nineteenth century when Neptune was discovered? I think we are probably less spiritual/religious, but on balance more sensitive and refined, certainly in the sense of being more collectively caring and compassionate (just think of Dickensian Victorian society). The world has evolved on the feeling level, and partly this has been through television. The transmission of powerful images of conflict into our homes has helped dispel lingering romantic notions about war. With the advent of televison the concept of a collective stratum of feeling has become more real. We think of events like *Live Aid* where there was a quite palpable sense of being united in fellow-feeling with humanity the world over. We are more aware than at any other time in history of the pain and suffering of the world. It has become our burden and, to varying individual degrees, we suffer anguish, feel guilt, or are moved to charity or service. This heightened social/global conscience, which is unique to our modern era, is perhaps the most positive manifestation so far of the Neptune principle.

The world of 2009 will be a different place to that of 1846. Life has evolved so there will be greater possibilities of expression. Because of this it is not wise to be too specific in projections. But I think Neptune will continue to equalise. It is the great leveller, and wherever there is great disparity of wealth, privilege and wellbeing it will be invoked. One hopes in the new cycle that the emphasis will be on compassion rather than political ideology, and that it will be truly global so that quality of life north and south of the equator is less starkly contrasted.

References:

1. Lois Rodden, *Profiles of Women*, AFA.
2. Thomas Mann, *Confessions of Felix Krull Confidence Man*, Secker & Warburg.
3. *Printers' Ink Monthly*, 1932.
4. *New Cambridge Modern History*, vol 11, p.15, Cambridge Univ Press.
5. Anthony Michael, *History of Technology*, vol 5, Oxford.
6. Roland Marchand, *Advertising the American Dream*, p.8, Univ of California Press.
7. Cited in above.

Pluto
in action

Pluto, the most recent addition to the planetary pantheon, was discovered in 1930, when it was positioned at 20 degrees of Cancer. A body of thought regarding its astrological nature has since accumulated, and we might first consider the planet's meaning.

The meaning of Pluto

In *The Literary Zodiac* I offer some ideas on Pluto, in the chapter on Scorpio, a sign that seems to have an affiliation with the planet. Pluto relates to the idea of a common 'feeling' stratum of life. It relates to those laws of nature through which we are born, have our being, and die. Associated with this is the awareness that we are a part of Nature at some basic level, that we are all rooted in some common sub-stratum. The plants in a given habitat are in some ways individual, and yet they are all composed of the same substance, drawn from the soil and the air, and the same fundamental law governs their growth cycle.

Pluto symbolises the experience of subscendence, a descent into this common level of being, and the subsequent sense of renewal and regeneration. There is a tension in Scorpio, which can be conveniently regarded in terms of a Mars-Pluto dipole: a contrast between detached and insular egocentricity, and surrender to the downward pull of the 'underworld'. Dane Rudhyar has described Pluto as 'the power which compels all separate individualisations ... to return to their collective roots or foundation of being.'[1] A book that condenses this side of Pluto very well is *The Fall*, by Albert Camus. The central figure of this book, Clamence, is sucked down into the underworld. What triggers his descent, his 'fall', is the recognition in himself of unsuspected dark and evil forces. He finds himself plotting a violent revenge, out of all proportion to the wrong that prompted it. This idea of hidden or repressed malignancy within the individual represents a common theme in Scorpio writing, with Stevenson's *Dr Jekyll and Mr Hyde* a good example.

Pluto, I believe, has a connection with power. Not individual power, but that which is rooted in the energies of a people and in the land itself. It seems also to have some connection with a nation's destiny. Pluto is a transformer. It functions as an agent of historical evolution. As we saw earlier, Uranus also relates to evolution, but at the Airy level of ideas. It is Pluto that does the dirty work. It is one thing to envision a better future, another to effect that change at root level, to prise people from entrenched thought patterns and ways of life, and drag them kicking and screaming into the future. It represents the dynamo behind historical evolution, a sort of collective libido pushing humanity upward and forward toward the Uranian vision.

One of the clearest and most in-depth expositions of Pluto's meaning is given by Liz Greene in chapters 2 and 3 of *The Astrology of Fate*. Pluto is pictured as something powerful and primal that can intrude into our lives. This intrusion might take the form of an upcurrent of dark emotion, or possibly the imposition of an inescapable fate on the individual. Pluto makes us aware of a more primal mode of existence, for it symbolises 'the rupturing of the psychic hymen, which protects us through our innocence.'[2]

In this book Pluto is once more equated to a psychic underworld. It symbolises that part of us that is a repository of emotional ugliness, resentments and ill-wills. To be drawn down into Pluto's abyss often means an 'agony of helplessness and futility', and a loss of our 'sense of willed potency and value.'[3] Ancient myths pertaining to the Underworld — of Sisyphus and Tantalus, for example — likewise hint at the Plutonic experience: eternal, repetitive cycles of hope or desire, finally frustrated by something beyond our control. Greene's thoughts as to how Pluto should be handled lead us once more to *The Fall*. Clamence, following his descent to the underworld becomes a 'judge penitent'. He acquires the ability to 'be with' someone, in a therapeutic sense. He becomes both a siphon and a receptacle for the poison of others. He does not condemn or judge the darkness that issues forth, and in this way he effects the Scorpionic task of purifying the world of its evil.

A king in the underworld.

The profiles section contains a number of examples of Pluto in action at the individual level. But we might here re-examine the case of Charles II, to illustrate some of the points raised so far. Charles's chart (see page 53) shows the Moon conjunct Pluto in Taurus, both squared by Mars; a 'Scorpionic' element in an otherwise light, Mercurial chart. The English Civil War represented to Charles a Plutonian 'rape', an unwelcome intrusion of powerful forces into his pleasant, innocent, regal world. They formed a reminder of his own mortality and his own smallness. He was made aware of a more fundamental level of being at which individuals and titles counted for nothing. In 1646 transiting

Saturn conjuncted his Moon/Pluto, heralding the start of a chronic Plutonic phase in his life. With the Royalist cause lost, Charles was sent to the Continent for his own safety, where he remained in exile, the victim of circumstances beyond his control, powerless to help himself or his father. On a straightforward level of interpretation we can see the close Mars-Pluto square as the signature of an intense frustration of will.

Charles made one attempt to win back his throne, but was defeated in battle, at Worcester. The transit of Uranus to oppose his natal Sun at this time is again a very accurate signature of his conflict with the demotic forces of the Parliamentarians. The aftermath of the Battle represented a further stripping away of externals. He was a fugitive in enemy territory. There was a price on his head, and had he been caught, he would likely have been executed. Life was about survival from day to day. Whether he lived or died depended largely on his own physical and mental resources. These served him well, and he escaped to live out the remainder of his exile in the shadow of failure. With transiting Pluto now moving to conjunct his Sun and Midheaven we can surmise that the experience of 'helplessness and futility' was intensified. Charles was restored to the British throne, and at the time of his coronation in the summer of 1661 Saturn had moved on half a cycle to oppose the natal Moon/Pluto conjunction. However, the frustrations and humiliations of his sojourn in the 'underworld' left their mark. The lightness of his youth was no more. He gained maturity, inner strength and courage, but at the same time a certain cynicism and melancholy.

Pluto robs of innocence by plunging into a raw level of existence. We observe the effect of the planet in those returning from wars, who have seen sights and experienced things that most of us will never have to. The forces that Pluto symbolises are normally contained. It is when social restraining forces, symbolised in astrology by Saturn and Venus, break down that the darkest side of human nature can find vent. Many nations in Europe at some point in their history have experienced the suspension of civilised values and the barbaric rape of marauding armies. One such period was the so-called Thirty Years' War (1618-28), which, significantly, was bounded either side by a Saturn/Pluto conjunction. It was a period when large areas of Europe (particularly Germany) were devastated by fire and sword. It was a holocaust as horrendous in its way as the one of our own century. If we consider the two World Wars as part of the same essential conflict (and there are grounds for doing so) then this dark period is likewise bound by a cycle of Pluto and Saturn, one conjunction falling in October 1914, another in August 1947. This second conjunction corresponded to a fresh release of human darkness, in Northern India following Independence, when years of repressed hatred and resentment came bubbling to the surface in a murderous frenzy.

The Pluto cycle.
As with the other outer planets, a Pluto cycle seems to be operative at the collective level, although so far we have experienced only a natal and a first quarter phase. The discovery of Pluto corresponded, as other writers have noted, with the rise of Naziism, with the blossoming of organised crime, and with depth psychology. The first quarter phase, which fell 1979-80, finds correspondences with the start of the AIDS pandemic, and in the strife that still torments the Middle East. For the remainder of this chapter, however, we will examine the workings of Pluto in a different historical context.

The curse of the Royal Stuarts.

Many who work with astrology are intrigued by the notion of a genetic dimension to their subject. Many have noticed that the charts of succeeding generations of a family often bear similar astrological signatures, suggesting that not only physical but also temperamental and psychological characteristics (and problems) are passed on down the line. It is not uncommon for astrologers to compile a sort of family album of charts, and when grouped together in this way it is easy to identify the recurrence of sometimes very specific astrological motifs. For example, in my own family, my mother has a Moon/Neptune conjunction; so did her mother and her mother's father. The conjunction does not appear in my generation (although the square does) but reappears in the next, in the chart of her grand-daughter. A Moon/Neptune conjunction is not a particularly common aspect. Allowing a ten-degree orb, it occurs in about one chart in eighteen, so to have four fall together in this way seems an unlikely chance happening.

The idea that astrology might function across generations is nothing new. Kepler for one subscribed to it. More recently, the Gauquelins examined the charts of tens of thousands of parents and children, and concluded that a person was more likely to have a planet in a key sector (that is, close to the ascendant or MC) if one or both parents also had the same planet similarly placed. Moreover, this likelihood can be expressed with a high degree of statistical significance.[4] In *The Astrology of Fate*[2], Liz Greene presents a case study involving the charts of the different generations of a family. She suggests that recurring astrological themes can describe a sort of family fate, a 'curse' passed on down the line in the form of unresolved (and often repressed) emotional difficulties, or life problems, which come to fall upon certain fated family members. These lives are then dominated, sometimes painfully, by 'the sins of the father'. This idea of something lying repressed until it finds issue in a concentrated and potent form when conditions are right is very Plutonian.

This genetic dimension of astrology is one which places the individual in a broader context of existence, and would seem to offer understanding where sometimes there seems to be none. It remains a relatively unexplored area of astrology and perhaps its precise value and application remains to be shown. The best way of determining this is through the accumulation of detailed case-studies, and I offer one here. It concerns royalty, because with kings and queens there is generally reliable birth data and ample biographical documentation. They are also often the agents through which the forces of history and the fates of nations operate in an overt way. It is a bonus that contained in the Royal Stuart Dynasty of Scotland are some colourful characters that still today grip the imagination.

The Stuart Dynasty

The Stuart Dynasty began in 1371, when Robert the High Steward (from which the name derives) was crowned king, becoming Robert II. The chart for this is shown, and might be regarded as a national chart for Scotland, from this time until the union of the Crowns. (We also note the two spellings, the French *Stu-* coming into effect with Mary.) The lineage is shown in figure 4., although the first two Stuart kings, for who no birth data and little biographical detail exist , are not included.

Despite the legends and the colour, the Stuarts are considered by historians to be an ill-fated line. Many of them came to bad ends, or suffered exile, or imprisonment. Figure 4 sums it up. James I was imprisoned in England for 18 years, and murdered by his nobles on his return to Scotland. James II was killed when one of his own cannons exploded. James III was murdered. James IV was killed in battle. James V died at the age of 30 of what has been described as an incurable melancholy. Mary Queen of Scots was a prisoner for 19 years and finally executed. James VI/I suffered no real problems; he enjoyed a contented enough life and reign. But then the 'curse' continues. Charles I was overthrown by his people and executed. His son, Charles II, suffered 14 years exile. His other son, James VII/II was likewise overthrown and exiled. James Edward, The Old Pretender, spent his whole life in exile. His son, Charles, Bonnie Prince Charlie, suffered military defeat, and likewise never reigned. It is a formidable catalogue of woe. I think the so-called Stuart curse can be related to a recurring astrological motif, and I propose to examine this in more detail. But first we might look at the charts of some of the individuals concerned.

The charts of four of the later Stuarts are presented in the main profiles section, and so are not dealt with here. Times are not available for all the characters, and where not, I have taken noon. In the case of James I, there is some doubt concerning the date. Such written evidence as exists dates it July 1394. In terms of this survey I am interested in the recurrence of the Mars/Pluto Stuart signature, and there was indeed a conjunction of the two planets in July of 1394. There is only sketchy character detail about James I, as indeed there is about the next two in the line. So we will move on to:

James IV: In terms of personal and regal qualities he is generally held in high esteem by historians. His chart shows a strong 'Mars' nature, with Sun in Aries and Moon in Scorpio, so it is perhaps not surprising to learn that he was one of the last great warrior kings, and certainly the last British king to die fighting at the head of an army. The Spanish ambassador of the time noted of James:

> He is courageous, even more than he should be ... I have seen him often undertake the most dangerous things. On such occasions he does not take the least care of himself. He is not a good captain because he begins to fight before he has given his orders.

Such impetuosity and primitive heroism is not uncommon when Aries is strong in a chart. He was a self-willed, forceful individual who had little difficulty imposing his kingly authority. He was possessed of the Stuart virility, begetting

Figure 4

Monarch	Dates reigned
James I	1406 — 1437
James II	1437 — 1460
James III	1460 — 1488
James IV	1488 — 1513
James V	1513 — 1542
Mary	1542 — 1567
James VI/I	1567 — 1625
Charles I	1625 — 1649
Charles II	1660 — 1685
James VII/II	1685 — 1688
James (the Old Pretender)	never reigned
Bonnie Prince Charlie	never reigned

Mars/Pluto in the birth-charts of the Royal Stuarts

Birth data (all n.s.)	Pluto/Mars contact	Fate
23.7.1394 (?)	Pluto/Mars conjunct	18 years imprisonment. Murdered by his own Nobles
25.10.1430	Close planetary complex of Saturn, Pluto, Mars, Sun, Jupiter.	Died when one of his own cannons exploded
19.7.1451	Pluto/Mars conjunct (and conjunct Sun)	Murdered after *coup d'etat*
26.3.1473	T-square of Mars, Pluto, Saturn	Killed in battle
evening 20.4.1512	Pluto/Mars conjunct	Died young of an 'incurable melancholy'
18.12.1542	Pluto/Mars conjunct, square Saturn	Imprisoned for 20 years, then executed
09.30 LT 29.6.1566 Edinburgh	None	Free of Stuart Fate. Not dominated by events.
23.00 LT 29.11.1600 Dunfermline	None	Overthrown and executed
12.00 LT 8.6.1630 London	Pluto square Mars (and conjunct Moon)	Military defeat; 14 years exile.
24.00 LT 24.10.1633 London	Pluto square Mars	Military defeat, overthrown and exiled
09.30 LT 20.6.1688 London	Pluto conjunct Mars	Lived whole life in exile
17.00 LT 31.12.1720 Rome	None	Military defeat; exile.

many illegitimate children.

However, he was not all Martial force, but a multifaceted man, in the Renaissance spirit of the time. He had a passion for architecture, and attempted, not wholly successfully, to vitalise learning in Scotland. He spoke several languages, and Erasmus said of him: 'He had a wonderful force of intellect, an incredible knowledge of all things' (which can not be total flattery).

James came to power by overthrowing his father. Against express instruction his father, James III, was murdered and the son felt eternally guilty about this. He refused absolution, and as a penance wore an iron chain around his waist to which he added extra links as the years progressed. Such a burden of guilt is suggested in the chart by a 'Piscean' overtone, Moon conjunct Neptune, and Mars in Pisces trine Neptune and square Jupiter.

If rash impetuosity was immediately responsible for his death, then it was bad-luck that seemed to embroil the country in a needless war in the first place. His reign did much to raise the status of Scotland in the eyes of the world, and his death was widely mourned.

James V: He was born in the evening of 20 April 1512, which puts the Sun just into Taurus, and which makes either Libra or Scorpio the ascendant (and the latter seems more likely). He did embody some of the more negative traits of Scorpio and Taurus in combination: he was lusty and acquisitive, covetous of men's wives and money; and under a superficial Venusian charm there was a violent, ill-tempered, vindictive nature. He was a great one for law and order, and often ruthless in his rooting out of malefactors. But if severe, he was also just. He founded the College of Justice in Scotland, which still exists. He did much to improve the finances of the Crown, increasing revenue by 50% over the course of his short reign. One commentator has noted: 'James longed to be a true prince of the Renaissance. For this he needed money, and money became his obsession. His policy at home and abroad, and his relationship with the Church were all linked to his insatiable thirst for funds.'[6] This side of his character seems an obvious reflection of the Sun in Taurus. The most lucrative source of revenue was his marriage, a fact suggested by the natal conjunction of Venus (a symbol of both wealth and female partners) and Jupiter (a symbol of abundance and good fortune). This same conjunction also mirrors his extravagant nature. He liked to live in style, and spent great sums building and improving royal palaces.

What was unusual for the time was that James V most often took the side of the people against the nobles, to which we should look to his Moon, placed in democratic Aquarius. He was known as the poor-man's king, and he sometimes wandered among his people *incognito*, in the guise of a simple farmer. However worthy this might seem, it was not wise policy given his circumstances. Essentially he antagonised those whose support he needed. The grudge he bore against his nobility was no doubt nurtured in his childhood and youth, when he was held prisoner by powerful families. The Pluto/Mars conjunction suggests the frustration of his will, and the development of a bitter resentment against those who sought to dominate him, which was later generalised into a broad hatred of the Scottish nobility (who, on the whole, were quite deserving of the spite).

When we read the letters he sent his wife we are left with a favourable impression. Despite the tone of weary despair, we are struck by his intelligence and his literacy. His concern for his people seems genuine, as was his anxiety to bring peace and stability to his country (as we might expect with his Sun in Venus-ruled Taurus). He comes over as a sensitive man — perhaps too sensitive for his times. Part of the experience of Taurus is having to come to terms with a 'fallen' world, one that is imperfect and which harbours evil; and having to struggle against the odds to extract something worthy from such a world. Taurus is often blessed with fortitude accordingly, though not enough in James's case, for he died worn out from his struggles against the powerful nobles. Events seemed to conspire to crush him further: he suffered defeat in battle; his two young sons died within days of each other. Transiting Pluto conjuncted his natal Moon, and it is said he lay on his bed, turned his face to the wall, and died, simply through lack of will to go on living. So it was that a girl-child, three days old, ascended the throne of Scotland.

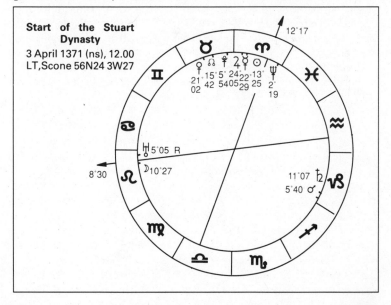

Start of the Stuart Dynasty
3 April 1371 (ns), 12.00 LT, Scone 56N24 3W27

Mary Queen of Scots: There is no recorded time for Mary's birth, and some disagreement regarding the day. She was born either the 7th or 8th of December 1542 (os), and most evidence points to the latter. The chart shown is drawn up for noon 18.12.1542 (ns). One of the most reliable astrological timers (though by no means infallible) is the

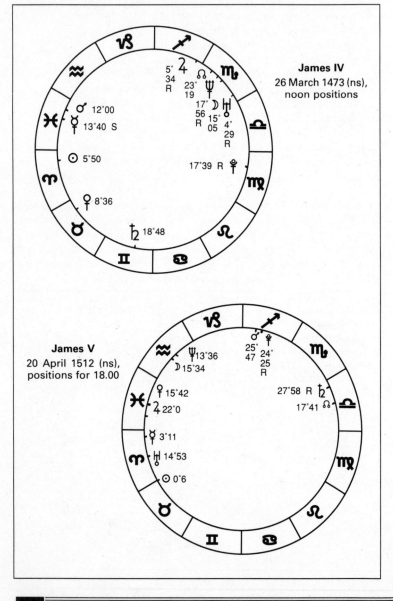

James IV
26 March 1473 (ns),
noon positions

James V
20 April 1512 (ns),
positions for 18.00

progressed new Moon. This often corresponds with the start of a significant new phase in an individual's life, and a number of examples are given in the profiles section. As often as not the change comes about in the run up to, rather than at the conjunction. The year 1568 was a watershed in Mary's life. Her life was very much one of two

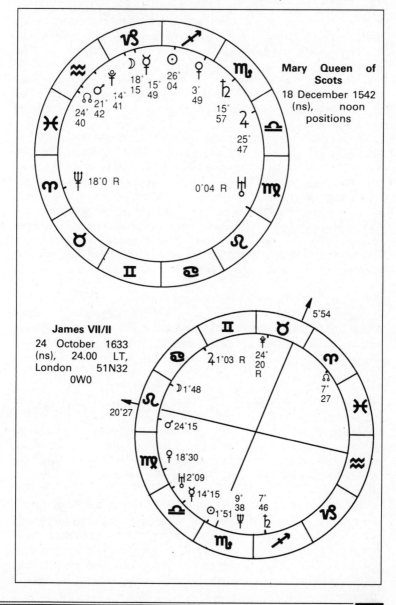

Mary Queen of Scots
18 December 1542 (ns), noon positions

James VII/II
24 October 1633 (ns), 24.00 LT, London 51N32 0W0

halves: into her first 26 years she packed an extraordinary amount of drama; the remainder were spent a prisoner. This is just the sort of major divide that often concurs with a progressed new Moon. The astrological evidence then, such as it is, suggests that Mary was born on December 8 (os), and later rather than earlier in the day, for this brings the required progressed new Moon within acceptable orb.

However, even without a time, and with the latitude of uncertainty, Mary's chart is worthy of study. There is a good deal written about her, and some of the biography probes deeply into her character and the meaning of her life (that by Stefan Zweig[5] is very good in this respect). We can concentrate on three things we do know for certain about the chart: the Moon is in Capricorn, the Sun in Sagittarius, and there is the Stuart 'signature', a Mars/Pluto conjunction, in this case, also squared by Saturn.

We see the Mars/Pluto combination revealed in a number of ways. She was a person whose own will was over-ridden by a larger fate, by the forces of historical destiny. In another way, death featured prominently in her life. The eddy of her fate seemed to suck in many who came to bad ends. She lost two husbands, her friend and servant Rizzio was murdered before her eyes, and there were many who were executed or tortured for association with her cause (or simply her person). On a more immediate level it suggests the courage, resolution and self-reliance that was very much part of her character (particularly in times of crisis), and an 'untamable and unbridled will to power'[5].

The Capricorn Moon in her case concurred with great ambition, and is suggestive of her early life, which was a long grooming for the public role she would have to play as Queen of France and Scotland. Usually when Capricorn is strong in a chart there is a foundation of practicality, shrewdness, and patience. But not in Mary's case. The Earth was overwhelmed by the Fire of the chart (which argues for a Fiery ascendant). There is a great contrast between Mary and her cousin Elizabeth I, who as we saw earlier was a strong Earth type. Elizabeth had a great impact on the world of political affairs. She contributed in a very real way to the subsequent prosperity and power of Britain as a nation. Mary made no impact on this level. Where she did make an impact, however, was in the realm of romance and legend. What she gave the world was her story. Thus the difference between Earth and Fire.

The nature of Sagittarius is very evident in descriptions of her character, for better and worse. She radiated the warmth of feeling of the Fiery personality. She was vivacious, and fun-loving to the point of frivolity. To her, life was a great game, an entertainment to be enjoyed. She had a love of risk, sport, and adventure. She was bold, proud, convinced of her superiority. She was easily taken with impractical and imprudent enthusiasms. Her passions were extreme. She loved and hated strongly, and was rarely lukewarm. She was very susceptible to changes in fortune, buoyed up or plunged into despair by the slightest turn. She was very forthright and turned people against herself with needless criticism. She was prone to self-deception, seeing people and events in the light of her romantic imaginings. She suffered accordingly from disillusionment, and the mortification that often accompanies this (particularly in Jupiterians). Her marriage to Darnley being a good case in point, an act described by one historian as 'the most foolish action of her life.'[5] The transits at the time of this romance are telling. Saturn opposes natal Pluto, while natal Venus is squared by Jupiter and opposed by Neptune. Plainly her judgement was clouded by romantic projections. This marriage also, in one sense marked the start of the end. She set wheels in motion, which is perhaps suggested by the Saturn opposition to the 'fateful' Pluto.

Mary, like Charles I, was an anachronism, which is why she ultimately failed in her ambitions. She went against rather than with the time (and the tides of change seemed to be quickening at this point in Western history). With her romantic notions of chivalry, her Catholic faith, her absolutist convictions, she was a medievalist. As a queen, she believed, she was answerable to no-one but God. As with Charles (likewise a Sagittarian) it was her beliefs which damned her. What also damned her, and what again is a mirror of her essential Sagittarian self, was a profound moral lapse. The challenge related to this sign is to associate with the human rather than the animal half of the centaur. Sagittarius must aspire to what is virtuous about the human condition, and shun what is base and ignoble. When confronted with this challenge, Mary failed. She surrendered to a violent passion for Bothwell, and was accomplice to the murder of her legal husband (of this there seems little doubt). It was this act that caused her people to rebel.

It seems in her long years in prison she suffered the torment of her conscience. The betrayal of her higher nature was her Centaur's 'wound', the knowledge of how base humans can be, how far short of perfection. The same sort of spiritual gloom that was Mary's we note in fictive Sagittarian characters. Lord Jim's wound, for example, was the bitter knowledge that he had acted the coward when heroism was called for. Kurtz's wound in *Heart of Darkness* was the sense of horror that came from abandoning his virtuous nature to the unrestrained gratification of lusts. (Both these characters are the creation of Conrad, a Sagittarian Sun).

When she chose her lower rather than higher self, fortune seemed to abandon her. The pampered, stage-centre existence was replaced by grey prison walls. She was executed 18.2.1587 ns, with progressed Moon square Mars (based on the noon December 8 chart).

The charts of James VI/I, Charles I, and Charles II are detailed in the profiles section. The next in line is:

James VII/II: James was born in London on 14 October 1633 (o.s.) at 24.00[7]. He was the brother of Charles II and ascended the throne on the latter's death. The two were similar in the abundance of their sexual energy, but in most respects they were different, the one lacking what was to the fore in the other. James had none of the wit, charm or intelligence of Charles, but a good deal of the energy and resolution his brother lacked. These qualities are suggestive of the Scorpionic Sun, as indeed is his military prowess. He was a good soldier, dominating military matters in his brother's reign (we note also Mars conjunct the ascendant).

This is a chart strong in Fire and Water, weak in Air and Earth (again, just the opposite of his brother's). Some of his better personal qualities seem to relate to the Leo Fire (Moon and ascendant in this sign). He had 'high standards of personal honour and integrity, from which he deviated only rarely.'[7] And he was a generous and a loyal man. His lack of Air came across as inability to reason or judge. He was slow-witted, and had an instinctive distrust of cleverer individuals. Being weak in the intellectual sphere he was most reluctant to let go of an idea once he had come to an understanding of it. Accordingly, he was judged a very stubborn man (as those with very Fixed charts are wont to be).

On top of this, he was a very self-willed man, utterly convinced of the rightness of his views. In a typical Martial way, he saw the world very simply, in terms of black and white with no room for shades of difference (and certainty only comes with such an extreme perspective). He had that type of vanity, an amalgam of Leo and Scorpio, that could not countenance views that differed from his own. His offensive certitude was compounded with a messianic quality, reflected in the chart, perhaps, by the exact trine of Jupiter to the Scorpio Sun. It was not just his will he was imposing on the nation, but God's will. However, he was not the first to misread the Almighty's will. As it was, it was the people's will that prevailed. He was forced to flee, and he never regained the Throne. He ultimately failed because his stubbornly held views on Catholicism and Divine Right did not accord with the time.

James Edward Francis (the Old Pretender) was titular king of Great Britain for some 63 years. However, he never reigned and spent virtually the whole of his life exiled in Europe. He was born according to the contemporary reports, 'between nine and ten in the morning'[8], 10 June 1688 (os), in London. Accounts of some of the 67 people who witnessed the birth make plain that it was nearer ten than nine, and the chart shown is drawn up for 9.30 LT.

James comes across as a pleasant and good-natured dullard. He had no great defects and no great merits, and undoubtedly would have made a good constitutional monarch. He was, among other things, pensive, conscientious, level-headed, tolerant, and possessed of a 'sweet reasonableness'. These reflect mostly the strong Mercury nature of the chart. Being strongly Mercurial he saw the merit of diversity. He had no desire to proselytize his subjects, but such was the prevailing fear of Papism that his own catholicism precluded the possibility of his becoming king. It seems that as a younger man he exhibited some Gemini sparkle and gaiety, but he was increasingly ground down by his frustrating circumstances, so that even by the age of thirty his demeanor was unsmiling and harassed. Again, we have the Stuart signature, a close Mars/Pluto conjunction symbolising frustration of will.

What James lacked was energy, enthusiasm, magnetism, resolution and self-confidence — necessary qualities for a man who has to inspire supporters and wrest a throne. It is not too difficult to see why he lacked in this area. There is no Fire in the chart, no Aries and no Scorpio. We see Mars is placed in Cancer, traditionally regarded as an unfavourable position. Moreover, it is, for the most part, poorly aspected. It receives a close trine from the Pisces Moon, and while this likely added to the pleasantness of his character, it must, given his destiny, be counted a debilitating influence. It likely defocalised the Mars energy — whatever else, a Pisces Moon is not resolute. It also

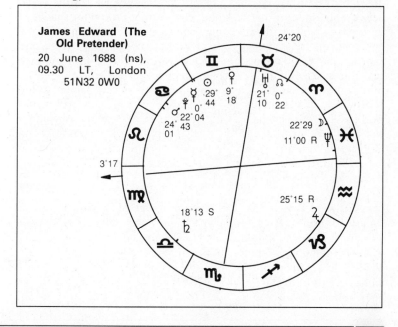

James Edward (The Old Pretender)
20 June 1688 (ns), 09.30 LT, London
51N32 0W0

seemed to preclude the decisiveness and ruthlessness necessary to lead armies. There is a strong 'Piscean' side to the whole chart, with the Moon in this sign, and Neptune conjunct an angle, and when there is such an overtone in a chart there is often an urge to remain behind the scenes (and this urge would be emphasised by the Virgo ascendant). At heart, he was probably content with obscurity.

The Stuart signature.

Across the twelve charts there is a remarkable recurrence of a specific planetary combination. In nine of the twelve there is a major aspect between Mars and Pluto — five conjunctions, two squares, an opposition, and an (exact) sextile. We note also that the chart for the start of the Stuart Dynasty contains an exact trine of the two planets. This represents a highly unlikely concentration of a specific aspect. If we consider the conjunction of Mars/Pluto, then it occurs in approximately one chart in 18 (allowing for a ten degree orb). But here we have five in twelve, more than seven times the expectation. What makes it the more interesting is that it is a meaningful coincidence. Mars and Pluto in combination do describe the actuality of the situation, as we will see shortly.

There are three charts where there is no aspect between Mars and Pluto. In two of the cases this seems to be as it should be; it mirrors the reality. There is a natural break in the history of the Stuarts, which came about when James VI/I left Scotland to succeed to the English throne, thereby uniting the Crowns of the two countries. James showed little inclination to return to Scotland. He found the relative security and prosperity of the English Court far more to his taste. It was a very real break with the past. He left behind not only his own, but his ancestral past. The Stuart curse stayed in Scotland. James's chart shows no Mars/Pluto combination, and he suffered no ill-luck. On the contrary, he lived out a peaceful and enjoyable reign.

The next of the line, Charles I, likewise has no Mars/Pluto signature, and when it comes to it, he was not really cursed or fated. In a sense he was the victim of events, but equally he brought about his own undoing. Had he acted sensibly he could very likely have saved his crown and his head. Kingship was still revered. As subsequent developments showed, it ran against the grain of the nation's consciousness to execute a king. It took a lot of pig-headedness on Charles's part to bring it about. He made his own fate. He chose his death at some level, and the accented Neptune on his chart's ascendant is pertinent here (he is sometimes known as Charles the Martyr). His death gave him the grandeur and heroism that his strong Sagittarian nature craved, but which he could not attain through his own actions. The Stuart signature reappears in the charts of both

Charles's sons, and in that of his grandson.

So, we have a clear pattern. The early Stuarts, from James I up to and including Mary were reaping 'karma' (for want of a better word). They seemed more the victims of bad luck, of something not of their own making. This bad luck was lain to rest through James VI's uprooting. His son, however, somehow re-activated the curse, and it appeared, albeit in a modified form in the charts of the next two generations. Bonnie Prince Charlie, the last of the line, was likewise ill-fated, but the Mars/Pluto combination does not appear in his chart (although it does show Pluto strong on the IC, and Mars closely conjunct Saturn). However, we should keep in mind that we are not dealing with mechanical systems here, and can not expect exactitude.

The Stuart fate.

In what way, then, does a Mars/Pluto combination describe the character and destiny of this royal family? In a straightforward sense, it corresponded to a strong sex drive in most of them, and in many to the experience of a great frustration of will. In a broader sense, it seems an apt symbol of the power struggles that beset the early Stuarts particularly. It was the struggle of an individual to maintain and assert authority against those who instinctively sought to undermine or arrogate it. Shakespeare based *Macbeth* on the Scottish history of the time we are talking about, and the play gives us a good taste of the prevailing atmosphere. Stability in Scotland depended on a precarious balance between the King and the powerful families of the nobility (who were anything but noble). The king was the focus of the nation's power, and this is a very Martial function. We think of the original glyph of Mars, an inverted Venus, the orb that still today is part of regal ceremony. Yet, in a sense, he could not rule without the consent of his nobility. They provided him with his armies, and with money from the lands he leased them. The king needed his nobility, but they also needed him. Only the king could confer titles and lands, and in many regards he represented the only method of enrichment and advancement.

It is true that such a power balance prevailed throughout northern Europe, but in Scotland it was more difficult for the monarch to control and retain power, partly because of the hostile terrain of much of the country, which precluded easy administration, and partly because of the clan system, which provided natural centres of cohesive resistance and power outside the Court. It required a strong individual on the throne, and this is where the Stuarts were unlucky. More often than not they ascended as minors, which was generally the signal for the jostling for power, and for rivalries to degenerate into naked aggression. Most often it was family against family, but the person of the king was not sacrosanct. Also, when there was internal strife in the kingdom, it was often the signal for a powerful and rapacious southern neighbour to march north. The Stuarts had to wrestle with power in this way, and just as it seemed an individual was getting the balance right, then bad luck, or fate would seem to intervene to upset the situation. This is the nature of the Stuart curse that so many historians have commented on.

But the Mars/Pluto combination symbolises, I believe, a more profound pattern to the Stuart destiny. We spoke earlier of Pluto as a transformer, as the driving force behind the processes of historical evolution. In social life as much as natural life, forms come and go, are born, grow, decay and die. Once an organism, biological or social, dies then the power it embodies can fire a new cycle. This association of Pluto with regeneration is familiar enough to astrologers. Pluto, then, associates with the changing patterns of history, not the nature of the patterns themselves, but that which determines that they do.

One of the more convincing models of social history is that proposed by P.A. Sorokin in his four-volumed *Social and Cultural Dynamics*.[9] He views the last thousand years or so of European history in terms of a dynamic interplay of two principles, which he calls *ideational* and *sensate*. In effect what he presents is a Taoistic model. His twin principles correspond very closely to what Eastern philosophy calls Yin and Yang, and he likewise recognises that it is the balance and tendency in change of the two poles that determine the quality of a particular 'moment' in history. This quality finds visible expression in the thought, art, religion and systems of government of a particular culture. In astrology we also have names for Sorokin's principles: Jupiter (ideational) and Mercury (sensate).

The essential characteristic of ideational times is that the ultimate reality is held to lie beyond the world of visible appearances. In sensate times the opposite holds, with this world considered more important than the next. Ideational cultures are essentially religious and collectivist. There is subservience to some higher, all-embracing thought or ideal. Faith is the truth system. In sensate times, empiricism becomes the dominant truth system. The emphasis is essentially pragmatic and secular, and high priority is placed on individual expression. Catholicism was the outcrop of an ideational spirit. A sensate culture has no real religion, just empty or degenerate forms. Protestantism, originally, was a sort of compromise. A pragmatic and natural approach to religion, an acceptance that God could be worshipped in the world and through His creations. The apogee of the ideational spirit was about the middle of the thirteenth century, at the height of the Middle Ages. Western culture was at its most sensate (according to Sorokin) at the end of the nineteenth century. The movement from the one to the other entailed a continuous metamorphosis, with periods like The Renaissance, The Reformation,

The Thirty Years' War, The Enlightenment, and The Scientific and Industrial Revolutions signifying critical points in the ongoing process of change.

The opposition of sensate and ideational does not exist wholly in time. It is only Western Europe that has undergone historic repolarisation. Today, the division is geographical. The East (including Russia) still by and large embraces the ideational mentality. Although at one level Catholicism and Communism might seem very different, they both reflect the ideational principle. To understand the anti-papist hysteria of late seventeenth century Britain, we have only to look to the anti-communist sentiment that permeates contemporary America. The forces that ousted James VII/II are the same forces that keep a communist from the Presidency. The characters are different, but the plot is the same: superpowers seeking ideological hegemony. In the seventeenth century it was Spain and Catholicism, today it is Communism and Capitalism. Why in Northern Ireland not even the characters have changed it is difficult to say. Perhaps geography plays a part; the Celtic consciousness lingered in this remote Isle centuries after it had been supplanted elsewhere. However, if we accept Northern Ireland as a region whose affairs are almost wholly dominated by an anachronistic struggle between sensate (Mercury/Protestant) and ideational (Jupiter/Catholic) principles, then the natal chart[8], which shows Sun closely conjunct Mercury in Sagittarius opposing a Gemini ascendant, and a wide conjunction of Moon and Pluto in Cancer, begins to make a lot of sense.

An important difference between the ideational medieval world, and the sensate modern lies in the concept of power. In the Middle Ages, the ultimate source of power was held to be God. Monarchs were His representatives on earth, answerable to no-one but Him. The modern concept of power is quite different. It is rooted in a sensate world-view. The source is not heaven, but the fruitfulness of the earth, and the energy, strength, and resourcefulness of the individuals that make up a nation. This power is vested in leaders elected from those who constitute a nation. In short, the medieval view is absolutist, the modern democratic.

The Stuart Dynasty started in 1371 and petered out with the death of Charles Edward Stuart in 1788. It spanned the turbulent change from the medieval to the modern world. As the leaders of nations it is natural enough that the Stuarts were involved in the processes of profound change. I do not subscribe to the view that individuals make history, or ultimately alter its course. What we judge as greatness is often only a measure of the extent to which profounder forces, of the sort we have been describing, find expression through individuality. Only in the sense that some are better suited than others to do this is character destiny. Significantly, it was those Stuarts with a strong

Jupiter nature who were ill-suited to further the waxing sensate, Mercurial tide. Charles I, Mary, James II all tried to pit their personal will and authority against the impersonal, immensely powerful 'will' of history. The outcome was inevitable.

References:
1. Dane Rudhyar, *An Astrological Triptych,* p.282, ASI.
2. Liz Greene, *The Astrology of Fate,* Unwin Paperbacks.
3. Sylvia Brinton Perera, *Descent to the Goddess,* Inner City Books (cited in reference 2).
4. Michel Gauquelin, *The Truth About Astrology,* p.38, Hutchinson.
5. Stefan Zweig, *The Queen of Scots,* Cassell Biographies.
6. Tom Steel, *Scotland's Story,* Collins.
7. John Miller, *James II A Study in Kingship,* Wayland.
8. *Gazette,* 10.6.1688, (no. 2354).
9. P.A. Sorokin, *Social and Cultural Dynamics,* American Book Co.
10. See page 434 of *Mundane Astrology,* M. Baigent, N. Campion, and C. Harvey, The Aquarian Press.

Other sources:
Bryan Bevan, *King James III of England,* Robert Hale.
Caroline Bingham, *James V King of Scots,* Collins.
Caroline Bingham, *The Stewart Kingdom of Scotland,* Weidenfeld & Nicolson.
Gordon Donaldson, *Mary Queen of Scots,* The English Univ Press.
Sir Archibald Dunbar, *Scottish Kings: A Revised Chronology of Scottish History 1005-1625,* David Douglas.
Antonia Fraser, *Mary Queen of Scots,* Weidenfeld & Nicolson.
R.L. Mackie, *King James IV of Scotland,* Oliver & Boyd.
Peggy Miller, *James,* George Allen & Unwin.
I.A. Taylor, *The Life of James IV,* Hutchinson.

Addendum

More astrological profiles

Astrological Index

Lady Isobel Barnett

Television personality.

Born: Isobel Marshall, 30 June 1918, 21.15 BST, Aberdeen 57N10 2W05 (birth certificate).

What's My Line? was the first television programme to become something of a national institution in Britain. Its success lay in the personalities of the panel members, not least in Isobel Barnett's. With her glacial elegance and aristocratic sophistication she seemed to early television audiences a superior creature from an elevated world remote from theirs. We note Sagittarius rising and Jupiter conjunct the descendant, and I think the image she projected is well described by these. Sagittarius relates to the idea of life lived at some heightened level of wonder and glamour, and amongst individuals of Olympian stature. It seems the world of television provided such a sphere for Isobel Barnett.

Her background was ordinary enough, and non-aristocratic (her title came through marriage). A middle-class Scot, she did well at school and went on to study medicine (which was not a common thing for a woman to do at that time). She specialised in obstetrics. She made her first television appearance in July 1953, and over the next couple of years rose to celebrity status. A progressed new Moon (exact in mid-1955) conjunct Neptune and Saturn symbolises this change of course, and her new life as a celebrated public figure.

Biography describes a fun-loving, enthusiastic, infectiously gay side, which suggests the strong Fire of the chart (particularly Jupiter). It notes also that she was snobbish — a great name dropper — and superficial. It seems she was a woman who repressed her feelings. She seemed determined to present to the world the composed and attractive mask that was her television image. There is a strong seventh house in the chart and this indicates a marked concern with what others think, and the need to appear admirable to others and the world at large. There is a 'Scorpionic' overtone to the chart — Sun conjunct Pluto, and a T-square of Moon, Mars and Pluto — and this suggests the obsessive nature of her concern.

As astrologers we can look at this chart and say Isobel Barnett was not what she wanted the world to think she was. Her mask has little to do with her core-nature, which is described by Sun conjunct Pluto in Cancer, and the Aries Moon T-square. These suggest a powerful feeling nature, but also that the Watery depths are rather dark, murky and forbidding. She can be forgiven her reluctance to stir them up. It seems likely that she contacted this 'Scorpionic' side in her early medical work, which took her to the Glasgow slums, and the world of birth, death, disease and dying. But some part of her rejected life at this raw level to pursue a Jupiterian show business sky-world. Cancer and Scorpio are both signs that relate to self-containment and reluctance to show the feelings. We have seen in many of the profiles in this book how those strong in Cancer often swathe themselves in a layer of insulation to anaethetise their own vulnerability. This Cancer shield is often austere and prickly, but not in Isobel Barnett's case. She mirrored the bright, bubbling, extrovert side of Sagittarius, and became so enthralled with it that she forgot about the rest.

The cost of Cancer's insularity is often isolation and loneliness. In the end these came to Isobel Barnett. Sometime in 1978 she started stealing from local shops. More than anything this seemed a cry for help, a plea for attention. She was eventually apprehended, and on 17 October 1980 prosecuted in the Crown Court. The ignominy proved too great, and she committed suicide two days later.

A somewhat exaggerated sense of propriety and an attendant determination to keep up appearances.

She had created her own protective barriers. The most effective of these was her ability to damp down her emotions before they reached the surface.

... beneath her overt gregariousness (she) was such an intensely private person that she could not share with anyone the darker, more uncomfortable emotions.

She never lost her anxiety about what other people thought about her and so carefully set about reconstructing her image to meet the expectations of the *What's My Line?* audience and of the press.

While she was always sympathetic to other people, she couldn't bear sympathy herself.

Source/reference:
Jock Gallagher, *Isobel Barnett, Portrait of a Lady*, Methuen.

Sir William Burrell
Businessman, art collector.

Born: 9 July 1861, 11.00 LT, Glasgow 55N53 4W15 (birth certificate).

Sir William Burrell was a successful shipping magnate who by his middle-life had amassed enough wealth to pursue full time a greater passion — the collection of *objets d'art*. The result of his ambition and labour was the famed Burrell Collection, since bequeathed to the city of Glasgow, and consisting of some 6000 pieces of antique stained glass, tapestry, bronzes, ceramics and paintings.

The broad pattern of Burrell's life seems to reflect his chart in quite straightforward ways. Cancer is noted for being a hoarder and collector, although generally not on such a grand scale as here. Common in the charts of connoisseurs is some sort of 'Venus' and 'Neptune' combination, and we note in Burrell's case Libra rising, with Venus conjunct the Moon, and Neptune strongly placed on the descendant. Cancer is traditionally related to the home, and Burrell spent more than a decade searching for the perfect home to house himself and his opulent collection.

As a businessman Burrell was very successful, and under his financial and his brother's technical expertise the company flourished. He was shrewd and practical and had great flair — a quality compounded of courage, self-confidence and intuition. This latter was particularly to the fore in Burrell, for he excelled at forecasting the ebb and flow of economic activity, and riding these times creatively: he knew when to buy, when to sell, and when to build ships. Perhaps his acumen is most clearly reflected in the strong Leo side of the chart — five planets in this sign, with Mars, Venus, Mercury and Moon bounded by only four degrees. Charles Carter[1] has suggested that this is a combination that reflects in a sound mind, and in enterprise and energy. Of Moon and Mercury in conjunction he notes: 'unusually active, penetrating understanding; a powerful brain and a fertile imagination'. Of Moon-Venus: 'strong mental effect ... a calm and steady view of things ... there is refinement, sometimes a love of luxury, or at all events of having things nice; the love of art is marked, and a cool, collected mental condition is common.' Of Mars-Moon he writes: Great energies, daring and enterprise characterise this position, and the native usually takes many risks, both physical and financial ... on the whole it is a healthy influence, which expresses itself freely and bravely as a ruler, teacher, reformer, or constructive man of business.'

His business skill applied to antiques as well as shipping. Although wealthy, he didn't possess the vast resources of some prominent collectors and he had to rely on shrewdness and judgement. A distinct Cancerian indirectness was evident in his methods and we are told he liked to 'circle round' a potential purchase, 'in order to avoid raising the price by alerting the dealer to his keen interest. On occasions he went to extraordinary lengths to conceal his intentions in the saleroom from rivals.'[2]

Burrell was a very private person, one who was 'careful to conceal his innermost emotions'. Despite his wealth, he lived a frugal existence, which degenerated in old age to an obsessive miserliness. He was healthy. He had a very good memory, a keen (if dry) sense of humour, and a notably unforgiving nature — all common Cancerian traits. He travelled a great deal. He was rather upright and moral, and a first impression was likely to be of an austere and reserved individual.

Sources/references:

1. Charles Carter, *The Astrological Aspects*, Fowler.
2. Richard Marks, *Burrell: Portrait of a Collector*, Richard Drew Publishing.

Sir Matt Busby
Football club manager.

Born: 26 May 1909, 03.50 GMT, Bellshill 55N50 4W15 (birth certificate)

Sir Matt Busby was manager of Manchester United from 1946 to 1970 and in that time made the club one of the most successful in the world. Under his managership they won the First Division championship five times, were runners-up seven times, and were the first English club to win the European Cup. However, for drama and trauma, the focal point in his life was none of these. Rather, it was the Munich air disaster (6 February 1958) which all but destroyed the team he built and left him critically ill for many weeks (indeed, he received the last rites three times). The transits and progressions of the period are quite striking. His Sun by secondary progression had moved to 20.46 Cancer, closely opposed to natal Uranus. Transiting Saturn opposed Pluto and Mercury, while transiting Pluto conjuncted the Moon/Jupiter midpoint and opposed Mars. The high point of success in his career was his team's victory in the European Cup Final, May 1968. At this time Jupiter transited natal Moon and Saturn returned to its own place.

A strong Leonine quality is evident in Busby's character, reflecting the Leo Moon and Sun conjunct the ascendant. When Prime Minister Harold Wilson said, 'Matt Busby is the symbol of everything that is best in our great national game' he was, in effect, referring to Busby's Leo side. For it is a sign that relates to what is

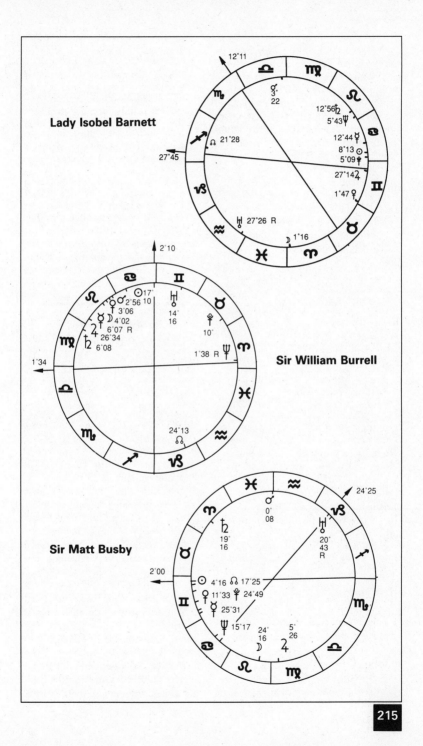

Lady Isobel Barnett

Sir William Burrell

Sir Matt Busby

good about human nature. When Leo is living this side of the sign it induces not only respect but also admiration and love. Leo has a marked paternalistic side. It encourages the young, seeks to bring out the best in them, to maximise their potential. This father/teacher approach was very evident in Busby's method. His policy was to seek out the best schoolboys in the land, nurture their individual talents, but at the same time mould them in accordance with his own grander designs. We can surmise that his Leonine intuition was to the fore here in this ability to recognise potential, to 'know' that a boy would develop into a great footballer. The result was the so-called 'Busby Babes', a team whose great promise was cut short at Munich.

It seems that Busby is a friendly man, but cool and detached at the same time — reflecting the strong Air of the chart. Biography describes him as somewhat reserved, tolerant, patient, calm, fair, unemotional, and balanced. There is some of the Leonine sensitivity to criticism. The accented Uranus (conjunct the MC) reflects in quiet as well as dramatic ways. He was an innovator in many respects. Perhaps most notably he altered the traditional role of the manager, becoming more closely associated with his players than with the directors. In short, he helped erode hierarchic distinctions in the game, a characteristic role of democratic Uranus. The quotes below speak a mix of Leo and Gemini (the third one, the adaptability of the Mercury ruled sign).

> He has always been ... a father to those around him ... he pervades both authority and security; there is a considered deliberate logic about all he does.

Busby, immensely warm yet somehow detached, has always been slightly remote from the players ... the economic severity of his youth and his preoccupation with his life's purpose have probably inhibited his capacity for the more casual involvement.

One of the most obvious and recurring factors in the life of Matt Busby has been his ability to turn almost every experience to profit.

Source/reference:
David Miller, *Father of Football, The Story of Sir Matt Busby*, Stanley Paul.

Jim Clark
Racing driver
Born: 4 March 1936, 15.25 GMT, Wester Kilmany 56N20 3W00 (birth certificate).

Scotland produces few racing drivers but in Jim Clark and Jackie Stewart has produced two of the highest calibre, each in their era dominating the sport. Clark was twice world champion, in 1963 and again in 1965.

One interesting feature of the chart is a close Sun-Saturn conjunction, for this is not an aspect one immediately associates with Formula 1 racing. Yet it is not so inappropriate when we recall that Saturn relates to achievement and ambition, and according to one piece of research[1] it is just this determination to succeed that constitutes the most significant factor in the make-up of racing drivers. The same research also concluded that they were likely to be more aggressive and independent than the average sportsperson; and to be cool, detached and emotionally stable.

These traits accord well enough with the astrological patterns that regularly turn up in the charts of racers, namely, some sort of emphasis on Aquarius/Uranus, Aries/Mars, sometimes Gemini and Sagittarius.

Again, Uranus is not a planet immediately associated with this sport, but it symbolises anything which overcomes the limitations of matter. This includes motor vehicles, which overcome human immobility, greatly increasing the distance that can be travelled in a given time — hence speed. Uranus is strong in this chart, conjunct the MC. It is also part of a midpoint set-up, with Mars conjunct the midpoint of Sun and Uranus. We perhaps have here a mirror of both Clark's vocation and his violent end. The midpoints of these three planets are generally active by transit at significant times in his life. When he first became world champion transiting Jupiter was stationary conjunct the Mars/Uranus midpoint. At the time of his second world championship, transiting Saturn conjuncted the Sun, and transiting Uranus opposed it. At the time of his death, on a practice run at Hockenheim April 7 1968, the Sun was close to the Mars/Uranus midpoint, and transiting Uranus closely opposed the Sun/Mars midpoint. By secondary progression Sun quincunxed Neptune, the Moon quincunxed Uranus, and Mars conjuncted Uranus.

There is a strong Leo emphasis in the chart, with both Moon and ascendant in this sign. This reflects in a certain endearing human quality that impressed itself strongly on those who knew him. The following quotation suggests some of this Leo nature, and also captures something of the Pisces Sun closely opposed by Neptune:

> Jim Clark represented for many people everything that is good about motor-racing ... he was polite, he was modest, he was kind-hearted, and calm to the point of wandering almost as if in a dream through the motor racing scene. Yet he was so talented as a driver, and that talent shone through.[2]

It seems that he was a rather shy, reserved person. He found it difficult to trust people and had few intimate friends.

Source/references:
1. K. Johnsgard and B. Ogilvie, *Journal of Sports, Medical and Physical Fitness,* (cited below).
2. Graham Gauld, *Jim Clark Remembered*, Patrick Stephens.

Lord Dowding
Military commander.

Born: Hugh Caswell Tremenhere Dowding, 24 April 1882, 12.30 LT, Moffat 55N20 3W27 (birth certificate).

Dowding, as commander of the Royal Air Force in the autumn of 1940 master-minded one of Britain's most important military victories, The Battle of Britain. This was a battle won through the skill and courage of individual airmen, but equally it was won by Dowding's foresight: his prewar decisions to develop certain aircraft, to establish an early-warning network of radar, and to develop an efficient organisational and administrative structure. Dowding's chart shows an accented Saturn, conjunct the Sun and midheaven, and as much as anything it was a Saturnian victory. We note also, that like another Taurean commander, Wellington, he excelled when stubborn resistance was the order of the day. When the air war became one of offence, Dowding stepped down.

The picture we get of Dowding is of a gaunt, deadpan, formal, rather severe sort of person. His nickname was 'stuffy.' This all reflects something of the strong Saturn, but also the Moon-Mars conjunction in Cancer. He was a person who would not express warmth or friendliness in public, lest it be construed as weakness or dereliction of duty. There is a lot of Feminine energy in the chart, with Taurus and Cancer accented, and yet as a military man it was not appropriate to express this. He lived behind a mask. The strong Saturn also suggests his ambition, integrity, capacity for self-sacrifice, and ability to shoulder tremendous responsibility. At the same time he was notably independent and unorthodox, often at odds with those around him, and this perhaps reflects the (equal) first house Uranus.

Dowding retired from public life at the age of 60, and was to change significantly in his maturity. Duty done, as it were, he could now relax, become more the essential person he was rather than a functionary of State. Saturn seemed to fade more and more into the background, allowing the gentler, Feminine side, the Venus and Lunar nature, to express. He became notably more personable, more tolerant of weakness, and more inward looking and contemplative. He underwent something of a religious conversion, becoming an active spiritualist and theosophist, even producing a number of books on the subject.

As is quite often the case when an individual's life is linked with a nation's destiny, we note strong and apposite cross-contacts between Dowding's chart and that of the UK. The UK Mars conjuncts Dowding's Sun/Saturn/MC set-up; the UK Moon conjuncts his Mars; the UK Saturn his ascendant. In the autumn of 1940, The Battle of Britain, Saturn was transiting his Saturn/MC. Essentially this was a time of testing, and ultimately a vindication of his qualities as man and commander. The nation reaped as he had sown.

Among those who had to do with him in his official capacity, who saw only the stern commander, ever zealous on behalf of the organisation under his control, quick to resent any move that seemed likely to weaken it, or make it less effective, Dowding had the reputation of a hard man, stubborn, self-opinionated, contemptuous of the views of others and merciless in pouncing on any weakness in an opponent's argument.

A man devoted to his duty and his country ... one whose dearest wishes centred around his eagerness to serve the public interest.

A disconcerting prickliness ... lack of pliancy ... lofty sense of his responsibilities.

His kindliness and generosity, his rather impish sense of humour were not apparent to those who did not know him well. His integrity and sense of dedication were obvious enough.

In reality a man of strong affections, kindly and generous to a fault, he passed at times — thanks partly to the protective armour gladly worn by the sensitive, but partly also to a less convenient inner barrier which sometimes checked a show of warmth when warmth would have been appropriate — for a cold, unfeeling cynic.

Source/reference:
Basil Collier, *Leader of the Few*, Jarrolds.

John Grierson
Film-maker

26 April 1898, 07.00 GMT, Kilmadock 56N25 3W26 (Birth certificate).

Grierson is sometimes known as 'the father of the documentary' because of his pioneering work in this field. We noted earlier that the planet Neptune has a connection with film, and it is accented in this chart, being conjunct the ascendant. Facility with image also relates to Taurus and Cancer, and in Grierson's chart we note an emphasis on both of these.

Grierson was not really interested in films as escapism or entertainment, but rather as a medium of communication — a reflection of his Gemini ascendant. His first film, *Drifters*, was about the North Sea fishing fleet. It was typical of his early work in its portrayal of working men toiling through hardship and against the elements to make a living, and to make the Earth yield up its bounty. It was typical too in its attempt to communicate some of the worth of the ordinary working person and a certain noble side to this kind of labour. His philosophy reflects his Taurean side: life might be hard, a struggle to the end, but there is value to be had in simply taking on the challenge.

His was a strongly etched personality. He was pugnacious, autocratic, and demanding. At the same time he was an inspirational leader and teacher commanding much affection and reverence. Most who came into contact with him were struck by his energy and dynamism. He had strong socialist leanings.

Most evident from biography, however, is his Gemini nature. He possessed considerable mental powers, loved debate, and was a fount of ideas. He needed movement and variety, and tended to move on to something else once a project had become routine. Perhaps most significantly, he was a communicator, intent on observing the world about him and passing on his observations in as powerful a way as possible.

A tremendous, continuous stream of ideas pouring from his mind.

(He) brought a charge and excitement to the business of communication which left its mark for many years to come, among two generations of film-makers.

He had a gift for refreshing and recharging his basic thinking with contemporary reference and example.

An insatiable appetite for travel and new experience.

It was the strength of mind, his mental power, which kept him alive.

Tremendous intensity of communication ... the meaning somehow burned through the complexities of his own speech and his own knowledge, which was encyclopaedic

Source/references:
Forsyth Hardy, *John Grierson A Documentary Biography*, Faber & Faber.

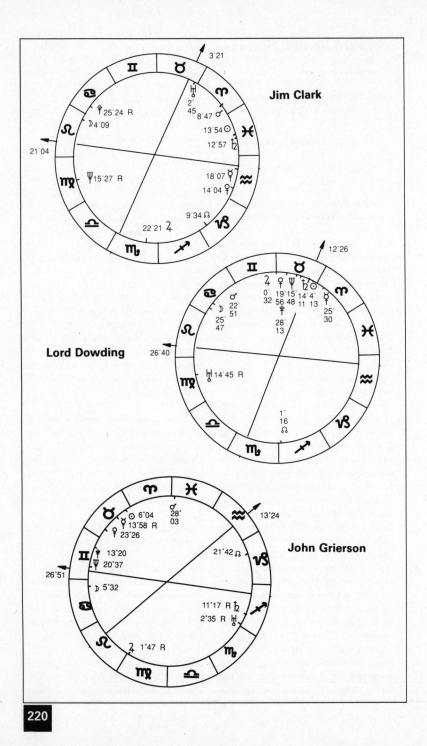

Jim Clark

Lord Dowding

John Grierson

Richard Burdon Haldane

Statesman, lawyer, philosopher

Born: 30 July 1856, 15.30 LT, Edinburgh
55N57 3W11 (birth certificate).

Lord Haldane achieved high political office in Liberal and Labour governments, as Lord Chancellor, and Secretary of State for War, in which position he carried through a major and far-reaching reorganisation of the army. His greatest passion, however, and what he considered his real work, was the expansion of higher education. He helped found Imperial College and The London School of Economics, and more generally encouraged a diffusion of learning away from Oxford and Cambridge. His chart supports the traditional view that higher education relates to Sagittarian factors for we see Sun and Venus in (equal) 9th house, a stationary Jupiter on the IC, and Sagittarius rising.

Haldane's chart is strong in Fire. This manifested, among other ways, as idealism and high-mindedness, qualities more a liability than an asset in the cynical world of politics. In professional life he came over as rather aloof, supercilious and pompous. Both Leo and Sagittarius can be elitist and Haldane was not always prepared to adjust himself to 'lesser' beings. There was also a certain naivety about him: he looked for the best in everyone, and had the Sagittarian habit of saying what he thought. All this made him easy prey for the Press and his political enemies.

Haldane possessed the Jupiterian shortcoming of not being able to adjust to differences (discrimination is the forte of polar Mercury). It is one thing to quote Schopenhauer to Cabinet colleagues, which he regularly did, and another to quote Goethe's *Faust*, at length, to a rally of Durham miners, which apparently he also did. His speeches were convoluted, long-winded and dry. The more he tried to explain something the more confused his listeners became. In short, he had a communication problem. Again, this seems to be a case of Jupiter overpowering Mercury, but I think also we should look to Moon conjunct Mercury in Cancer. The Moon, Cancer's ruler, symbolises the associative faculty and the attempt to express half a dozen related ideas at the same time, does not make for clarity (although it can make for fine literature — we think of Proust, who was a Cancer Sun).

Haldane's multistranded professional life is suggested by the Mutable strength of the chart: the Jupiter overtone, and the Moon/Mercury conjunction. He built up a successful career in law, and had a passion for philosophy (again, both traditionally related to Jupiter, its sign and house). His metaphysic, with its ideas of progressive levels of being, mirrors his Leo Sun. His approach to law seems more Jupiterian, for his was the ability to grasp the underlying principle in any case, no matter how complex the surface detail.

Beatrice Webb, who knew Haldane well, seemed to tune into his Cancerian side. She talks of warmth and kindness, and of his need for intimacy. For although he had a very successful professional life, and an enviable social life, it seems he was an essentially lonely person. Following a painful disillusionment in love, he never married. He was jilted by his fiance. This plunged him into deep depression for seven years or so, during which time he nurtured the hope that she would return to him. The engagement and subsequent jilting occurred in March/April 1890. We note at this time progressed Moon opposite Jupiter, transiting Neptune on the descendant, and transiting Jupiter opposed to natal Sun. The emphasis on Jupiter suggests the element of shattered dream that is often at the root of Sagittarian pain.

Haldane entered Parliament in December 1885. The nadir of his political career was in May 1915, when he was excluded from office in humiliating fashion. The emphasis on Neptune in the transits and progressions of the time — transiting Neptune conjunct Sun/Moon, and progressed Moon opposite Neptune — are apt in the sense that he was a victim of events, even of treachery. It seems that Haldane was sacrificed so that the Government and the incumbent Prime Minister would have a better chance of retaining power.

It would be out of place here to follow out further the kind of idealism that has throughout had hold of me. It is enough to say that its essence led me to the belief in the possibility of finding rational principles underlying all forms of experience, and to a strong sense of the endeavour to find some principles as a first duty in every department of public life.[1]

Haldane's relationship with his mother should not be underestimated as a source of his inspiration and resolve. Many of the decisions of his career ... can be ascribed to a desire to make his mother proud.[3]

He was a genial and outgoing person who accepted the misfortunes that befell him and who learned to abide them. Despite his essential loneliness, he had a zest for life and a capacity for gracious living, an unbounding enthusiasm for his work and a warm devotion to his friends.[3]

The rank and file of his own party dislike him intensely, partly because he detaches himself from party discipline and acts according to his own light and partly because he is dominated by some vague principle which they do not understand and which he does not make intelligible. His ... pompous ways, his absolute lack of masculine vices ... and 'manly' tastes, his intense superiority and constant attitude of a teacher, his curiously woolly mind would make him an unattractive figure if it were not for the beaming kindliness of his nature, warm appreciation of friends and a certain pawky humour with which he surveys the world.[2]

Sources/references:
1. Richard Burdon Haldane, *An Autobiography*, Hodder & Stoughton.
2. *The Diary of Beatrice Webb vol 2*, Virago.
3. Stephen Koss, *Lord Haldane, Scapegoat for Liberalism*, Columbia Univ Press.

Cosmo Lang
Archbishop.

Born: 31 October 1864, 15.55 LT, Aberdeen 57N10 2W05 (birth certificate).

Lang was an ambitious man and from an early age was determined on a career at the Bar. His personal qualities seemed well-suited to this. He was energetic, attractive, magnetic, and an excellent orator. He was a 'man most likely to succeed' type. He did succeed, although not at the Bar for in his mid-20s a religious experience altered the direction of his life. In the early summer, probably May, of 1889 he felt an overwhelming urge to be ordained. The climax of this was hearing a voice saying, 'you are wanted, you are called. You must obey.' Lang recounts the aftermath of this climax:

> The burden of the long struggle dropped. My mind was free. I don't want to write emotionally, but it is only recording a fact to say that a wave of such peace and indeed joy as I have ever known before filled my whole being ... I felt like a man who had suddenly been set free from chains ... all I know is that the experience itself was more real than any other in my inward life and more abiding. If there be a personal God ... He then and thus spoke to me.

There is a strong Scorpio quality to his experience. This is a dual sign, of tension between surface and root; between a detached, intellectual side, and a compassionate, feeling nature. Part of the Scorpio experience is the sense of being drawn down into the underworld of the feeling nature. Scorpio is a sign of sub- rather than transcendence. Characters created by Scorpio writers often undergo a 'fall' of this nature, and it is interesting to compare these to Lang's.

An aspect in the chart more traditionally associated with religion is the Jupiter/Venus conjunction in Sagittarius. It is this conjunction that is active by transit and progression at the significant phases of his life and career. At the time of his religious experience the Sun had progressed to about three degrees of Sagittarius, the midpoint of the conjunction. Transiting Pluto also opposed the midpoint, and transiting Neptune opposed Jupiter. Transiting Jupiter was conjunct the MC, and transiting Saturn square the Sun/Moon midpoint. Taken together these seem descriptive of a powerful emotional experience translated into Christian terms, and in a desire to be ordained.

Lang's ambitions carried over to his Church career. He rose rapidly within the hierarchy, becoming Archbishop of York (the Number 2 spot in the Church of England) 21 January 1909, and Primate, the Archbishop of Canterbury on 4 December 1928. The ambitious nature is suggested by the Aries ascendant and Saturn conjunct the descendant.

The strong 'Mars' nature of the chart reflected in a powerful presence. He could hold an audience, whether from the pulpit, or more informally. He had great energy and drove himself very hard. He was noted for his dignity and sense of the dramatic. He never married. He carried a strong sense of dissatisfaction, a disappointment with his own life (perhaps an outcrop of the high idealism of the Jupiter/Venus conjunction). He had a snobbish side, an undisguised liking for the company of the powerful and famous.

In 1916 he underwent a period of rapid aging. He lost his hair and some of his vigour. Significantly or coincidentally the progressed Sun entered Capricorn in September 1915. At a deep level the experience seems to have been another Scorpionic transformation. It marked an overall mellowing. His sharpness and energy were tempered, but in compensation there was increased gentleness and kindness. He died of heart failure 5.12.1944.

A compelling sense of duty ... an exceptional capacity for sustained effort.[1]

Complicated, introspective, emotional person.[2]

He took few into his confidence.[2]

I have never found it easy to exchange deeper thoughts, even with the many friends of later years.[2]

As a boy and young man, he had been intensely ambitious, absorbed in the business of getting on, carving a career, making a name. He could and must win his way to the top; his will was fixed on success and all his thoughts revolved round it.[2]

His self-consciousness and lifelong habit of introspection.[2]

Sources/references:
1. *The Dictionary of National Biography*, Oxford Univ Press.
2. J. Lockhart, *Cosmo Gordon Lang,* Hodder & Stoughton.

Sir Harry Lauder

Star of Music Hall.

Born: 4 August 1870, 02.45 LT, Edinburgh 55N57 3W11 (birth certificate).

In his day Sir Harry Lauder was a very popular entertainer, particularly in the United States, a country he toured 22 times. He was probably the highest paid entertainer of his day, at his peak earning something like $10000 a night. He was another Leo who was lionised, that is, made a fuss of, treated as something special by the public. And like other Leos, Lauder enjoyed the applause of the crowd.

His universal popularity is likely a reflection of a strong Uranus (conjunct the ascendant), a planet that often enough concurs with a capacity to penetrate the popular consciousness. Uranus relates also to the capacity to transcend barriers of time and culture. The songs he wrote, mawkish as they are, still echo in

Caledonian societies the world over, not to mention Sauchiehall Street on a Saturday night.

At the basic level, his fame rested on his ability to propagate a racial archetype. On stage Harry Lauder became a larger than life mythic figment: not just himself, but All Scotsmen. It is Leo that relates to this idea of racial archetype, that pattern or substance embodying that which is unique about a race. Just as, at the individual level, Leo and the Sun symbolise that unique figment that characterises an individual and which seeks outward creative expression. There is also a strong Cancer element in the chart, with the ascendant, Venus and Mars in this sign and this seems to reflect in the rather sentimental and patriotic nature of his performances, and in the warm empathy he seemed able to establish with his audiences.

He was an ambitious man, and always willing to take a chance to further his career. He had the energetic drive of a Scorpio Moon, and the personal magnetism and presence that is often to be found with Leo and Scorpio in combination. He was by all accounts a conceited man, but was noted also for his honesty, simplicity, sincerity, and piety.

He first toured America in mid-October 1907. This represented the real take-off point of his career, and corresponded to transiting Jupiter conjunct the Sun, transiting Saturn on the MC, and progressed Moon conjunct the MC. He married 18 June 1896. He was taken ill in the autumn of 1949 and died 26 February 1950.

Star quality on the stage is indefinable; roughly it means that its possessor has a magnetic, even a mesmeric, power which holds

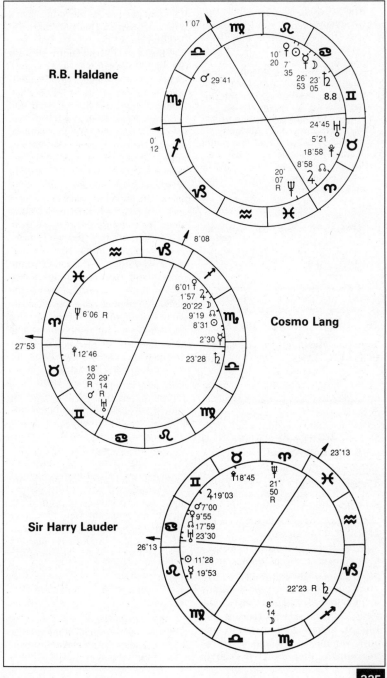

R.B. Haldane

Cosmo Lang

Sir Harry Lauder

the audience immediately and maintains that grasp whatever the performer may be saying or doing. Lauder had that quality to the full.[1]

His authoritarian command of the stage, and of everyone involved in his act, developed in him the pomposity of a conductor. Off-stage, he carried himself with the air, not of a comic, or even of a star, but of a prominent public figure, on the level of a prime-minister at least, and not far removed from royalty.[2]

Harry Lauder believed in himself. He set his sights high, and he was always aspiring to bigger things. He kept ambition under control, but he made the most of his constant wish to improve himself.[3]

Sources/references:
1. *Dictionary of National Biography 1941-50*, Oxford Univ Press.
2. Albert D Mackie, *The Scotch Comedians*, Ramsay Head Press.
3. Gordon Irving, *Great Scott. The Life Story of Sir Harry Lauder*, Leslie Frewin.

James Maxton
Politician.

Born: 22 June 1885, 05.30 GMT, Glasgow 55N53 4W15 (birth certificate).

James Maxton was chairman of the Independent Labour Party, and part of the wave of 'Red Clydeside' MPs who assailed Westminster in 1922. He held his parliamentary seat for 24 years.

Maxton was noted, among other things, for his oratory and for his personal qualities. He was considered kind, charming, and humorous, and had a marked flair for friendship. Even his political opponents considered him the most likeable of revolutionaries. Venus on the ascendant (and conjunct the Sun/ascendant midpoint) is the most obvious reflection of these qualities.

He was a politician of the heart rather than the head, which is what might be expected with a strong Watery chart such as this one. There was passion, compassion, evangelic fervour, but often little consistency or logic. He was too contrary, individual and subjective — too Cancerian in short — to be a successful career politician. He was not a party man. He was unwilling to compromise, to take political responsibility, or to work patiently toward realising ideals. Indeed, he was often overcritical of those who worked in a lower key, but with more realism to the same political ends. His greatest asset to the Labour Party was undoubtedly in the area of public relations: his personable nature demonstrated that working-class socialists could also be pleasant human beings, while his compelling oratory helped sell the Socialist message.

Maxton was a pacifist and his principles here brought conflict with authority. In May 1916 he was tried under the notorious Defence of the Realm Act, and sentenced to a year in prison (which he seemed to bear well). We note at this time progressed Moon opposite the Saturn/Mars midpoint, and transiting Pluto conjunct Sun. He was first elected to Parliament in November 1922 (transiting Jupiter conjunct Moon, progressed Moon opposite Jupiter). He married in June 1919, but his wife died 31 August 1922 (progressed Mars conjunct Saturn, progressed Moon square Mars and Pluto, transiting Pluto conjunct Venus and Sun/ascendant midpoint). He died 23 July 1946.

He was indeed a born orator. His quick mind, almost feminine in its intuitiveness, readily adapted itself to all circumstances and to every kind of audience ... he had an instinct which enabled him to steer his course so that he carried almost any audience with him.[1]

His natural sympathy with children and with animals is not the least likeable of the many exceedingly human traits in Maxton's make-up.[1]

In spite of his humanitarianism and other fine qualities, Maxton was prone to bouts of excessive emotionalism and sentimentality which clouded his judgement on occasion. Intellectual indolence was another of his failings and this increased his reliance on others to provide the theoretical underpinnings of many of his utterances.[2]

... his eloquence, his humour, and his pathos. He had become the super-propagandist for socialism and what he lacked in persuasive argument ... he made up in persuasive charm. For that is one of the greatest things about Maxton; he had the gift of courtesy in an extraordinary degree.[1]

Sources/references:
1. Gilbert McAllister, *James Maxton: the Portrait of a Rebel*, John Murray.
2. *Scottish Labour Leaders 1918-32*, Mainstream Publishing.

Edwin Muir
Poet

Born: 15 May 1887, 01.00 GMT, Orkney 59N10 3W30 (birth certificate).

Muir enjoyed a happy upbringing on remote Orkney. His parents, he recounts, were kind and loving, not given to the rigorous treatment of children common at the time. However, his health was poor, and consequently his schooling was broken.

There were two particularly impressionable periods in his childhood. The first of these was at the age of seven when he experienced a strong awareness of a loss of innocence. He became aware for the first time of guilt, fear, death, and, more generally, of the evil and disharmony present in the world. He talks of 'the destruction of my first image of the world', and of a sense of some unseen tragedy being played out around him. He realised later in his life that many of his poetic images were drawn from this innocent early period. What Muir seemed to be experiencing at this time was the myth of The Fall. As I wrote in *The Literary Zodiac*, this is a myth that relates to the meaning of Taurus. Themes of a Lost Eden, of disharmonious worlds are common amongst Taurean writers (including Muir).

An essentially similar event occurred in January 1902, when the Muir family uprooted and moved to Glasgow. This was a much more concrete manifestation of 'the Fall' compared to the earlier subjective experience. Orkney was 'Eden', rural, timeless, where life flowed to the swing of the seasons, and according to time-honoured ritual. It represented a harmonious, meaningful and protective natural order. By comparison Glasgow was a fallen world, rotten and askew, a chaos rather than a cosmos, with its sprawling industry, its squalor and violence, and where capitalist competition reigned, rather than the Venusian co-operation that permeated his Orkney community. For Muir it was the start of one of the worst periods of his life. The next years were dogged by illness — notably by stomach complaints — and passed in unpleasant menial work (which perhaps reflects the sixth house Saturn in Cancer).

His mother and brother died within two years of the move, and Muir associated their deaths with the psychological jolt of the family's uprooting. At the time of the first 'fall', in 1894, we note a progressed new Moon, conjunct Pluto. At the time of the move to Glasgow, Jupiter transited his ascendant, and progressed Venus had moved to conjunct natal Saturn, an appropriate indicator of a more concrete manifestation of an essentially Venusian experience.

The 1920s and early 30s were times of optimism and new ideas in Europe, and Muir was very alive to these currents. He had a marked intellectual and cosmopolitan nature, suggested by the Aquarian Moon. In later life he was to work as cultural attaché for the British Council in a number of European cities, and once more this is suggestive of the Aquarian Moon. Freud was in vogue in Muir's social circle and, encouraged by friends, he submitted himself for analysis, under Maurice Nicol (better known to astrologers for his lucid writings on occult and religious subjects). It was a painful period for Muir, but ultimately a fruitful one. It cleared the path to his becoming a poet. Muir always dreamt profusely, indeed sometimes experienced waking visions. The analysis seemed to bring up a lot of material from his deep unconscious, and some of it alarmed the analyst. It seems that the whole period 1920, 1921, 1922 was one of inner transformation. Muir underwent a number of these during his life, which is suggested in the chart by Pluto on the IC and Mars conjunct

the Sun (giving a 'Scorpionic' overtone to the chart).

Dates are a little vague for this period, but apposite are: progressed Moon conjunct Mars (September 1921), and then Sun, Neptune, IC, and Pluto between this date and the end of 1922. There was a progressed new Moon (conjunct Venus) in September 1924, which is a good symbol of the completion of his transformation. It was about this time that he took seriously to writing poetry. But he was a late developer creatively (which is common when Capricorn is strong, as it is here, as the rising sign), much of his best work not coming until his fiftieth year or so.

He met his wife in the autumn of 1918, and they were married in June 1919 — 'the most fortunate event of my life'. Muir's chart lacks Fire, but his wife seemed to provide this for him, giving him confidence, hope in the future, and more generally helping him become a fuller person. The quotes below mostly reflect his basic Venusian nature.

Beneath the story of his life he saw the fable of man — Eden, the Fall, the journey through the labyrinth of time. He made much use of his dreams and of myths for in them the fable is most clearly seen.[1]

Muir was a man of complete integrity; gentle, unassuming, and vulnerable, but with firm tenacity of purpose; sometimes abstracted, but strongly affectionate and quick in sympathy.[1]

... beneath the gentleness (was) a core of steel ... he attracted people with a mothering instinct ... he was vastly attractive to women.[2]

He had great tenacity of purpose,

but not the ability to push for himself.[2]

...modest, considerate, religious, utterly sincere ... grounded in love.[2]

His overruling positive yearning for harmony rather than discord, for gentleness rather than violence, for tolerance, compassion and love rather than hatred and punishment.[3] .

Sources/references:

1. *The Dictionary of National Biography 1951-60,* Oxford Univ Press.
2. P.H. Butter, *Edwin Muir, Man and Poet,* Oliver & Boyd.
3. Willa Muir, *Belonging, A Memoir,* The Hogarth Press.
4. Edwin Muir, *An Autobiography,* The Hogarth Press.

Lord Reith

First Director General of the BBC.

Born: John Charles Reith, 20 July 1889, 16.30 GMT, Stonehaven 56N38 2W13 (birth certificate).

When the BBC came into being in January 1927 Lord Reith was appointed its first Director General. He ruled autocratically for some eleven years and set a general tone and standard which lasted for many more. Cancer (Reith's Sun sign) can be very paternalistic. We have noticed this in other profiles, that of James VI/I for example. But unlike James, Reith was not an indulgent and pampering father. He comes across, rather, as a stern Old Testament patriarch, obsessed with the moral wellbeing of the Corporation and the nation in general. He didn't hesitate to sack those who impugned his strict moral code (and things like divorce constituted a transgression). This side of him, his strong religious-moral nature and compulsion to impose it on others is a reflection of his Sagittarian ascendant and (in part) the Taurus Moon.

He was criticised for using the power of monopoly to foist a Christian morality upon the viewing population, and there is some basis at least for this view. On the positive side, however, Reith established lofty standards for the Network. These have been maintained over the years and we have been spared the worst of the trivia and bad taste that infests commercial channels the world over. Sagittarius at its best relates to what we call the higher self, the more dignified, noble, high-minded, aspects of human nature, and Reith sought to make the BBC worthy in this respect.

There is often something of the misfit or loner about Cancer. It is a strongly individual sign and one that feels the weight of its own uniqueness. More than any other sign, it experiences difficulty in finding its place in the world, that is, in harmonising its individual talents and desires with the demands of the socio-economic structure. This was a pattern evident throughout much of Reith's life. 'Even among his brothers and sisters', we are told 'he was like an unarmed scout cut off in hostile territory.'[1] Cancerian shyness and sensitivity hampered his efforts at sociability, and like many strong in this sign, he seemed to find sanctuary in an inner world of his own imagining.

It was only as head of the BBC that Reith felt he belonged. The BBC was his 'child', one reared in his own

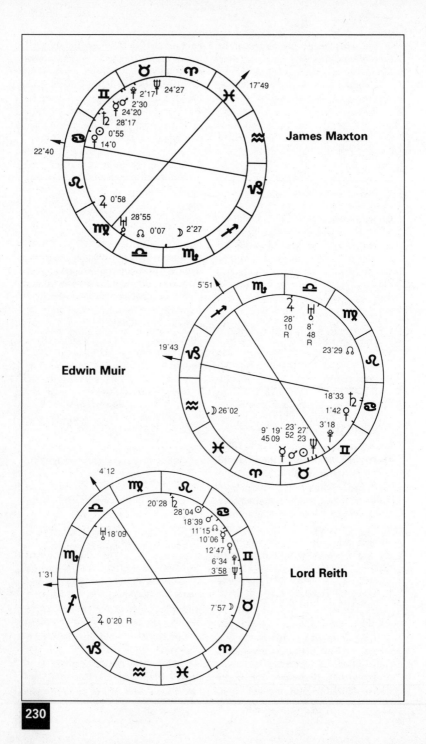

James Maxton

Edwin Muir

Lord Reith

image, and like any Cancerian parent, he was mortified when it declared its independence and cast him off.

It seems that Reith was a good organiser and administrator. He possessed determination, energy, and the (Jupiterian) power to think big. More than most at the time, he saw the manifold possibilities of television, and his belief in it provided a firm foundation and the impetus for growth. In biography he comes over as a rather austere, morose, moody, cantankerous sort of figure, and there is the peculiar Cancerian combination of aggressiveness and shyness. He was an obsessive diarist and had an 'exceptionally retentive memory'.[1] For much of his life he suffered morbid religious fears — the conviction that he was damned.

On 7 October 1915, on active service, he was hit in the head by a sniper's bullet. He was seriously wounded and fortunate to survive. We note at the time transiting Mars conjunct natal Sun, and transiting Saturn conjunct natal Mars. He married on 14 July 1921, and became General Manager of the British Broadcasting Company on 18 December 1922 (transiting Jupiter opposite natal Moon). His mother died 28 December 1935 (progressed Moon opposite Mars, transiting Pluto conjunct Sun.)

(Of his inner world): As he grew older ... everything served as fuel for the furnace; and by some enchanted process of alchemy, everything touched by his vivid fantasy could be turned to fairy gold. Time had no meaning or terrors for him in this private universe where the people and the realities of everyday existence were not excluded but simply transmuted and made more

tolerable. As architect and supreme controller of the dream domain the young John Reith could enter or leave it at will.[1]

His refusal to be rebuffed by anyone, one of the facets of Reith's touchy pride.[1]

(His) moral principles had the tensile strength of steel and extended to everybody, high and low alike.

Sir John Reith, far from regarding himself as a man of outstanding achievement, still felt at times like a stranger in a hostile land ... This feeling was by no means novel. It squared with the almost atavistic sense of inadequacy which had possessed him at intervals since adolescence.[1]

He saw far and clearly ... He had too a zest for the development of freshly discovered possibilities.[2]

The hard, strong, yet basically shy personality of Reith.[1]

Sources/references:
1. Andrew Boyle, *Only The Wind Will Listen: Reith of the BBC*, Hutchinson.
2. *Obituaries from the Times 1971-75*.

William Soutar
Poet.

Born: 28 April 1898, 05.15 GMT, Perth 56N25 3W26 (birth certificate).

William Soutar's life was dominated by serious illness. For the last ten years of his short life he lay bed-ridden, crippled by a form of spondylitis. The accented 12th house is likely a mirror of this helplessness and enforced passivity. Also of the sacrifice involved. He believed his body had been sacrificed in order that his poetic self could develop. He produced in all some twelve volumes of verse, which have attracted a good deal of critical acclaim.

Transits and progressions point to a Neptunian influence in his physical affliction. There was an illness related to this in December 1918, when Neptune squared the Sun, and progressed Venus (Sun and ascendant ruler) conjuncted Neptune. For the next six years the illness remained a mystery. It wasn't diagnosed correctly until the end of November 1924 (with transiting Saturn opposite Sun). At his death in October 1943 the Sun had progressed to 21 degrees of Gemini, close to natal Neptune. At the same time, transiting Mars conjuncted

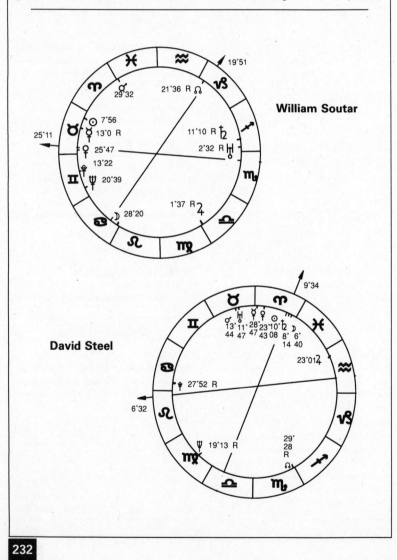

William Soutar

David Steel

Neptune, and Pluto squared the Sun. The onset of illness was also marked broadly by a progressed new Moon (exact in 1920, opposite Uranus). From this time onward he was to be increasingly burdened by illness.

This is a chart strong in Taurus, with Sun, Venus, Mercury, and ascendant here. Venus also conjuncts the ascendant. He seemed to embody particularly the stoic side of the sign. Taurus relates to that brand of courage we call fortitude, a chronic rather than acute manifestation of the quality. When Soutar wrote 'man who is truly man must accept the challenge of circumstances and give it meaning, if but for a moment' he was expressing the meaning of Taurus at a fundamental level. Through his creation of poetry Soutar left the world more harmonious and more conscious than when he entered it. He formed the unformed with his individual archetype.

This is a strong Venus chart and yet Soutar was a person who harboured serious doubts about his capacity to love. 'When a person comes too near me,' he wrote, 'my blood instinctively cries out, stand back, stand back.' It seems as if all the Venusian warmth might be chilled somewhat through an opposition with Uranus (which also conjuncts the 7th house cusp). Likewise, the Moon is in grand trine with Mars and Uranus, which suggests an *instinctive* coolness. Uranus demands detachment and independence, and yet, in his infirmity, Soutar was wholly dependent upon the welfare of others. We have suggested an intolerable tension from which the only release was retreat to an inner world where he could in spirit be a free, creative individual.

Soutar had the Taurean appreciation of physical beauty in all its forms. He speaks of a 'full-blooded virility' that it was necessary to come to terms with (in view of his physical incapacity). His libido had to find other channels. He exhibited another characteristically Venusian trait: he was haunted by a romantic figment from his past. He had, for want of a better word, a fetish for women in black, and he put this down to an unfulfilled adolescent passion for a girl in black stockings. The original experience impressed itself so firmly on his consciousness that even in dreams 20 years later he could invoke the precise feeling associated with it (a reflection also of the strong Moon, in Cancer conjunct the IC).

Sources/references:
1. William Soutar, *Diaries of a Dying Man*, Chambers.
2. Alexander Scott, *Still Life*, Chambers.

David Steel

Politician.

Born: 31 March 1938, 12.15 GMT, Kirkcaldy 56N7 3W10 (birth certificate).

The focal point of David Steel's chart is the close Sun/Moon/Saturn conjunction in Aries on the MC. Among other things it symbolises the strong ambition that propelled him rapidly up the political ladder. Both Saturn and Aries relate to the need to achieve, and the need for recognition. Saturn is rather plodding in the attainment of it, but Aries inclines to rapidity, as it did with David Steel. He became leader of the Liberal Party at a comparatively early age, on 7 July 1976, as Saturn conjuncted his ascendant, and Pluto opposed the MC stellium.

This is a strong Fire chart, with five planets in Aries and Leo rising, and yet he is not a Fiery politician. There is little obvious emotion or spontaneity. Neil Kinnock, the Labour Party leader, who also has Sun Aries and Leo rising, is more typically Fiery in his style, and often demonstrates the characteristic aggression of Aries. There is passion, energy, and drive in David Steel, but for the most part it is very toned down. What it is that cools his Fire is the dominating Saturn. He comes over as controlled, calm, polished and reasonable. He is a pragmatic politician. He values what works. He prefers stability and gradual change to radicalism.

Basically Saturn has worked well for him. It provides anchorage for an otherwise unbalanced chart. It provides patience and staying power. It gives an adeptness at operating in the public world. Saturn usually concurs with integrity, and Mr Steel is more easily believed than most politicians. The quotes below suggest the mix of Saturn and Aries that is the main overtone of his character.

In reality, Steel is a political hard case, one of the toughest in Britain today. The gentle demeanour, the softly spoken voice, the air of sweet reason, mask an inner core of sheer political determination.

He is quiet, tough, slightly shy and disciplined.

He is not so much shy as reserved. He is naturally a very private person ... he has emotions, and very strong emotions on some subjects, but they are channelled and controlled by a formidable intellect.

... a single-minded determination to get what he wanted, despite the wishes of others.

Source/reference:
Peter Barton, *David Steel, His Life and Politics*, W.H. Allen.

Astrological Index

212, 213, 214, 218, 219, 221, 224, 226, 229, 231.

Leo/Sun
43, 56, 70, 76, 82, 86, 101, 102, 115, 139, 143, 153, 154, 213, 214, 216,217, 221, 224.

Virgo/Mercury
32, 49, 67, 88, 89, 96, 97, 110, 114, 127.

Libra/Venus
52, 107, 116, 117, 138, 139, 150, 157.

Scorpio/Mars/ Pluto
50, 54, 56, 57, 73, 76, 81, 107, 111, 113, 115, 146, 149, 150, 156, 160, 212, 223, 224, 228.

Sag./Jupiter
32, 33, 43, 47, 51, 52, 61, 65, 90, 91, 96, 112, 113, 125, 145, 212, 217, 221, 229.

Capricorn/Saturn
33, 43, 49, 60, 61, 68, 73, 80, 81, 90, 99, 100, 102, 109, 110, 120, 121, 127, 216, 217, 218, 228, 233, 234.

Aquarius/Saturn/Uranus
35, 48, 56, 64, 65, 72, 82, 86, 99, 120, 123, 124, 128, 145, 146, 148, 150, 216, 217, 218, 224, 233.

Pisces/Jupiter/ Neptune
33, 50, 52, 53, 56, 57, 58, 61, 88, 89, 90, 91, 96, 97, 100, 102, 104, 105, 111, 115, 117, 118, 126, 127, 139, 143, 144, 198, 206, 219, 231, 232.

Element types

Air: 62, 64, 105, 216.
Weak Air: 73, 204.

Earth: 42, 48, 49, 54, 60, 68, 73, 109, 121, 202.
Weak Earth: 82, 204.

Fire: 33, 40, 70, 73, 82, 116, 204, 212, 221, 234, 282.

Weak Fire: 205.

Water: 50, 56, 73, 160, 204, 226.
Weak Water: 64, 105.

Houses

1st: 33, 35, 42, 102, 149, 159, 160, 218.
2nd: 35.
6th: 228.
7th: 66, 212.
8th: 39.
9th: 125, 221.
10th: 43, 60, 90.
11th: 35, 86, 157.
12th: 64, 85, 90, 91, 92, 100, 143, 231.

Midpoints

48, 70, 156, 214, 217, 223, 226.

Progressions

Of Sun: 35, 62, 75, 134, 160, 217, 223, 232.
Of Moon: 62, 74, 80, 91, 94, 145, 149, 150, 160, 203, 217, 222, 224, 226, 228, 231.
Pr. Full Moon: 35, 72.
Pr. New Moon: 37, 40, 55, 60, 71, 74, 91, 115, 123, 128, 137, 146, 148, 153, 157, 201, 202, 212, 228, 233.
Of Mercury: 36.
Of Venus: 36, 91, 228, 232.
Of Mars: 156, 217, 226.

Signs

Aries
Sun: 45, 88, 140, 196, 233, 234.
Moon: 45, 212, 233.
Mars: 124.
Saturn: 233.
asc: 106, 223.

Taurus
Sun: 37, 42, 48, 90, 198, 199, 218, 233.
Moon: 54, 56, 65, 68, 77, 79, 102, 139, 140, 160, 192, 229.
Mercury: 233.
Venus: 54, 90, 233.
Mars: 90, 121.
asc: 42, 233.

Gemini
Sun: 65, 76, 81, 104, 110, 120, 205.
Moon: 43, 133.
Mercury: 65, 104.
Venus: 65.
Mars: 43, 68, 104.
Saturn: 43.
asc: 77, 104, 219.

Cancer
Sun: 50, 92, 93, 143, 212, 213, 221, 229.
Moon: 41, 85, 100, 124, 133, 218, 221, 233.
Mercury: 92, 221.
Venus: 224.
Mars: 205, 218, 224.
Saturn: 66, 228.
asc: 37, 77, 90, 146, 159, 160, 224.

Leo
Sun: 35, 43, 70, 72, 84, 101, 115, 221, 224.
Moon: 42, 114, 157, 204, 213, 214, 217.
Mercury: 115, 213.
Venus: 115, 213.
asc: 56, 76, 86, 115, 116, 135, 139, 204, 217, 234.

Virgo
Sun: 67, 95, 96, 125, 146.
Moon: 127.
Mercury: 96.
asc: 32, 33, 35, 40, 41, 51, 110, 120, 121, 150, 206.

Libra
Sun: 106, 116, 138, 150, 151, 157.
Moon: 51, 52, 104, 105.
Mercury: 68.
Venus: 33, 68.
Mars: 97.
Saturn: 104, 105.
asc: 213.

Scorpio

Sun: 56, 57, 148, 204.
Moon: 35, 81, 111, 115, 128,
   129, 196.
Mercury: 56.
Mars: 35, 49, 149.
asc: 49, 50, 111, 140, 155,
   198.

Sagittarius
Sun: 32, 51, 133, 202, 203.
Moon: 70, 90, 91, 116, 146.
Mercury: 32, 51.
Venus: 51, 223.
Mars: 51, 154.
Jupiter: 32, 90, 133, 223.
Saturn: 125, 130, 154.
asc: 46, 64, 84, 212, 221, 229.

Capricorn
Sun: 33, 60, 77, 94, 99, 109,
   110, 135, 153.
Moon: 33, 37, 49, 73, 109,
   110, 121, 202.
Mercury: 109.
Mars: 33, 37, 113.
Saturn: 113, 133.
asc: 66, 81, 96, 228.

Aquarius
Sun: 33, 107, 123, 124.
Moon: 33, 64, 77, 82, 107,
   154, 198, 228.
Mercury: 99.
Venus: 99, 154.
asc: 99, 102, 148.

Pisces
Sun: 79, 125, 160, 217.
Moon: 50, 88, 96, 149, 150,
   151, 205, 206.

Venus: 50, 125.
Mars: 198.
Jupiter: 128.
Saturn: 160.

Transits

Of Sun
To Uranus: 70.

Of Moon
To Saturn: 91.

Of Mars
To Sun: 231.
To Moon: 91, 134.
To Venus: 91.
To Uranus: 91.
To Neptune: 38, 232.
To MC: 74.

Of Jupiter
To Sun: 72, 74, 91, 110, 130,
   145, 146, 222, 224.
To Moon: 44, 110, 141, 156,
   214, 226, 231.
To Venus: 203.
To Saturn: 71, 89.
To asc/desc: 44, 110, 129,
   228.
To MC: 123, 223.

Of Saturn
To Sun: 52, 79, 80, 133, 141,
   156, 217, 232.
To Moon: 55, 91, 193.
To Mercury: 214.
To Mars: 38, 156, 231.

To Saturn: 84, 90, 110, 137,
   141, 149, 156, 160, 214,
   218.
To Uranus: 146.
To Neptune: 79, 84.
To Pluto: 55, 134, 156, 160,
   193, 203, 214.
To asc/desc: 110, 156, 233.
To MC/IC: 38, 90, 110, 141,
   156, 218, 224.

Of Uranus
To Moon: 149.
To Venus: 91.
To Mars: 38, 74.
To Saturn: 75.
To Uranus: 121.
To asc/desc: 91, 103, 123.

Of Neptune
To Sun: 35, 38, 52, 149, 222,
   232.
To Moon: 222.
To Mercury: 52.
To Venus: 203.
To Mars: 149.
To Jupiter: 223.
To asc/desc: 141, 145, 222.
To MC/IC: 58, 75, 160.

Of Pluto
To Sun: 40, 52, 62, 86, 133,
   156, 193, 226, 231, 233.
To Moon: 75, 199, 233.
To Venus: 226.
To Mars: 74, 124, 145, 149,
   156, 214.
To Saturn: 157, 233.
To asc: 71, 157.
To MC: 156, 193, 233.

The Literary Zodiac

by Paul Wright

THIS IS SUPERB. *It is beautifully written and its content is worth being studied by the most experienced astrologer as well as the student. . . . This is a first class book. Paul Wright must be congratulated. This will surely become an astrological classic.*—Considerations Magazine

Very impressive! If there were universities that gave degrees in astrology, the author would have a Ph.D. by now.—Stephen Arroyo

Extremely interesting, well researched and original. . . . I found his analysis deep and insightful.—Liz Greene

The Literary Zodiac is the outcome of a seven year project by the author in which he examines the work of a great number of writers. He compares writers on the basis of the sign of the zodiac under which they were born and demonstrates, with many examples from well-known works of literature, that there is a remarkable consistency of creative theme to be found among writers of the same sign, and that the themes themselves correspond to the meanings of the signs. It is a book that demonstrates not only the validity of the signs of the zodiac, but also clarifies and illumines the individual sign meanings.

Since its publication in Autumn 1987, many have commended *The Literary Zodiac* for its originality, its insights, and its significant contribution to astrological knowledge. If you are serious about astrology, then the book is essential reading.

Available in paperback from bookshops, price $14.95

CRCS Books

THE ANCIENT SCIENCE OF GEOMANCY:Living in Harmony with the Earth by Nigel Pennick
$12.95. The best and most accessible survey of this ancient wholistic art/science,
superbly illustrated with 120 photos.

AN ASTROLOGICAL GUIDE TO SELF-AWARENESS by Donna Cunningham, M.S.W. $6.95. Written in a
lively style, this book includes chapters on transits, houses, interpreting aspects, etc.
A popular book translated into 5 languages.

THE ART OF CHART INTERPRETATION: A Step-by-Step Method of Analyzing,Synthesizing &
Understanding the Birth Chart by Tracy Marks $7.95. A guide to determining the most
important features of a birth chart. A must for students!

THE ASTROLOGER'S GUIDE TO COUNSELING: Astrology's Role in the Helping Professions
by Bernard Rosenblum, M.D. $7.95. Establishes astrological counseling as a valid and
legitimate helping profession. A break-through book!

THE ASTROLOGER'S MANUAL: Modern Insights into an Ancient Art by Landis Knight Green
$10.95, 240 pages. A strikingly original work that includes extensive sections on
relationships, aspects, and all the fundamentals in a lively new way.

THE ASTROLOGICAL HOUSES: The Spectrum of Individual Experience by Dane Rudhyar $8.95.
A recognized classic of modern astrology that has sold over 100,000 copies, this book
is required reading for every student of astrology seeking to understand the deeper
meanings of the houses.

ASTROLOGY: The Classic Guide to Understanding Your Horoscope by Ronald C. Davison $7.95.
The most popular book on astrology during the 1960's & 1970's is now back in print in a
new edition, with an instructive new foreword that explains how the author's remarkable
keyword system can be used by even the novice student of astrology.

ASTROLOGY FOR THE NEW AGE: An Intuitive Approach by Marcus Allen $7.95. Emphasizes self-
acceptance and tuning in to your chart with a positive openness. Helps one create his
or her own interpretation.

ASTROLOGY IN MODERN LANGUAGE by Richard Vaughan $12.95, 336 pages. An in-depth inter-
pretation of the birth chart focusing on the houses and their ruling planets-- including
the Ascendant and its ruler. A unique, strikingly original work.

ASTROLOGY, KARMA & TRANSFORMATION: The Inner Dimensions of the Birth Chart by Stephen
Arroyo $10.95. An insightful book on the use of astrology for persoal growth, seen in
the light of the theory of karma and the urge toward self-transformation. International
best-seller!

THE ASTROLOGY OF SELF-DISCOVERY: An In-Depth Exploration of the Potentials Revealed in Your
Birth Chart by Tracy Marks $8.95, 288 pages. Emphasizes the Moon and its nodes, Neptune,
Pluto, & the outer planet transits. An important and brilliantly original work!

ASTROLOGY, PSYCHOLOGY AND THE FOUR ELEMENTS: An Energy Approach to Astrology & Its Use in
the Counseling Arts by Stephen Arroyo $7.95. An international best-seller, this book
deals with the use of astrology as a practical method of understanding one's attunement
to universal forces. Clearly shows how to approach astrology with a real understanding
of the energies involved. Awarded the British Astrological Assn's Astrology Prize. A
classic translated into 8 languages!

CYCLES OF BECOMING: The Planetary Pattern of Growth by Alexander Ruperti $12.95,
274 pages. The first complete treatment of transits from a humanistic and holistic
perspective. All important planetary cycles are correlated with the essential
phases of personal development. A pioneering work!

DYNAMICS OF ASPECT ANALYSIS: New Perceptions in Astrology by Bil Tierney $8.95,
288 pages. Ground-breaking work! The most in-depth treatment of aspects and aspect
patterns available, including both major and minor configurations. Also includes
retrogrades, unaspected planets & more!

A JOURNEY THROUGH THE BIRTH CHART: Using Astrology on Your Life Path by Joanne
Wickenburg $7.95. Gives the reader the tools to put the pieces of the birth chart
together for self-understanding and encourages creative interpretation by helping
the reader to think through the endless combinations of astrological symbols.

THE JUPITER/SATURN CONFERENCE LECTURES: New Insights in Modern Astrology by Stephen Arroyo & Liz Greene $8.95. Talks included deal with myth, chart synthesis, relationships, & Jungian psychology related to astrology. A wealth of original & important ideas!

THE LITERARY ZODIAC by Paul Wright $12.95, 240 pages. A pioneering work, based on extensive research, exploring the connection between astrology and literary creativity.

LOOKING AT ASTROLOGY by Liz Greene $7.50. A beautiful, full-color children's book for ages 6-13. Illustrated by the author, this is the best explanation of astrology for children and was highly recommended by SCHOOL LIBRARY JOURNAL. Emphasizes self-acceptance and a realistic understanding of others.

NUMBERS AS SYMBOLS FOR SELF-DISCOVERY: Exploring Character & Destiny with Numerology by Richard Vaughan $8.95, 336 pages. A how-to book on personal analysis and forecasting your future through Numerology. Examples include the number patterns of a thousand famous personalities.

THE OUTER PLANETS & THEIR CYCLES: The Astrology of the Collective by Liz Greene $7.95. Deals with the individual's attunement to the outer planets as well as with significant historical and generational trends that correlate to these planetary cycles.

PLANETARY ASPECTS: FROM CONFLICT TO COOPERATION: How to Make Your Stressful Aspects Work for You by Tracy Marks $8.95, 225 pages. This revised edition of HOW TO HANDLE YOUR T-SQUARE focuses on the creative understanding of the stressful aspects and focuses on the T-Square configuration both in natal charts and as formed by transits & progressions. The most thorough treatment of these subjects in print!

THE PLANETS AND HUMAN BEHAVIOR by Jeff Mayo $7.95. A pioneering exploration of the symbolism of the planets, blending their modern psychological significance with their ancient mythological meanings. Includes many tips on interpretation.

PRACTICAL PALMISTRY: A Positive Approach from a Modern Perspective by David Brandon-Jones $8.95, 268 pages. This easy-to-use book describes and illustrates all the basics of traditional palmistry and then builds upon that with more recent discoveries based upon the author's extensive experience and case studies. A discriminating approach to an ancient science that includes many original ideas!

THE PRACTICE AND PROFESSION OF ASTROLOGY: Rebuilding Our Lost Connections with the Cosmos by Stephen Arroyo $7.95. A challenging, often controversial treatment of astrology's place in modern society and of astrological counseling as both a legitimate profession and a healing process.

REINCARNATION THROUGH THE ZODIAC by Joan Hodgson $6.50. A study of the signs of the zodiac from a spiritual perspective, based upon the development of different phases of conciousness through reincarnation.

RELATIONSHIPS & LIFE CYCLES: Modern Dimensions of Astrology by Stephen Arroyo $8.95. Thorough discussion of natal chart indicators of one's capacity and need for relationship; techniques of chart comparison; using transits practically; and the use of the houses in chart comparison.

SEX & THE ZODIAC: An Astrological Guide to Intimate Relationships by Helen Terrell $7.95, 256 pages. Goes into great detail in describing and analyzing the dominant traits of women and men as indicated by their Zodiacal signs.

THE SPIRAL OF LIFE: Unlocking Your Potential with Astrology by Joanne Wickenburg & Virginia Meyer $7.95. Covering all astrological factors, this book shows how understanding the birth pattern is an exciting path toward increased self-awareness.

A SPIRITUAL APPROACH TO ASTROLOGY: A Complete Textbook of Astrology by Myrna Lofthus $12.95, 444 pages. A complete astrology textbook from a karmic viewpoint, with an especially valuable 130-page section on karmic interpretation of all aspects, including the Ascendant & MC.

For more complete information on our books, a complete booklist, or to order any of the above publications, WRITE TO:

CRCS Publications
Post Office Box 1460
Sebastopol, California 95473
U.S.A.